Integrating Literature
and Writing Instruction

Integrating Literature and Writing Instruction

First-Year English, Humanities Core Courses, Seminars

Edited by
Judith H. Anderson and Christine R. Farris

The Modern Language Association of America

New York   2007

For information about obtaining permission to reprint material from MLA book publications, send your request by mail (see address below), e-mail (permissions@mla.org), or fax (646 458-0030).

LIBRARY OF CONGRESS CATALOGING-IN-PUBLICATION DATA

Integrating literature and writing instruction: first-year English, Humanities core courses, seminars / edited by Judith H. Anderson and Christine R. Farris.
    p. cm.
    Includes bibliographical references and index.
    ISBN-13: 978-0-87352-948-8 (alk. paper)
    ISBN-10: 0-87352-948-0 (alk. paper)
    ISBN-13: 978-0-87352-949-5 (pbk. : alk. paper)
    ISBN-10: 0-87352-949-9 (pbk. : alk. paper)
    1. English language–Rhetoric–Study and teaching (Higher). 2. Academic writing –Study and teaching (Higher). 3. Literature–History and criticism–Theory, etc. 4. Critical thinking–Study and teaching (Higher). 5. Humanities–Study and teaching (Higher).
    I. Anderson, Judith H. II. Farris, Christine R., 1949- III. Modern Language Association of America.
PE1404.I526 2006   2006031279
808'. 0420711–dc22

Published by The Modern Language Association of America
26 Broadway, New York, NY 10004-1789
www.mla.org

Contents

Introduction

Literature and Composition: Stakes and Issues of Relationship

Our volume aims to make available to a professional audience of college teachers and scholars in the discipline of English an account of courses taught in various institutional contexts that use literature in teaching first-year college students how to read, write, and think critically. While such courses may include potential majors in English, they are mainly for nonmajors. Our contributors both describe and assess the use and viability of literature in teaching academic literacies to college students. These courses attempt to pair composition and literature in ways that are basic to textual interpretation and production across the curriculum.

Our volume is also about integrating the concerns of English departments. Arguably, these concerns were never successfully integrated in the twentieth century, and the vexed history of their lack of integration reaches back into the nineteenth century and beyond to a much earlier time when the vernacular achieved rival status with Latin. These days, even to mention the relation of literature to composition is to trigger larger issues in the politics of English studies. Most composition scholars agree on a narrative of the history of English studies in which the powerful position of literature depends on its opposition to composition, the teaching of which has paradoxically enabled the privileging of literary specialization within large English departments (Berlin, *Rhetorics* 3; Crowley 11; S. Miller 2). In contrast, many literary historians and institutional critics elide the role of composition, even as some condemn exploitation of the contingent teaching labor that built the industry in which their own scholarly work accrues capital (Nelson; Guillory). Despite repeated arguments for and attempts at altering the relation between rhetoric and poetic discourse configured variously

Christine R. Farris and Judith H. Anderson

throughout decades, if not centuries, of American academic politics, composition specialists still find themselves having to argue the intellectual place of composition in English departments or in departments reconfigured as rhetoric or cultural studies, even as credit hours in composition instruction continue to fund assistantships in large graduate programs. Thus there are those for whom the inclusion of literature in composition courses or programs would signify the loss of political ground. For some, such inclusion would also signal the return of literary interpretation at the expense of the production of students' texts.

Theoretical and Historical Background

Since the 1960s, the turn toward an emphasis on students' personal growth and experience, along with attention to the writing process, largely displaced literary texts in composition courses as rhetorical models and as the sources of ideas for writing. As Joseph Harris notes, this change occurred around the time of the 1966 Dartmouth Conference on the Teaching and Learning of English (*Subject* 3). While some participants in this conference called for a redefinition of the subject matter of English that would justify the coherence of language, literature, and composition, others, opposing this body-of-knowledge model, argued for, and helped usher in, an emphasis on personal and expressive forms of writing and of response to literature. Harris argues that this emphasis, which might have led to an integration of goals for English studies, particularly for first-year college students, became relegated to teaching methods like freewriting, drafting, and peer-group work (*Subject* 13–14). In some versions of literary theory, it led to heightened claims for affective and acculturated subjectivity in reader response.

In composition studies, the relegation to method that Harris describes led to a heightened concern with the mental processes of student writers and with stages of the writing process, which was embraced by researchers and "authentic voice" advocates alike. This concern became in turn more important than the texts — those with which students might engage and those they might produce as a result of their engagement. As composition studies, influenced in part by empirical studies of successful writers, sought disciplinary credibility in the 1980s, many first-year courses made student writing the only texts in the classroom. In the process movement, the focus on writing—not just as a product but as an activity involving discovery, audience awareness, teacher and peer intervention, and revision—made possible a theorizing of writing tied to a pedagogy emphasizing these activities (Olson 7). Central to this theorizing was the notion that the activities of successful writers would form the basis of a model that could be generalized to all writing—in effect, then, an essentialized model of composition.

While the basic tenets of this process movement remain central to composition pedagogy, postmodern suspicion of a universal model of the writing process apart from context has led to attempts to reestablish links with revitalized historical, textual, and cultural inquiry in the rest of English studies, where various historicisms continue to be much in evidence (Farris and Anson). What has been termed postprocess theory now assumes that writing is a situated, public activity requiring interpretive interaction with others (Kent 1). Such an interpretive turn might allow for the reintroduction of literary texts in the first-year classroom, insofar as literature is a situated, public representation. Yet in shifting attention to the larger forces that affect writers, whether on principle or in practice, many first-year courses avoid or displace literature to focus exclusively on nonliterary, noncanonical texts and artifacts that more directly address and more simply contextualize historical and social issues.

Arguments that first-year courses ought to focus on analysis and production of discourse common to a variety of disciplines students will encounter have tended to view literature more as a category of text than as specific critical language practices applicable to disciplines other than English. Essential to Erika Lindemann's position in her landmark essay "Freshman Composition: No Place for Literature" that imaginative literature does not belong in required first-year writing is the need for the transferability of composition writing skills and genres to other courses in the college curriculum (312). The now familiar debate that ensued between Lindemann and Gary Tate over whether to include literature in a composition course was featured in two issues of *College English* in the early 1990s. Cited by a number of our contributors, it centers, according to Lindemann, on the goals and values that other disciplines give the course. "Freshman English," she posits, "offers guided practice in reading and writing the discourses of the academy and the professions. This is what our colleagues across the campus want it to do; that is what it should do if we are going to drag every first-year student through the requirement" ("Composition" 312). Her opponent, Tate, laments the extent to which composition, by replacing literature with rhetoric, has been turned into the "ultimate 'service course' for all the other disciplines in the academy" ("Place" 319). Tate, himself a professor of rhetoric, asks partly in jest whether we gave up too much when "we allowed the Rhetoric Police to drive literature out of our writing courses" ("Place" 118). Echoing a growing complaint about the demise of the liberal arts, he resists "the increasing professionalization of undergraduate education in this country," preferring to help composition students join "conversations . . . *outside the academy*, as they struggle to figure out how to live their lives" ("Place" 320).

Responses to the Lindemann-Tate debate followed, including a sequel issue of *College English* in March 1995, in which Tate and Lindemann refined and at least slightly modulated their arguments. Lindemann repeats her concern with the real purpose of a writing course, qualifies her claims for English-based composition teachers' knowledge of disciplinary discourse outside the humanities, and acknowledges the existence of various approaches to the teaching of writing in the profession, making a bit more space for the role of reading and texts in a writing course ("Views" 298). Tate, in support of his position, revisits historical evidence that the use of literature in composition courses never disappeared, even with the return of rhetoric. Nevertheless, referencing workshops at the annual Conference on College Composition and Communication (CCCC), he acknowledges that professional claims made for the benefits of using literature in composition classes did not change from 1950 to the mid-1970s and were exaggerated, unsupported, and undeveloped ("Notes" 306). As Harris remarked so tellingly of the period in the 1960s and 1970s after the Dartmouth Conference and as these later views of the still mainly disagreeing Lindemann and Tate even begin to suggest, opportunities were missed to develop connections between engagement with literature and rhetorical and cognitive approaches to the teaching of writing.

Sharon Crowley has characterized the Lindemann-Tate exchanges specifically and the debate about the use of literary texts in composition more generally as being not so much about curricular content as about how much literary study and composition have, or do not have, in common (21). She views first-year English as having merely provided a convenient site for defending a humanist, as opposed to a postmodern, approach to literary texts. Her view would explain why most of the responses to the Lindemann-Tate debates argue for the connection of literature to life instead of making the point that literary studies offers students practice in a specialized discourse that might be transferable to other disciplines. Along with Tate, Crowley also questions the extent to which composition teachers can "anticipate every discursive exigency their students will be asked to meet in college or in life" (28). Unlike Tate, however, she advocates no longer striving for or requiring the teaching of a nonexistent universal discourse in first-year English. Arguably, she does not realize the extent to which literary studies can afford practice in a specialized discourse that might be generalized to other disciplines. We will return to the questions of whether and how English can be at once a specialized discourse and an exportable one.

Before leaving this retrospective on the Lindemann-Tate debate and its sequel — indeed in its light — and before turning to the emergence of cultural studies and its effects over the last fifteen years, however, we would caution that at present, as in the 1990s, composition is no more a monolithic entity than literary studies is. While we can locate dominant trends and positions, there will always be vestigial, emergent, and otherwise exceptional ones. Life comes in messy, fuzzy-edged forms rather than in neat frozen packages. Compositionists do not necessarily agree with one another, let alone with their colleagues in literature, about the goals and best practices of first-year composition, which can also include workplace writing, multiculturalism, and service learning.

The growing importance of cultural studies over the last fifteen years has brought a further, related development: less attention to the concerns of rhetorical and linguistic studies. Separately yet simultaneously, it can be argued that composition and literature have drifted away from their roots in rhetoric and language and thus from their own media and most basic raison d'être, particularly when it comes to the justification for a required first-year English course. Ironically, even while the concerns of many practitioners have found a common bond in cultural relevance and social effect, this commonality has needlessly been accompanied by a reciprocal devaluing of either literature or composition as the locus of rhetoric and language, whether as subject matter or as technique. Influential voices on both the composition and literature sides have urged the avoidance of literature as a distraction from the business at hand, insofar as literature, by its very artfulness, insistently invites attention to its medium as well as its message. Attention to the medium leads to the reintroduction of canonical texts, and soon the real purpose of literary study or of composition is lost, or so the fears go.

Arguments—both conservative and radical—for the abolition of first-year composition or for its liberation from the vexed relation between literature and composition have been many over the years (Hairston, "Breaking"; Lindemann, "Composition"; Crowley). Likewise, arguments have been plentiful for unification, given the attention of both literary and composition studies to the ways in which what we know and value is shaped by language and material conditions (Horner; Clifford and Schilb; Tate, "Place"). More prevalent than efforts at unification in English departments, however, has been the development of tracks and subdisciplinary programs. As James Seitz observes, this development "allow[s] faculty to teach what they know best and students to take a range of courses within a single realm of an expansive discipline"(154). Seitz adds, however, that "separate programs lead faculty to identify themselves all the more forcefully with their areas of specialization—and with their own marketability within those areas," often resulting in turf wars and struggles for power, resources, and students (155). Ideally, these difficulties would eventually give way to recognition of the need for what Seitz describes as "a collectivist curricular practice, one in which faculty from different programs in the English department articulate a curriculum whose vision is larger than that of any single program" (160).

It was an effort at curricular collaboration across programs, such as Seitz advocates, that inspired this volume. Our collaboration, first as colleagues in the separate subdisciplines of composition and literature and now as editors, has resulted from participation in an initiative supported by our graduate school and the program Preparing Future Faculty, to integrate the teaching and scholarly experiences of doctoral students—mainly teaching composition but mainly studying literature—with the diverse specialties of faculty members. Christine Farris, director of composition, who is responsible for preparing new graduate instructors in the teaching of writing, codesigned with several faculty colleagues a pedagogy seminar in the teaching of literature and culture. Judith Anderson subsequently volunteered to teach one of these seminars, in which she collaborated with experienced graduate instructors of composition in the design and eventual implementation of a first-year English course for nonmajors that would integrate literature and composition. We will have more to say about both course and program in the final section of our volume.

Writing across the Curriculum

But here, we must move from a general history of stakes and issues of relationship that has reached our own situated present to focus on what ties the subcultures of literature and composition together and what relation this tie has to the social purpose of English as an institution and as a discipline. The relation of our volume to writing across the curriculum, or WAC, now comes to the fore. In the last twenty years, as we have noted, a number of forces have worked to undermine the perceived division between literature and composition, including postmodern considerations of the social construction of knowledge, recognition that textual interpretation is situated, and the rise of composition studies as a subdiscipline reshaping preparation in the pedagogy of English and spawning the WAC movement. As Art Young and Toby Fulwiler observe in their introduction to *When Writing Teachers Teach Literature: Bringing Writing to Reading*, graduate students today are trained not only in literary scholarship but also in writing pedagogy that focuses on the process of students' learning (Introduction 2). Both their volume and this one attest to the fact that the increased attention to active student learning and to the reflective practice characteristic of composition teaching has produced significant changes in the pedagogy of literature. These include a more fully integrated and progressive use of writing to bridge student response and academic discourse.

Young and Fulwiler's involvement with WAC, which typically emphasizes writing as a mode of learning and active engagement with the disciplinary making of meaning, is, they assert, what led them back to English to reexamine the potential of literature pedagogy to be "not the mere transmission of knowledge but the transmission of the means of creating knowledge and the excitement that accompanies it" (2). Most of the contributors to their 1995 volume, who identify themselves primarily with composition studies, emphasize in teaching literature the student-centered tenets of the process approach to writing, which also forms the basis of many WAC-sponsored interdisciplinary workshops. Designed to disrupt the transmission-of-knowledge model of learning, the pedagogy of Young and Fulwiler's contributors includes strategies of invention intended to help students individually and collectively to "create literary knowledge" and to produce their own creative and critical, "professional" literary publications (5). These contributors tend to deemphasize academic conventions and their own interpretations and stress instead the intersection between professional literature and students' personal experience, the coauthoring of meaning, and the contributions their students have made to their own understanding of literature. Here it is worth reemphasizing that the view of Young and Fulwiler still bears predominantly on the pedagogy of process rather than on disciplinary content, on method rather than subject.

Linda Peterson breaks rank with the other contributors to the Young and Fulwiler volume by suggesting that the dichotomy between the transmission and the creation of knowledge that English-based WAC programs typically export to other disciplines is an oversimplification (263). Peterson cites Susan McLeod's categorization of the approaches WAC programs take as being either "rhetorical" and emphasizing "the discourse community and its conventions" or else "cognitive" and emphasizing writing to learn, and she recognizes the value of both (269). She argues that the rhetorical approach to literature, which is a critical methodology for working with texts, does not necessarily run counter to the writing-to-learn agenda. She is more willing than most of Young and Fulwiler's contributors to reenvision the discipline of English through WAC eyes and to introduce students "to the discourse conventions of literary studies and to the *process* by which disciplinary knowledge is [there] developed and put to use" (Introduction 9; emphasis added). Although Peterson directly addresses an upper-division, intensive writing course in English, her argument has broader and more significant implications. We can harvest these for the present volume: the critical methodology in use today with literary texts does not automatically or necessarily contravene the goals for first-year reading and writing courses that presume to prepare students for work in more than one discipline (Peterson 263). In fact, it is an effective way to further them.

Textuality and Intertextuality

Like Peterson, Robert Scholes would demystify for students how English academic discourse works rather than demonize it. In both *Textual Power* and *The Rise and Fall of English*, Scholes laments the schism in departments between literature and writing instruction and proposes instead "a discipline based on rhetoric and the teaching of reading and writing over a broad range of texts," including "poems, plays, stories, letters, essays, interviews, books, magazines, newspapers, movies, television shows," and the like (*Rise* 130, 179). But such an integrated discipline, according to Scholes, requires that we deconstruct the "invidious binary opposition between writing teachers and literary scholars" (*Rise* 35) by "denying the special mystical privileges we have accorded to 'literature'" (36) and that we "reconstruct our efforts as students and teachers of English around the notion of textuality" (36), that is, around the rhetorical discipline described just above. Thus Scholes emphatically defends, not a bifurcated curriculum, but one that embraces literary and nonliterary texts in an effort to provide students with analytical tools for college and beyond.

It might be useful here to pause over a fuller definition of *textuality*, since it is central to our argument. Harry Berger, Jr., describes it as linguistic play and difference, in which differential structuring enables *"the discourse of the other,"* defined as an instance when what is said escapes authorial intention and becomes instead the expression of "a collective or structural agency: *différance*... or the unconscious, or the unconscious as language, or heteroglossia, or language-games, or the collective discourses shaped by a society's cultural and institutional practices" (416). *Textuality*, in Berger's helpfully composite conception, also includes interpretation and therefore a degree of reference that at least minimally stabilizes linguistic play and moves toward the limitation of semiosis, or, in Berger's open-ended conception, toward provisional and always potentially temporary "countertextuality."

While Scholes agrees with Stanley Fish (*Professional Correctness*) and others who call for English to "maintain a distinctive disciplinary core" (*Rise* 179), he believes that textuality best serves this function because it focuses attention on the means and media of expression and communication (*Rise* 179–80). Scholes's argument has two immediate ramifications for our volume. In our view it rightly suggests, first, that the unqualified centrality of literature in the English curriculum is outmoded and, second, that the justification for this centrality's shaping opposition like Lindemann's to literature in composition is outmoded as well, since such opposition is based on the assumption that the exegesis of texts for content, be it spiritual, moral, ethical, social, or political, will necessarily crowd out attention to the writing skills students need in a variety of disciplines and professions. Textuality can thus be a part of, rather than separate from, the interdisciplinary service responsibility of English. In fact, it is fundamental to it.

Our mission, says Scholes, should be to provide students with a flexible understanding of language and texts that is connected to their intellectual growth, "a useful mental discipline that [they] can draw upon... for the rest of their lives" (*Rise* 87). If now we really believe that "texts are made out of other texts, intertextuality should be central in any attempt to do what is usually called 'teaching writing'" (*Rise* 89). Intertextuality, as Scholes uses it, is comparable to the philosopher Andy Clark's use of scaffolding in the context of cognitive science (32–33). Or at least it is so if we understand this scaffolding necessarily to involve language, the conceptualization that human language enables, and the situatedness of both these conditions. Intertextuality is the living evidence, subject to inspection and discussion, of the operation of language and in a vital sense of intelligibility in human history and human culture. An intertext thus results from the play of the various cultural discourses that constitute its message. As Roland Barthes explains in a classic passage that characterizes intertextuality, the text is "a multi-dimensional space in which a variety of writings, none of them original, blend and clash." For Barthes, a text, itself by definition intertextual, is "a tissue of quotations, drawn from the innumerable centers of a culture" (Barthes 146, 148; Culler 32–33). With variations, Michel Foucault, Jacques Derrida, Mikhail Bakhtin all agree.

Composition has long had experience with a simpler version of intertextuality. In this version, textbook anthologies provide decontextualized formal models (mostly literary essays) for students to imitate as expository modes (narration, description, definition, persuasion) or to use as springboards for response. Too often such use has been belletristic instead of analytical, however. But those who have studied the relation between students' writing performance and their habits of misreading and misusing sources as both cognitive and cultural phenomena, compositionists such as David Bartholomae, Mariolina Salvatori, and Patricia Bizzell, have refined the practice of textuality and intertextuality by making creative and productive use of texts and contexts in writing instruction.[1] The textbook of Bartholomae and Anthony Petrosky, *Ways of Reading*, whose seventh edition appeared in 2005, invites students to expand and complicate their positions in a series of responses to provocative juxtapositions of different readings, both literary and nonliterary. "The issue," Bartholomae and Petrosky agree, "is not only what students read, but what they can learn to do with what they read" (v). Like several of our contributors, they are interested in working with texts in a writing course that do not "solve all the problems they raise" and thereby turn reading into "an act of appreciation" captured easily in student writing (vi). Instead, they want to teach students that initial confusion when faced with a complex text is not "a sign of failure" but the start of how expert readers construct interpretations, that is, "by writing and rewriting—by working on a text" (vii). In this sense, as well as in an interpretive one, the student's own text itself becomes an intertext. Like Scholes, Bartholomae and Petrosky have no apologies to make for teaching academic writing by directing students to read and write as we do in the academy, or, in Scholes's words, to operate "at the boundaries of our knowledge where discoveries may be made" (*Rise* 98).

Scholes's view, consistent with that of most compositionists, advocates a revision of practice in English that starts "with the needs of our students" (*Rise* 84), but he also challenges the assumption of Lindemann's argument against the use of literature in writing courses, namely, "that we in English departments are properly responsible for all the possible kinds of writing in English" (*Rise* 34). Specialists both in English-based first-year writing and in WAC defend the transferability, or translatability, to other disciplines of the writing strategies and conventions they advocate. In doing so, however, they exaggerate, perhaps in the interest of territory, what English as a discipline can teach about writing in another discipline, such as economics, biology, political science, or history. (Farris, "Giving"). Once again, Scholes is useful: he reminds us that what faculty members in other disciplines respect about our expertise in English is not so much "that we will teach . . . how to write like social scientists or engineers" as that "what we can teach about writing involves mainly those elements of it that are literary or rhetorical" (*Rise* 34). Here Scholes either identifies the highly rhetorical features of literature with rhetoric itself or signals by the word *literary* the necessary concern of imaginative writing with the medium of its own craft, namely, *litera*, "the letter," or language.

Writing pedagogy that operates out of a sense of textuality like Scholes's understandably reflects the ways in which the discipline of English has changed, not only in composition but also in literary and cultural studies. The courses our contributors describe reflect their awareness that first-year students both in English and in interdisciplinary courses will not necessarily put literature, much less literary scholarship, at the center of their lives. Nevertheless, in various ways, they believe that even students who are not English majors can benefit as writers, readers, members of the academic community, and citizens of the world from a better understanding of how various texts in our culture are constructed through language and visual image. Particularly since first-year college students are increasingly likely to have been introduced earlier in their schooling to strategies of the writing process, such as prewriting, free writing, drafting, and revision, they are positioned to acquire a critical methodology that not merely allows but actively encourages the analysis for themselves of how both literary and nonliterary writers use rhetorical language to construct intellectual arguments. In addition, the contributors to our volume conspicuously, more subtly, or even somewhat tentatively enact in their courses what entrenched colleagues in both composition and literature are often reluctant to acknowledge, or at least to acknowledge in practice as well as in theory: that the field of English has changed, that our individual course designs and teaching practices reflect that change, and thus that curriculum design and department configurations can and ought to reflect that change as well.

When we consider the makeup of first-year courses, we need not always imagine worst-case scenarios rather than best ones: for example, the literature instructor concerned only with nonnegotiable exegesis; the renegade composition instructor who, if allowed to assign literature, will not devote enough attention to revision; or the anti-intellectual first-year student who only wants his college ticket punched. We should also recognize that the academic culture has changed and that institutional reconfigurations, such as first-year seminars and first-year interest groups and cotaught interdisciplinary first-year courses, now put literature and writing to uses consistent with the best in postmodern and new-historicist paradigms in any number of fields.

Our contributors do more than balance the teaching of writing and the teaching of literature in their courses, although they do this in the various ways and combinations suitable to their institutional contexts. They offset the top-down dissemination of static interpretation by allowing students to proffer their own experience as readers in their own voices, but they also do more. They enact postmodern or postprocess theory by encouraging students to work with acknowledged binaries, tensions, and contradictions in their reading and in their writing: for example, between their own voices and interpretive frames and those typical of literary discourse, between historical and fictional narratives, between contemporary and earlier treatments, between and within generic conventions and between these and social change, between and within representations of gender and race, between their own readings and those of their peers. It is this sort of work, says Gerald Graff, along with the "contingent, constructed, and negotiated" nature of literature and the tensions between nonacademic and academic discourse, that can become the textualized object of study in a course that "brings the concerns of literature and composition together" (Afterword 325, 333).

Invoking the congenial view of Seitz, we earlier explained that local conditions and circumstances have made possible our own collaboration in an integrated first-year program at Indiana University that makes wider use of literature than critics of its use in composition typically fear. In conceiving of a collaboration of literature and composition, our readers ought not to imagine only a canonical literature frozen in time and aimed merely at the cultivation of taste or self-expression, any more than they need imagine a vacuous composition dealing only with form and mechanics. Composition need not be a "secondary act," if, indeed, it *is* possible to study literary texts as having been "produced in the same way that all texts are produced: by means of composition" (Crowley 85). Since our own program at Indiana University has permitted the more generous understandings of literature and composition as discourse analysis and production and as complementary sets of critical practices with literacy implications across the curriculum, we have also wondered how this might be the case in courses and programs at other institutions, particularly those in which the teaching of literature and the teaching of writing are not conceived and necessarily structured as separate or hierarchical enterprises. Our present volume has thus been conceived.

The combination of local conditions and practices, of curricular options and actual courses, has enabled some notable progress in integration at our institution by moving us beyond the impasse of theories premised on the allegedly great divide of literature and composition. If integration has been deferred and debated on the national scene to the point of theoretical paralysis, in various provocative ways it has been achieved in practice in many courses at diverse colleges and universities. To our minds, a bottom-up rather than a top-down approach, thoughtful praxis rather than political imperative, at present has a better chance of bridging this supposed divide. Our volume has been launched in this spirit.

The Contents of This Volume

As we turn from the broader aims of this volume to the representative courses that substantiate them, the concept operative in the fourteen essays selected for inclusion needs emphasis. *First-year English*, as we use the term, employs literature in introducing college students to critical reading, thinking, and writing. Our volume thus focuses on the viability of utilizing literature to teach these fundamental literacies in courses foundational to interpretation across the curriculum. It is about first-year courses that introduce nonmajors and majors alike to these literacies, rather than about introducing the English major. Ours is a focus on literate understanding and, inseparably, on the expression that both informs and communicates it. Each contributor has combined literature with composition in actual classroom practice, and for this volume each has been asked to consider the aims, the forms of learning, the kinds of analysis, and the production of student writing that have made her or his course a worthwhile first-year experience. We have also asked contributors to identify the nature of the programs in which their courses play a role, including the kinds of academic institutions in which they currently teach or have taught the courses they describe.

By *literature*, we primarily mean imaginative writing, but we do not intend imaginative writing to exclude other pertinent kinds of writing, such as essays, from the representative courses in our volume, and by the term *imaginative* itself, we certainly do not mean canonical in the sense written before 1950, let alone before 1900. A number of the courses integrating literature with composition in our volume have presentist reading lists, but several attend broadly to history, and nearly all to diversity, whether multicultural or focused on a single country or race. Many also include attention to other media, such as graphics, film, or the Internet. We consider imaginative writing itself not only and inevitably a representation of culture but also an active, influential, provocative contributor to it. Language, the sine qua non of any specifically written expression and the substance—the very being—of poetic and prosaic fiction, is, after all, the most fundamentally enabling condition of human culture itself. For this reason, we no more subscribe to a theoretical opposition of language to human culture and history than we do to one between literature and composition.

No single course described in this volume is or could be the monolithic model for all first-year English courses. No one size fits all institutions and traditions of higher learning or all times and individual instructors. First-year courses that integrate literature with writing instruction, moreover, do not even begin to fit into a single size themselves. Accordingly, we have not sought out programs and courses that have arrived at an identical or hypothetically ideal balance between literature and composition or that have achieved their balance by the same methods. To have endeavored to do so would have been to deny what actually exists and really works in the field and, quite simply, to kid ourselves. Representation of a variety of courses, programs, and academic institutions, with the hope of future cross-fertilization among them, rather than homogeneity, is not the least of the purposes of our volume. The courses and programs described here offer imaginative assignments and innovative pedagogical techniques, as well as concepts, that could either be adopted whole or, more likely, adapted profitably, in whole or in part, to other courses and institutional contexts attempting the integration of literature with writing instruction.

There are also different methods and even various conceptions of learning in this volume, some largely participatory and others combining small-group discussion with large-group lectures, for example. Ranges and amounts of reading and writing also vary. Some contributors set the bar high with apparent success, and others set it lower to be effective, doing so for reasons credible within their institutional contexts. As editors, our task is not to determine which choice is right (even if we supposed we could) but to offer reasoned, working alternatives for consideration. We believe that this kind of presentation will encourage a better discussion in the field than would our generation of a one-sided pronouncement.

We would like to dispel one mistaken assumption about our project that has proved distracting, however. We do not intend the inclusion of literature in writing courses to solve all writing or pedagogical problems, and this is one reason that we have asked our contributors to provide some contextual sense of the institutions and programs in which their courses are situated. In most of these, explicit attention to developmental or basic instruction in grammar and syntax is found, as needed, elsewhere in the system: for example, either in an alternative track in the first-year program or in an additional option, such as a course in grammar or individual tutorials at a writing center. All these options exist at Indiana University, for an example from the Big Ten whose writing program is represented in our volume. For an example from a small institution whose humanities program is also represented in our volume, Centre College in Danville, Kentucky, offers special, writing-intensive humanities sections that feature an additional weekly writing lab for those needing further or more basic instruction. Again, the primary focus of our volume is on courses integrating literature and writing instruction, rather than on developmental courses or on pedagogical methods per se.

We also believe that in education (from Latin *educere*, "to lead") models, whatever their origin, that offer alternatives, opportunities, breadth, and intellectual stimulation have relevance both for students whose educational backgrounds are strong and whose academic programs are privileged and for those whose backgrounds and programs are neither. We have therefore included a variety of schools and programs in this volume, including small and selective ones. The essay by Faye Halpern affords a representative example. She writes tellingly about a gifted student at Harvard who has not mastered argumentation. This student has a great deal in common with the first-year audience of David Rosenwasser and Jill Stephen's admirable *Writing Analytically*, a textbook used in elementary composition and in first-year courses combining literature and composition at Indiana University. Experienced teachers of composition know that the representative mistakes of the best paper in the class, rather than those of the worst one, often demonstrate effectively where improvement is needed. In other words, although Halpern's story and the course in which she addresses argumentation may not transfer whole cloth to a less selective classroom, they are full of insight and ideas about content and method. In this way, the conception of her course invites and provokes imaginative modification.

Particularly in the first part of our introduction and to a lesser extent in the final group of essays and in our conclusion, we have sought to frame our volume with theory, but our major focus nonetheless remains on practice. We have not tried to level the tone of every contributor or required the same extent of reference to composition theory, literary theory, or cultural theory from each. We take a bottom-up approach — one based on informed, reflective practice — rather than a top-down approach based mainly on theory. Not least, in fact, we hope to question disembodied pronouncements that are insufficiently informed by practice. Whereas we often hear that in theory the combination of literature and first-year writing instruction does not work or proves counterproductive, we see that it can and often does succeed. In some of our essays, practice is imbued with composition theory; in others, it is more informed by experience and exposure: for example, in earlier graduate training in composition and pedagogy and in current classroom practice, but also in such informative departmental activities as the review of portfolios by tenure, promotion, and recruitment committees. In some courses, practice is informed by literary theory or by the broadly cultural theories — psychological, sociological, philosophical, rhetorical, linguistic — that composition and literary theory share: witness Foucault, Barthes, Derrida, Judith Butler, just for example.

Even common sense, it is said, is, if not a theory in disguise, at least an ideology: no course — indeed, no cultural practice — is innocent of such orientation (Belsey 3). That granted, accomplished teachers of first-year English may not explicitly invoke composition theory or other kinds of theory and may not even be specifically aware of or specifically affected by theory. This is not to dismiss theory or to disavow its importance but to deny it the status of indispensability in all situations. Ideally, teaching and courses are a perfect combination of theory and practice, including course concept, design, and method, with equal representation of the theories and practices of composition and literature. At the present time, however, the privileging of theory over practice is more likely to further identity politics and to reinscribe the separation of composition from literature than to disrupt it, as we wish to do.

We have not attempted to be exhaustive in our coverage of courses, academic institutions, and geographic areas represented, but these considerations helped guide our selection of essays. In the final mix, we have (with categories overlapping) at least three Research I universities, two of them public; two additional state universities, both large; three selective, small colleges; two colleges and a small university with religious affiliations; a college of public affairs in another large state university; a state college founded as a normal school; and a polytechnic institute. Some contributors also represent broader experience: for example, one now teaches and directs writing in a two-year college, and four others have recently moved to different institutions from the one about which they have written. Another contributor also reports that a version of her course in a Big Ten university has twice been adapted for successful teaching in two-year colleges.

Groupings of Courses

Like the categories of institutions, the three groupings into which we have divided the essays overlap considerably, yet they identify dominant foci. The first group, of four essays, highlights core programs in the humanities in which literature plays a central or vital role. In the second group, also of four, literature is the source of discovery and the locus of examination—the source of what is focal in writing. While the writers of this group are variously aware of the interweaving of text and larger context, their courses suggest a conceptual model that moves from text to context and privileges generic, rhetorical, and linguistic conventions. Such conventions, which are themselves implicated in culture, participate in and shape content. With the exception of the final essay in this group, "Reading Detectives," which originates in a large state university, these contributions come from teachers at more select, yet also quite diverse, institutions.

Where the second group of essays starts with literature, our third group starts with the larger culture and discovers that literature is useful for engaging with it. Three of these essays originate in state universities, one in a technical institute, and one both in a state college and in a small sectarian university, since it is coauthored by teachers at two such institutions. In this group of five courses, the analysis of language and rhetoric, or textuality, is less focal. The relation of literature and culture motivates writing, but often the writing does not center on the text. Again, our characterization of each group of essays sketches notable tendencies and dominant foci, not extremes and exclusions. Neither the second nor the third group of essays is without some of the interests of the other: in group 2, for example, the essays by Tamara Goeglein and by John Cyril Barton, Douglas Higbee, and Andre Hulet engage history and culture, and in group 3, the essays of Allison Berg and Jeanne Marie Rose in particular engage linguistic or rhetorical conventions. We might have organized the volume in a more neutral way—alphabetically or by size of institution, for example. The patterns and differences we emphasize are the ones we found most salient and provocative and least likely to misrepresent or oversimplify our contributors' generally complex points of view. We imagine and indeed hope that readers will discover other provocative combinations of essays, especially those crossing between and exceeding our sectional groupings.

The final section in our volume, which has been contributed by the editors themselves, shares characteristics with all three earlier groups of essays and represents what both editors are inclined to regard as an especially promising model. More exactly, Anderson's course is, like the humanities core courses in our first group, multisectioned, and it is part of a larger program, which her coeditor, Farris, oversees and describes; while Anderson's is not actually a humanities core course, its range of texts and concerns is also broader than those in our other earlier groupings. It shares with the courses in group 2 a focal interest in texts and in their analysis, but it also shares with group 3 a direct interest in and engagement of the broader social and cultural world, since for Anderson's essay this world is a referential reality that is not only ever-present but also necessarily textualized—that is, linguistic and rhetorical to its conceptual core. We therefore place this course at the conclusion of our collection and intend it as an integral part of our final statement. Like the volume as a whole, it is a conclusion answering to praxis.

Courses: Group 1

Heading the first group of contributors, Michael Clark and Elizabeth Losh describe a complex and ambitious Humanities Core. This year-long course seeks to counter what they perceive as the "centrifugal tendency" evident both in many models of first-year curricula focusing on specific cultural content and in the separation of such cultural analysis from composition. Core readings have interdisciplinary, historical, geographic, and racial and ethnic range. Sites of discursive activity vary from lectures to discussions in sections and through e-mail. Research is library-based, as well as Web-based, and writing progresses systematically from techniques of analytic and rhetorical analysis to the more advanced use of textual and cultural evidence, generally in accordance with B. S. Bloom's ordering of cognitive skills. The work of Lev Vygotsky, A. R. Luria, and Jerome Bruner further inspires correlation of composition with "other educational goals for conceptual development" in each core course. Analysis of multimedia texts is also "approached in the spirit of Roland Barthes's writerly text," that is, "as a hybrid of reading and writing, reception and production, passive and active literacy."

The first-year English program Margaret Vandenburg describes is more literary in cast than the humanities sequence of Clark and Losh, but, like theirs, it is also cross-cultural and broadly historical. Each aesthetic and cultural tradition the course features — Mediterranean, feminism, the Americas — undergoes examination "through the prism of revisionist critical methodologies, especially the new historicism and feminism." Although most entering students whom Vandenburg's program serves are technically proficient writers, she reports that "the distinction between description and analysis eludes them." In this important respect, which is vital to successful academic writing, first-year writers in her program resemble those whom many of us teach. Invoking the philosophic views of Hélène Cixous or Derrida as readily as those of Lindemann, Peter Elbow, Bartholomae, or Don Bialostosky, Vandenburg explains that the first-year English course she has devised challenges students with difficult texts to develop complex forms of conceptual and analytical expression. Revision in the course of the writing process, as Vandenburg characterizes it, is embedded in the revised treatment of course materials and thus a variation on Hayden White's "content of the form" or, indeed, of Fredric Jameson's "ideology of form" that is actualized in practice (White, *Content* ix–xi; Jameson 76, 145–47).

Gordon Thompson also characterizes a multisectioned, multicultural, and multidisciplinary program, but where Vandenburg's is recent in conception, his has existed in roughly the same form, with regular changes in common texts and writing assignments and with the addition of new instructors, for almost fifty years. An attraction of Thompson's description is the sense of pedagogical texture it conveys — the feeling of lived experience. This texture itself speaks volumes and does much to compel assent to the goals of "passionate, thoughtful, and articulate engagement with challenging texts" on his campus. Thompson also offers a thoughtful and revealing analytic history of his program.

The final essay in this group has been contributed by six multidisciplinary faculty members teaching in a humanities program that includes not only literature, history, philosophy, and the like but also the performance and plastic arts, taught by all instructors. Like the other programs in this group, it is a two-semester sequence with a common syllabus. Recently it has also become the required writing course for all students, rather than just for the more competent writers. For weaker writers, there are writing-intensive sections within the same humanities program. The contributors of this essay tell us that the students who enroll at their relatively small campus tend to have little experience of the wider world of humanistic culture and that the humanities program seeks to introduce them to it in a meaningful way.

Courses: Group 2

In our second group of courses, each focuses on a single genre or subgenre: poetry, satire (and irony), historical novels, detective fiction. The course integrating first-year writing instruction with literature that Helen Whall describes is so traditional that it seems radically new. Its reading consists entirely of poetry. Whall identifies the early written exercises in her poetry course as best characterizing what is unusual about it. These are "literalizations," or "literal comprehensions," often focusing first on one of Shakespeare's sonnets. Incrementally, the course attends to more complex analyses, credibly relating reading and comprehension to writing and doing so in evidential detail. It moves as well from language and grammar to argument, from literalization to larger context, and from local analysis to "the discipline of critical thought and conscious information retrieval."

Faye Halpern, the next contributor, posits that the wealth of detail in a literary text can provide "an excellent forum for debate" since it can be shaped into different readings, some of which prove more convincing than others. In her view, this potential for multiple, plausible interpretations is exactly why literature is well suited to foster students' academic writing. Literary texts, especially satiric and ironic ones, help students "recognize the possibility for debates" and offer them "the means to argue" a case effectively.

Goeglein's first-year seminar on historical fiction is a striking reminder that using literature to enable effective writing instruction need not entail the exclusion of historical or cultural context. Examining the truth in historical fiction and the fiction in "real" history, her seminar focuses first on the Battle of Gettysburg in the Civil War and then on four other historical subjects, one from sixteenth-century France and three from twentieth-century America: respectively, the identity of Martin Guerre, the turn of the twentieth century in America, the assassination of President Kennedy, and the life and times of Malcolm X. The stated aims of such seminars in her college are to develop critical skills in thinking, reading, writing, and oral communication.

The final selection in this group, written by Barton, Higbee, and Hulet, employs detective fiction as a heuristic analogue to textual interpretation. As the authors explain, the detective's search for clues approximates the students' performance of textual analysis to reach an interpretive conclusion. This analogy extends from the students' eventual recognition of generic conventions in detective fiction to their grasping how other genres, such as academic writing, employ conventions to understand and order the subject. Through progressively structured readings and writings, the students thus begin to perceive how social conventions similarly structure experience in the actual world. The writing assignments that Barton, Higbee, and Hulet discuss and the examples of student writing they analyze substantiate the analogy between detective work and textual analysis. Their course successfully translates discursive content and fictive form to the practice of composition. To bolster their argument, they invoke and at times adjust or refine the views of Maxine Hairston, Bartholomae, Bizzell, Harris, Anis Bawarshi, Charles Bazerman, Ann Berthoff, and Kenneth Bruffee.

Courses: Group 3

An essay on cultural "boundary writing" by Lori Robison and Eric Wolfe introduces the final group of essays, whose content variously derives from cultural studies. In Robison and Wolfe's account, Stephen Greenblatt's essay "Culture" provides the critical model both for students' seeing how implicit arguments in a piece of fiction work against "the dominant beliefs and social structures of its culture" and for their written analyses of such textual response to cultural ideologies (Greenblatt 231). The aim of this course is thus "to position literary writing as part of a larger cultural conversation" in which the students participate as well. In the authors' account, while pedagogy is no more self-conscious or participatory than in the accounts in our second grouping, it is seen explicitly in politicized terms and focally thematized. In this way it appeals to the postmodern pedagogue in many of us.

Noting with Elizabeth Latosi-Sawin that literature is used for instruction in business, sociology, psychology, history, and religion, Clyde Moneyhun argues in the second essay of this group that it is used because "literary texts provide a better means . . . of teaching students to interpret texts, to make meaning from texts." His point, a telling one, is shared by other contributors, conspicuously Halpern and Barton, Higbee, and Hulet in group 2. In its light, Moneyhun devises three writing assignments, or "games," based on literature that are designed "to make students aware that meaning is as much a product of an interpretive framework as it is a property of a text." Moneyhun, again like Halpern and Barton, Higbee, and Hulet, makes a claim for the transferability of interpretive insight from literary to nonliterary texts.

Like several other essays in the volume, including our introduction, Moneyhun refers to the catalytic Lindemann-Tate debate regarding the use of literature in composition courses, and he, too, summons to the table a host of contributors to relevant aspects of its legacy, such as Crowley, Salvatori, and Michael Gamer. In this way he provides a reprise of these issues in the later pages of our collection and affords a variant perspective on them. The advantages of reprise include the readmission of challenge to our project within its very confines.

Rose's essay, the third in this group, originated in her discoveries in graduate school both of the Tate-Lindemann debate and of Bakhtin's assertion that literary and nonliterary language share a common medium. The first-year English course she describes, which reflects these discoveries, asks students to recognize the provisionality of their personal writing—to recognize that the confessional mode is itself a rhetorical choice and uses rhetorical conventions and strategies. A second unit in her course focuses on the mediation of all narratives through language and finds models of this mediation in the storytelling of oral cultures, in fairy tales, and in the revision of myth in novels. This unit also investigates discourse communities and language standards. The final unit of the course treats the e-mail epistolary novel as an instance of language in the virtual world. Throughout, Rose thus relates literary language to a real world that at least pretends to be nonfictive.

Berg's essay, like Rose's, is concerned with education outside a college of arts and sciences. Her seminar seeks to integrate first-year writing instruction with African American literature in a way that will speak to students majoring in public affairs. She wants them to see that literature really matters, that it helps shape social, cultural, and political aspects of public life, and the relative visibility of rhetoric and politics in African American literature greatly assists her effort. While Berg acknowledges that her course "might at first glance pass for an abbreviated survey of African American literature," she argues persuasively that its design also bridges the aims and concerns of literature and composition. Salvatori, Lindemann,

Donald McQuade, and the collection of Young and Fulwiler are among the theorized resources orienting her essay.

Whereas Berg frankly acknowledges that she is interested more in what literature can bring to the composition classroom than in the reverse, Rona Kaufman and Lee Torda are compositionists so leery of literature that they will admit only to the use of reading, "not literature," in their classrooms. Nonetheless, like Bartholomae and Petrosky, they argue eloquently for the necessity of teaching reading in conjunction with composition and propose the use of required, supplementary book clubs outside (or if need be inside) the classroom to do so. Their persuasive account of these clubs, which consist exclusively of students in their standard composition classes, unapologetically privileges literary texts.

A Derridean pun therefore may best convey the relation between composition and literature that Kaufman and Torda propose: a relation of the one a-part from, but also of, the other. Their combination of concerns, while sensitive to the skeptical views of Lindemann and Elbow, derives support from a plethora of such authorities as Hans-Georg Gadamer, Wolfgang Iser, Michel de Certeau, Mary Louise Pratt, Louise Rosenblatt, Ann Berthoff, Kenneth Bruffee, Elizabeth Long, and Karen Burke LeFevre. Like Moneyhun's view, theirs is noticeably marked by Salvatori's theory of reading and writing about a difficult text, as well as by the other relevant authorities just enumerated. Their account offers a promising model for some degree of integration of literature as reading with the standard composition classroom. Since Kaufman and Torda are situated not only on opposite coasts but also in classes enrolling very differently situated students, their account goes beyond attesting to the adaptability — that is, the translatability with modification — of models in this volume to instantiate it in practice.

Concluding Section

In this section, Farris's description of an initiative to integrate literature with writing instruction more effectively in an English department provides a preamble to Anderson's contribution as part of this initiative. Anderson then describes her two interdependent courses, first one for the graduate students who would subsequently join her in teaching literature with composition and then one for the first-year undergraduates, a course for which the syllabus results from collaboration in the graduate course on pedagogical technique, linguistic and rhetorical theory, and the selection of texts to be taught to the undergraduates. That is, the graduate course provides the pedagogical and theoretical underpinnings, as well as the syllabus itself, put into practice in the subsequent course for first-year students. In final concept and actual practice, this particular first-year syllabus thus belongs to everyone who teaches it.

In an effort to reach what matters most fundamentally in first-year English, Anderson's entry-level undergraduate course has its basis primarily in language per se and secondarily in metaphor, eventually enlarging a sustained focus on these to cultural metaphors in science and political and racial history, with a conclusive return at the end to fictive language. Literature weaves in and out of every unit of her syllabus but shares this ground with a variety of other kinds of texts, including other media. An argument for the basis of reading, writing, and conceptual thinking in language and for the integration of composition and literature under its aegis thus returns as well in the final essay of the volume.

Note

1. Bizzell's textbook with Bruce Herzberg, *Negotiating Difference: Cultural Case Studies for Composition*, is a multicultural reader focusing on various texts associated with conflicts in American history, such as slavery, women's rights, Japanese American internment, and Vietnam. John Schilb and John Clifford's *Making Literature Matter* is both a literary anthology and a writing text that helps students use methods of argumentation to develop their responses into positions on literary issues. Scholes's own *Text Book: Writing through Literature*, edited with Nancy Comley and Gregory Ulmer and now in its third edition, explores the connections between the features of literary and nonliterary texts, for example, narrative, metaphor, and intertextuality. Many of the suggested writing assignments call for students to revise or transform literary texts.

Group I

Core Courses in the Humanities

Intellectual Community and Integrated Curricula in the First-Year Experience: The Humanities Core Course at the University of California, Irvine

*O*ur understanding of "English" as an object of study and as an academic field has grown increasingly inclusive and diverse since the 1980s. Along with this expansion has come an even greater range of opinion about the proper content and pedagogical objectives for courses offered to (and often required of) first-year students at colleges and universities. Most first-year courses in English have opened their curricula to a heterogeneous span of texts and topics far beyond what anyone would call literature in a traditional sense, and writing is often treated as a separate course, or even a separate requirement, especially for students whose familiarity with academic discourse and Standard English is limited. The objectives for these courses have also expanded beyond the traditional introduction to — and indoctrination in — a relatively stable literary canon and fixed set of cultural values. They now encompass an eclectic congeries of social and pedagogical ambitions that are often overtly opposed to the values and practices of earlier models.

Opening up our curricula to a wider range of cultures and media has resulted in incontrovertible social and intellectual rewards for students and teachers alike. Too often, however, the newer curricula in first-year English are characterized by an inherent centrifugal tendency that divides courses in terms of their specific cultural content by race, ethnicity, and gender. They further distinguish between cultural analysis and the teaching of composition as an academic skill or tool to be acquired from experts and applied as needed to the various contents. Though ostensibly valorizing the whole range of such content, this tendency replicates, albeit along different lines, the fragmentation associated with traditional national and disciplinary boundaries, including a pedagogical gap between reading and writing just as

Michael P. Clark and Elizabeth Losh

pernicious as the misleading hierarchy of literature over composition that it replaced. Consequently, these reforms, whether cultural or disciplinary, fail to produce any principle of intellectual or pedagogical coherence that can make much sense of the collocation of texts and methodologies offered to first-year students under the optimistic rubrics of first-year English, humanities, or writing.[1]

This lack of coherence has important institutional consequences. The courses that serve as first-year English are often the only courses taken by all students, and so they form the basis for whatever intellectual community may — or may not — exist before students are well into the curricula of requirements for their majors. When courses lack a sense of larger purpose beyond their immediate content, it is difficult for students (and, indeed, often faculty members) to see any value in or connection among the courses beyond the requirements they fulfill, and few institutions even pretend to pursue broad liberal arts education into the upper-division curricula of academic majors. Failure to connect these courses in a coherent program and to connect that program integrally with the general objectives of the institution virtually guarantees that the isolation and incoherence of the typical first-year curriculum will be writ large across the educational experience of all students at all levels.

This loss for the students can be reflected in equally dire consequences for the faculty and departments associated with ineffectual programs. Large introductory courses in the humanities are often the only venue in which systematic pedagogical training is offered to new instructors and in which faculty members from different fields can engage in collaborative reflection and planning about a common curriculum. Programs in first-year English that lack coherence and comprehensive scope provide few opportunities for either of those activities. Furthermore, since first-year English is often a significant source of graduate-student support and other funding for units that offer the courses, the failure to meet institutional expectations can lead universities to explore alternative avenues to fulfill those needs and to shift resources and institutional influence.[2]

If some version of first-year English is to retain its place at the center of the first-year experience, the courses must not only be coherent and comprehensive; they must also address social, institutional, and academic functions associated with the role of these courses in the students' general education and with the institutional functions of the courses in the university as a whole. As we argue below, meeting this objective can entail formidable pedagogical and intellectual challenges and involve considerable organizational innovation and commitment. At the same time, it can open up opportunities for collaboration among the faculty, graduate students, and postdoctoral instructors that can extend beyond the classroom to link scholarly research to a larger public sphere.

Interdisciplinary Collaboration and Institutional Networking

At the University of California, Irvine, the full range of these objectives is addressed by the Humanities Core course. A year-long course, Humanities Core challenges incoming freshmen from across the campus with a multidisciplinary introduction to humanist inquiry. It integrates the study of literary, historical, and philosophical texts, the visual arts, and music, using canonical and noncanonical works from various national and cultural traditions. The course offers a coherent educational experience that exposes students to a diverse range of materials, disciplines, interdisciplinary methods, and opinions. It equips them with the cognitive, discursive, and technical skills necessary to make sense out of that experience through discursive activities that include lectures, oral argument in class, electronic discussions, library-based and online research, and formal academic writing. Reading, writing, research, and technological facility are closely connected in practice, and that practice provides a foundation of active literacy and critical thought that students take into upper-division classes.

These goals are supported by a highly articulated course structure and extensive institutional engagement that bring together representatives from departments throughout the School of Humanities and, occasionally, even the natural sciences. Each week, students attend two hours of lectures by a team of faculty members from departments of literature, history, philosophy, and art history. Students also meet for three hours each week in small discussion sections taught by faculty members, postdoctoral instructors (with the formal title of lecturers), and graduate-student teaching associates. Humanities Core meets two breadth requirements in humanist inquiry and in multicultural and international studies. With its curriculum in composition, designed by the writing director, a professional composi- tionist, the course also satisfies the lower-division writing requirement. The sequence of writing assignments begins in the fall quarter with structured essay templates that focus on close reading. Over the course of the year the writing curriculum guides students through progressively more complex assignments in which they must integrate primary sources with historical context, etymological or philological information, and scholarly criticism. The year culminates in a formal research paper that requires multiple print and electronic sources and an original scholarly argument.[3]

Humanities Core thus links what would otherwise be isolated categories of breadth courses and presents them as strategic approaches for address- ing the intellectual and cultural issues raised in the course. Furthermore, students receive twice the usual credit hours of a single course, making Humanities Core one-third to one-half of the normal course load for most first-year students. Since the course enrolls about twelve hundred students, roughly one-third of each freshman class at UCI, Humanities Core occu- pies an equally prominent place in the collective first-year experience of the whole student body, providing both a common curriculum and an intel- lectual community for students from their first day on campus. At the same time, because the instructional staff combines three professional cohorts, all of whom contribute to the staff meetings, handbook, online resources, and electronic mailing list, the course serves as one of the few sites for collaboration among instructors whose professional lives are usually segre- gated not only by departmental boundaries but also by the hierarchies of expertise and credentials typical of all research universities.

This interaction among the instructors takes place most directly in weekly staff meetings where the lectures and readings for the week are discussed, strategies for approaching the writing exercises and assignments are considered, and appropriate standards for grading essays and examina- tions are reinforced by discussion and norming sessions. Faculty members and other instructors also contribute to a large collaborative Web site, which now contains hundreds of lesson plans, exercises, and handouts that supplement the formal pedagogical training in the weekly staff meetings. The Web site is grown and sustained by a lively electronic discussion list in which the central argument of the lecturing professor for the week is elaborated—and sometimes challenged—from the perspective of different fields of disciplinary expertise. These activities help ensure a reasonable degree of consistency in teaching and grading across all the sections and serve as a forum in which different disciplinary expectations can be aired and coordinated to avoid potentially confusing contradictions as students move from one instructor to another each quarter.

This transdisciplinary dialogue begins with the faculty members lecturing in the course, who model methodological, thematic, and conceptual approaches to the assigned material that are associated with different humanist disciplines. Comparisons among the disciplines are facilitated by team-teaching particular works each quarter, a practice that contrasts the viewpoint of a professor from a department of literature with one outside a literary field. In the cycle of Humanities Core discussed in detail below, for example, Plato's *Euthyphro*, Joseph Conrad's *Heart of Darkness*, and Daniel Defoe's *Robinson Crusoe* are all taught by at least two faculty members from different disciplines so students can compare literary analysis with the analytic practices of philosophers and historians who do not necessarily foreground the language of the text as the privileged object of knowledge in their reading.

Perhaps the most concrete and visible form of collaboration among the three cohorts on the instructional staff occurs in the interdisciplinary teaching of writing. A common syllabus of thirty weekly writing topics coordinates instruction across individual sections, and weekly topics are broadly construed so that the many instructors who come to Humanities Core from disciplines other than English can contribute their expertise to the training in composition pedagogy that is provided in the weekly staff meetings by the writing director. The aim of this syllabus is to build a pedagogical culture among the fifty instructors of the course and to promulgate a common discourse on reading and writing that can be sustained during the four-year experience of UCI undergraduates.[4] The Humanities Core course is organized to present a full-year writing and literature experience that builds on argument, textual analysis, and research with a sequence of essay assignments that are closely coordinated with lectures from nine professors from different fields in the humanities.

Since the 1980s, as composition has gained credence as a research field, many universities have introduced programs with writing-across-the-curriculum (WAC) courses or writing-in-the-disciplines (WID) courses. Unfortunately, these top-down administrative proposals for WAC and WID often lack a substantive commitment from research faculty members in disciplines outside composition. Humanities Core offers a different paradigm. Scholars from various areas of the humanities discuss the process of producing an academic essay in lectures on the assigned readings. They often explicitly model expository strategies by identifying the thesis statement for a particular lecture, noting that they are defining key terms as necessary, explaining the connection of particular passages, and referring frequently to material in the custom-published *Core Writer's Handbook* (Clark and Losh) that supports the curriculum in composition for Humanities Core (*The Handbook* also circulates widely among high schools and community colleges in the area around UCI). The incorporation of terms from the *Handbook* into the lectures is reflected conversely by the inclusion in the *Handbook* of published scholarly prose by those lecturing in the course, alongside articles by other faculty members, graduate students, and postdoctoral lecturers who serve as instructors in the small sections. In addition, the *Handbook* contains samples of student writing and the annual winner for the best essay written in Humanities Core, making it a concrete manifestation of the discursive community created by the course.

At all scales of magnitude, writing and reading are closely integrated in Humanities Core, whether the student is working alone at a computer, conferencing with an instructor or peer, discussing course material in the classroom, or responding to the lectures that model academic discourse. The practice of textual analysis is foregrounded throughout the year because Humanities Core defines a text to include many genres and media of expression and because analysis is approached in the spirit of Roland Barthes's writerly text, that is, as a hybrid of reading and writing, reception and production, passive and active literacy. In writing activities, students practice close reading of historical narratives and write reports on their own oral histories; they analyze the structure of philosophical argument and compose their own Socratic dialogues; they listen to music and sing along with operas in the large lectures; they view films and can manipulate clips from the films online as part of their analytical papers; and they incorporate their online research into their Web-based hypertexts. By the time students write the research paper that serves as a capstone experience for the course, their research, analysis, and incorporation of published scholarly essays into their work occurs less as an arcane academic ritual than simply one further step in the broader range of humanist inquiry the course encourages.

Above all, Humanities Core is committed to developing undergraduate research skills in the context of a research university whose primary purpose is the production of knowledge and its reproduction in an intellectual community that extends beyond the campus. The Humanities Core course is particularly well situated at UCI, where campuswide and national initiatives for promulgating undergraduate research have gained considerable attention. Consequently, all students in Humanities Core must complete a year-long curriculum on research methods, and research itself is treated as a meaningful object of study throughout the year. Humanities Core promotes undergraduate research through two major collaborative efforts: joint curricular projects with information specialists from the library, and faculty direction to help students formulate research questions. To guide instructors and their students through the research process, campus librarians serve as curricular consultants and coauthor assignments on research methodology with the faculty and writing director of the course. These assignments provide students with online worksheets in library skills that are directly related to reading and writing assignments from faculty members. A corresponding virtual research project helps students learn to use print and electronic resources available in the UCI library and from the California Digital Library, the UC Digital Cultures Project, and Web-based archives from universities and libraries across the country. In addition to expanding the amount of primary and secondary material available to the students, these online assignments provide self-paced instruction in research methods outside class, thereby allowing instructors to focus class time on how to use and evaluate the material rather than simply on how to find it. The global expanse of the Internet also encourages students—and, of course, their instructors—to think of themselves as part of an international scholarly community dedicated to the discovery and dissemination of knowledge for all levels of users—an analog in practice, in other words, of the international scope represented in the readings, images, and lectures. This ideal of a multilayered, participatory intellectual community among the students, faculty members, graduate students, and postdoctoral lecturers is reinforced by an effort to improve undergraduate teaching through a close connection between scholarly research, pedagogical practice, and community outreach, often to local schools whose students seldom plan on attending college. Many of these faculty members and graduate students commit to K-12 outreach programs in local schools, and they approach the first-year experience of Humanities Core as a critical transition from the students' home culture to an academic setting and hence as a connection between academia and the broader communities that surround it.

History and Pedagogical Theory of the Course

The general format of the Humanities Core course has remained constant for over thirty years, but the topics, assigned reading, writing assignments, and the faculty members giving the lectures have changed on a regular basis. The course was first offered in 1970, five years after the University of California, Irvine, was founded. The transdisciplinary and collaborative nature of the course reflected a campuswide emphasis on interdisciplinary study that resulted in new organizational forms in several fields including biological sciences, social ecology, and information and computer sciences, as well as the humanities. Originally imagined as a rather typical course in Western civilization, by 1973 the Humanities Core course had taken on the topical structure and extensive range of works and cultures that it retains today.[5]

Based on the quarter system, each year focused on three topics (e.g., in 1973-74, The Quest for Freedom; Obedience, Disobedience, and Authority;

and The Quest for Freedom in the Twentieth Century; and in 1975–76, Classical Athens, Mass Society and Its Discontents, and The Nature of Evil). As suggested by these titles, the organizational principle of any given year was less that of cultural unity and ideological coherence than of a dialectical or agonistic confrontation among competing cultures and systems of thought.[6] Conflicts among these systems thus emerged as an explicit pedagogical focus, sometimes in a single lecture and sometimes through literal dialogues when two or more lecturers took the stage to engage in a debate. The principle itself remained constant as an important source of continuity across all three quarters and over the years. Each set of topics was repeated two or, later, three times to allow lecturing faculty to get more use out of the extensive preparation required for each lecture and for the supporting material that is distributed to students and the instructional staff. On the other hand, regular changes in the topics and faculty members resulted in an unusually broad and inclusive set of readings that cumulatively reinforced the agonistic dialogue over the years.[7] The changes also anticipated most recent challenges to Eurocentric culture, the canon, and prejudices of class and gender in traditional humanist study that created such controversy in core curricula at Stanford, Columbia, and many other universities in the 1980s and 1990s, and they have facilitated a continuing adjustment to the changing interests and cultural backgrounds among the students at UCI, which now has one of the most diverse groups of undergraduates in the country.

The teaching of writing has been an essential part of Humanities Core from its beginning. The writing director for the earliest cycles of the course was Albert O. Wlecke, who was one of the first to emphasize process as part of pedagogy in composition (see Rohman and Wlecke). Wlecke's process model at times created some tension with the more conventional text-based pedagogy familiar to most of the instructors, but his theoretical sophistication and direct attention to composition pedagogy professionalized the teaching of writing in Humanities Core to a degree that was unusual for the time. In addition, as one of the faculty members lecturing in the course, Wlecke also introduced the practice of teaching writing from the podium as part of his lectures on the reading assignments. That gesture reinforced the connection between reading and writing for the students and offered a point of departure for the more sustained attention to composition in the small sections of the course.

Theoretical models for the teaching of writing in Humanities Core came and went with changes in the field and with new writing directors, who were usually professional compositionists but whose tenure in that position was generally limited to three or four years. Consequently, writing assignments in the course changed frequently and were often designed as a series of discrete exercises that reflected competing pressures from the interests of different writing directors, the topics and readings for each cycle, the expectations of the instructional staff, and the needs of students. Furthermore, the logistics of such a large course with a common set of readings inhibited the incorporation of genuine research into assignments. (Just the idea of sending over one thousand first-year students to the library seeking information about the same books and topics in the same week provoked doomsday scenarios among librarians reminiscent of scenes from *Conquest of the Planet of the Apes*, which had been filmed partly on the steps of the main library building in the early 1970s.) As a result, the writing component of Humanities Core was at times perceived to lack the sense of purpose and intellectual substance associated with the "content" of the course, and writing instruction was often subordinated to discussion of the lectures and reading assignments in sections and staff meetings.

In the late 1990s, the writing component was revised significantly to address these issues. A year-long curriculum in writing was created that is conceptually coherent and provides a clear sense of pedagogical continuity across all three quarters. First, instead of merely encouraging students to "learn to write" independent of other educational goals for conceptual development, the writing assignments were sequenced based on a radically different write-to-learn paradigm first introduced to composition pedagogy through the work of Lev Vygotsky, A. R. Luria, and Jerome Bruner and through compositionists' arguments for a broader analogy between writing and successful learning strategies (see Emig). The write-to-learn philosophy assumes that writing is a highly specialized mode of learning that has particular cognitive features distinct from—although complementary to—oral forms of communication. It also assumes that written composition maximizes the reinforcement of learning objectives because it uniquely associates process with product. Thus a successful write-to-learn curriculum links stages in conceptual development to stages in discursive development through an iterative process in which the writing assignments reinforce the analytic foci of the lectures throughout the year. The sequence begins with close readings of specific arguments and texts in the fall quarter and concludes in the spring quarter with topics that require the assimilation of information and perspectives from many sources to produce an original (or at least syncretic) argument of the students' own making. Students thus experience reading and writing as poles of a discursive continuum that makes the writing component an integral part of instruction throughout the course, and the culminating research project offers the students an opportunity to assume a more active role in their own learning modeled on the scholars and creative artists they have encountered in their reading.

Second, after analyzing student evaluations and portfolios from years past, course administrators found that explicit writing-in-the-disciplines assignments sometimes had the unintended consequence of barring first-year students from making any claims to expertise or authority in their writing activities and fragmenting the composition curriculum in the course as a whole.[8] The aim of these assignments had clearly been to familiarize students with expectations of different academic fields and to facilitate the academic equivalent of code switching among historical, literary, and philosophical discourses. Unfortunately, disciplinary differences were often perceived as exclusionary regulations that barred novices from speaking with even provisional authority and that undermined the very interdisciplinary dialogues WID is supposed to encourage. To solve this problem, pedagogical stakeholders from different disciplinary and theoretical perspectives—represented by the lecturing faculty members and section leaders in the course—were still encouraged to acknowledge and to articulate their individual instructional expectations for writing in their own departments or disciplines. However, they then worked together with the writing director to develop a consensus about rhetorical competence for the humanities at large that included general structural principles, shared analytic processes, rules of evidence and citation, a sociolinguistic account of Standard English as the prestige dialect for academic prose, and other specific transdisciplinary discursive practices that were recognizable within discipline-specific writing but not confined to the regulatory apparatus of any single field. Far from a generalized metadiscourse, this highly articulated and concrete set of shared goals and expectations for student writing now serves as the pedagogical focus for the writing component of the course, and in the hands of the best students (and instructors) it can even serve as a foundation for genuinely interdisciplinary reflection on the topics of the course.[9]

Third, technological advances in Web-based archival and reference sources alleviated many of the logistical problems associated with teaching research papers in a large class, which allowed for the inclusion of a genuine research paper as the capstone experience of the course. In addition to extending the range of material available to the students, the integration of online research into the course thus greatly enhances the scope and sophistication of assignments that can be coordinated centrally. At the same time, instruction in research methodology for print and electronic sources leads the students out of the classroom into the world through the library and the portal of the Web, thereby reinforcing the larger philosophical ambition of the course to produce more informed and engaged citizens.

Organization of the Curriculum

The first three-year cycle of the Humanities Core course fully to integrate Web-based instruction and research into the lectures and assignments occurred in 1998–2001.[10] The topic for the cycle was Exploration and Discovery, a motif intended to connect the intellectual adventure of scientific and cultural discovery that drives life at a research university with fictional and historical accounts of geographic exploration and discovery that were recounted in the assigned readings and viewings. The year was loosely organized to emphasize one general field of humanist inquiry each quarter—philosophy in the fall, literature in the winter, and history in the spring—but the lecturers and readings for each quarter were chosen to illustrate the various ways those general fields might be approached by scholars in any of the disciplines represented in our School of Humanities. So, for example, in the fall quarter a philosopher and a rhetorician lectured on Plato's *Euthyphro*; in the winter, a historian lectured on Puccini's *Madama Butterfly* and *Heart of Darkness*; and in the spring a literary historian lectured on the British colonies in New England while a historian lectured on *Robinson Crusoe*.

Fall quarter instruction for this cycle focused on rhetorical modes of literary analysis and, by emphasizing competence in argument and analysis, anticipated difficulties that students would face in the transition from writing in high school to academic writing at a research university. An opening series of lectures on intellectual discovery focused on logic, rhetoric, narrative, and image in texts by Plato, David Hume, William James, Frederick Douglass, and Sigmund Freud and in films by Alfred Hitchcock and Alain Resnais. Each work was presented as an explicit or implicit argument that was designed to persuade an audience in a particular historical context.

In this first quarter, the composition curriculum used the voyage metaphor of the course to introduce the idea that arguments could be ways to explore or discover ideas rather than merely conventional exercises for leading readers to preordained conclusions. Students learned to formalize an argument in the opening writing assignment on definition.[11] By writing a sustained argument that defined a term that might otherwise be considered self-evident — *red*, for example — students had to grapple with the complexities that an act of definition entails. To challenge the simplistic writing formulas that many students brought with them to the university, such as the abstract structure of the five-paragraph essay, this first assignment used a unique fill-in-the-blanks template in which the first paragraph was largely written by the professor of philosophy lecturing on the material for that portion of the course. Then, with each succeeding paragraph, the student was responsible for more of the required prose. Students who began the assignment merely writing clauses to finish the given sentences eventually had to write uninterrupted sequences of entire sentences in succession. Finally, as the essay approached the conclusion, students wrote the final paragraph without any language cues from the template. This essay challenged students to identify the functional characteristics of logical argument and academic discourse and then to reproduce them with increasing degrees of independence and freedom. Students who naively idealized originality were forced to consider critically the knowledge necessary to work within the parameters of a particular written form and the extent to which established academic models can facilitate the production of original argument. Because this assignment also required students to understand the basic logic in the argument of Plato's *Euthyphro*, in many ways it served as a write-to-learn exercise in which the students reenacted in their papers the logical process they were analyzing in Plato's dialogue. A less specific template and similar write-to-learn strategies were used in the second writing assignment, a counterargument responding to Hume's *Dialogue concerning Natural Religion*, and in subsequent assignments the templates grew increasingly schematic and general as the students became more experienced with the features and expectations of academic discourse. Both of these introductory writing prompts in the Exploration and Discovery cycle were produced by a team composed of a professor of philosophy, a faculty course supervisor from a department of literature, and a writing program administrator. All writing assignments presented during the course of a given year were produced by a similar process of interdepartmental collaboration, which was designed to present different disciplinary perspectives over the course of the year as a coherent set of analytic alternatives by emphasizing one approach in dialectical tension with another. For example, the two assignments described above deliberately subordinated the language of the texts to their argumentative structures, an attempt to challenge the predisposition of many students (and instructors with literary backgrounds) to treat all canonical or "serious" writing, whether literary, philosophical, or historical, as self-contained textual objects for aesthetic appreciation and formalist analysis instead of considering the logical structure of their arguments or the validity of any claims to truth they might contain.

The philosopher's reading of Plato was then followed by a professor of rhetoric, who analyzed the same text but stressed the pragmatic rhetorical motives behind Plato's choices of certain terms, examples, and argumentative strategies. That transformation of the text as an object of study prepared the students for the third writing assignment, a rhetorical analysis in which they applied the constructs of ethos, logos, and pathos from Aristotle's *Rhetoric* to a reading of a passage from *Narrative of the Life of Frederick Douglass.*

The fourth writing assignment applied the techniques of sustained and systematic analysis to visual images in Hitchcock's film *Rebecca*, with the objective of having students extend the psychoanalytic interpretation of the film proposed in lecture through a close reading of a particular scene. The transition from analyzing verbal passages to analyzing visual images was difficult for many students, but it was supported through the use of Web-based RealPlayer and QuickTime software that enabled students to view scenes repeatedly; stop, start, and review them at will; and even enlarge specific frames for more detailed viewing of particular frames or shots to search for an assigned motif such as women's costumes or the consumption of food.[12] These clips allowed the students to study the cinematic scenes repeatedly as they would a printed text. On the basis of Web traffic logs that indicate thousands of visits to the sites with the film clips, it appeared that students were much more likely to focus on details of cinematic form when they had Web-based media to supplement their initial viewings of the film in the traditional setting of an auditorium, and the ability to freeze frames and replay whole scenes produced essays that approached the detail and precision of more conventional textual analysis.

In the winter, the syllabus for Voyages of Discovery presented fictional narratives of mythic and imaginary journeys from literature around the world in conjunction with historical, geographical, and ideological analysis and research. Whereas students in the first quarter focused on building the analytic and rhetorical skills to make arguable claims about literature, in the second quarter they focused on the language and literary devices of the works to develop detailed links between abstract argumentative claims and the linguistic features of corresponding textual evidence. In this quarter, literary texts were presented not only as arguments but also as cultural artifacts in dialogue with the world at specific historical moments. That dialogue both articulated and contested the norms of the cultures in which they were produced, while dramatizing the ambiguities of cultural contact with others in both canonical and noncanonical texts: the *Odyssey, Journey to the West, The Tempest, Heart of Darkness, Madama Butterfly, M. Butterfly,* and *Second-Class Citizen.* In their presentations, the faculty members lecturing this quarter worked closely with specific passages from the text and modeled connections among different kinds of literary and historical analysis, often by way of illustrating effective strategies for approaching the essay assignment and formulating arguable theses. Many of the lectures focused on the role of gender relations in cultural contact, but the thematic continuity of feminist criticism was varied by the marked disciplinary differences in lectures by a twentieth-century historian, a Shakespearean scholar, and a specialist in Chinese literature and language.

In the writing assignments, students began the quarter by performing a pair of related close readings, which constituted the fifth and sixth assignments in the year-long sequence.[13] The general series of assignments on writing about literature followed the traditional order of B. S. Bloom's hierarchy of cognitive skills: knowledge, comprehension, application, analysis, synthesis, and evaluation.[14] In the first of these close readings, a textual analysis of twenty to thirty lines from the *Odyssey*, students were expected to focus on specific features of the language in the passage to make claims about a particular aspect of cultural contact. As they were able to do in the assignment on *Rebecca*, students could use the Web to support their close reading with information that would otherwise be inaccessible to these inexperienced scholars. They could access information from etymological reference works, classical encyclopedias, and concordances to better understand the original Greek in which the *Odyssey* was performed and eventually written down. In making tools of classical philology and linguistics available even to the novice reader of a translated text, the course facilitated an intellectual process that Gregory Crane has called "deep reading," which supplements New Critical methods of close reading by integrating information from linguistics, history, and cultural studies. Through hyperlinks to the Perseus Project, students could access a range of morphological aids and archeological evidence to understand better the denotative and connotative significance of words in the original Greek. With the electronic interface they could also study the frequency

of particular phrases and locate other passages that used similar vocabulary. Using this hypertextual scholarly material, eighteen-year-olds could
speak with at least some authority on subjects usually too sophisticated
for first-year students, as this writer does in her analysis of Odysseus's isolation at the moment of building a makeshift shelter in the land of the
Phaiakians:

> He "heaped [himself] a bed to sleep on," made primitively with his own bare
> hands (V.482). In the translation, Odysseus gathers dead leaves to make him-
> self a cushion to sleep on. It is interesting, however, that Homer chose the
> word *eunen*, a bed, rather than the Greek word *stibas*, meaning a makeshift
> bed of straw or leaves. It seems to be that *stibas* would be the more fitting
> choice of words; however, Homer chooses to keep his depiction of the bed
> vague and simple. In doing so, Homer is allowing the possibility that the bed
> Odysseus made is much more complicated than a simple pile of leaves. Such an
> uncivilized and primitive bed does not show much about individuality, whereas
> Odysseus' complicated design is yet another expression of his identity. Homer
> uses the same word, *eunen*, when speaking of Telemachus' bed, a bed of great
> importance and honor (I.427). The word is used again by Circe as she speaks
> to Odysseus about going to her bed (X.297). Here, *eunen* refers to a divine bed
> worthy enough to belong to a goddess. Homer uses this word to describe beds
> that are honorable and important. Unlike his bed at Ithaka that is described as
> *lechos*, or a marriage bed, this bed that he makes out of leaves has no sexual
> value; it is purely one of honor.

This student's reading follows a chain of possible linguistic substitutions
suggested by exploring the electronic features of the Perseus database to
make an argument about the connotations of a particular instance of language choice. While obviously lacking the authority of a genuine classicist
and translator, the student nonetheless can begin to experiment with some
of the scholarly practices associated with such expertise and thereby significantly extend her familiarity with what scholars in humanities do when
they read and write. Even at this relatively naive level, her work joins the
tools of reading and writing to epitomize what George Landow, Michael
Joyce, Nancy Kaplan, and other theorists of electronic intertextuality and
high-tech pedagogy have argued: the experience of hypertext itself challenges and obviates distinctions between production and reception—and,

we might add, between the capacities of expert and novice to make use of the resources available to scholars in the humanities.

In the second assignment of the quarter, a close reading of a scene from William Shakespeare's *The Tempest*, students went beyond the analysis of specific linguistic features of the text to grapple with the ways that texts may use literary devices to present more than one point of view. If in the fall the emphasis was on abstracting a single argument from the readings, then in the winter lecturers showed how the language of texts may be read against their explicit or overt claims. A unit on textual explication guided students through the problem of characterizing what a text doesn't say using evidence from what it does, and then it focused their attention on the complex functioning of tropes, ambiguity, and omission in literary texts. The results are evident in this student's analysis of Caliban's curse:

> Caliban's initial attempt to defy Prospero's power via a verbal curse actually gives Prospero more authority as master in that the curse acknowledges the duke's ultimate power. Caliban begins his speech with the vengeful request that all the evil "infections" (2.2.1) under the sun "fall" (2.2.2) upon the "tyrant" (2.2.160) Prospero. While Caliban wishes for Prospero to be so harmed by sickness, the slave does not have the power to make this happen. Instead, he must request that these evils "fall" (2.2.2) of their own accord upon Prospero. Caliban's lack of authority because of his condition as a slave is immediately contrasted to that of Prospero the master, who can "bid" (2.2.7) or literally command not just diseases but powerful "spirits" (2.2.3) to harm Caliban. Caliban's agents of destruction are inanimate infections that only have the power to rise and "fall" (2.2.2) from the earth. The slaves under Prospero's command are immortal spirits who can "bite" (2.2.10), "hiss" (2.2.14), and take action against Caliban.

Like the student who wrote about the *Odyssey*, this student pays close attention to the denotations and connotations of language in the text, but here the writer must also address the ambivalence of the curse and the aspects of Caliban's speech act that are merely implied rather than stated explicitly. (A variation of the prompt encouraged students to write about different possible stagings of the speech and consider how performance and particular explication strategies are related.)

After two assignments based on close readings of passages assigned from individual literary works, students progressed to reading an entire text in conjunction with a second text. This assignment asked them to choose multiple passages from Buchi Emecheta's *Second-Class Citizen* and read them alongside Conrad's *Heart of Darkness*. It emphasized the move from analyzing discrete passages to creating synthetic accounts of complete narrative structures in both novels. To keep students from retreating to truisms inherent in conventional comparison and contrast assignments, the prompt described a particular situation in which an argument about cultural value in a postcolonial context must be made, and it then asked students to assume a persona other than their own to write within that situation.

In the spring quarter, Discovering America, the lecturers discussed the history and literature of Spanish and English conquest and colonization; they provided historical readings of literary texts and, conversely, literary readings of historical texts. This combination of literary and historical analysis was reflected in the writing assignments for this quarter, which joined analysis, argument, and research. While students previously focused almost exclusively on close readings that used direct quotation to comment on specific passages or images in the assigned texts, in this quarter students began to use research, secondary sources, and paraphrase to link texts to specific historical events.

In the first assignment, students were asked to take a position about who was the better historian between two manifestly flawed scholars from the 1950s and the 1970s, respectively the Columbus booster Samuel Eliot Morison and the Columbus critic Hans Koning. Students used both a primary source and a scholarly secondary source other than those by Morison and Koning. Presented with a large database of articles about Columbus from Millersville University, students had to differentiate between scholarly academic articles and news stories, and the task of locating an appropriate secondary source was facilitated by exercises on evaluating sources from two Web-based tutorials.[15]

In the next writing and research assignment, students wrote an essay based on causal analysis that examined historical narratives of conquest by Bernal Díaz and Álvar Núñez Cabeza de Vaca. Students were asked to explain the cause of a particular historical event described by these conquistadores, and each class generated explanations and permutations in discussion as part of a larger dialogue on causality carried out by the historian and literary scholars lecturing on these texts. Although these sixteenth-century authors often provide theological or nationalistic causal explanations for the events they describe, students were encouraged to draw on the work of contemporary historians and literary critics to consider alternative possibilities that might only be implied or suggested by the text of the primary source. As in the previous assignment, students had to integrate a scholarly secondary source, generally an electronic journal article from JSTOR, and be able to paraphrase its argument accurately. In this assignment, however, causal analysis was treated as an interpretive activity that approached cause and effect relations within particular disciplinary methodologies. Students read one chapter in the *Core Writer's Handbook* on causal analysis by a team of philosophy graduate students; this was then juxtaposed with another chapter on causal analysis by a historian serving as a postdoctoral discussion leader in the course.

This causal analysis assignment is, in many ways, a model writing task in the Humanities Core course in that it

> draws attention to methodological differences involved in interpretive activity;
> presents literature in the context of disciplinary approaches outside the English department;
> requires the writer's engagement with scholarly secondary sources and multiple primary sources;
> makes the positioning of the author in an academic debate central to the writing activity; and
> capitalizes on the availability of new technology to create connections between reading and writing.

The final assignment was a documentary research project that required students to apply these skills in the analysis of an early American British text, such as Mary Rowlandson's captivity narrative. This capstone assignment was a cumulative paper in which students were expected to be able to use all the techniques and modes covered throughout the year, including definition, rhetorical analysis, counterargument, image analysis, textual explication, comparison and contrast, application, evaluation, and causal analysis, as well as the research methods from the discovery tasks. The following example from a student's essay on Rowlandson's text shows the integration of primary and secondary source material and the degree of her facility with both direct quotation and paraphrase:

> The reference to the second week, in which Rowlandson's "stomach grew very faint for want of something" and yet she struggled to "get down their filthy trash" (79), is clearly the most significant aspect of the passage, as during this week evolves an important struggle between the starvation of the body and the starvation of the soul. Prior to this week, the Soul was strong and neutral; after this week, the stomach identified certain aspects of Native American culture not only as an acceptable substitute for their trespasses, but also a delicacy and divine taste. However, during this week, Rowlandson's conflict between stomach and soul reaches an impasse. This evolution is essential to understanding Rowlandson's views toward food preparation and consumption and how they are frustrated and tested during her captivity. The connection between food and religion within the Puritan tradition is an important one for Rowlandson at this juncture in her captivity. Susan Mizruchi argues that food becomes "a language for expressing God's wisdom (when God himself is consumed especially); and food is a language for articulating boundaries" (Mizruchi 471). This is a very important point, in terms of taking the Eucharist and in the Puritan tradition of mirroring every meal after the Lord's Supper.

This student's analysis of Rowlandson's captivity narrative combines literary modes of analysis with material history, the study of cultural products and lifestyles associated with the production and consumption of material goods, and theology and anthropology. In the paper as a whole, however, these other forms of analysis are clearly subordinated to a literary reading that focuses on the language of Rowlandson's narrative and the discursive conventions of the Puritan Eucharist on which Rowlandson operates. This focus appropriately reflects the emphasis of Humanities Core on the centrality of language and precise methods of reading and writing in all forms of academic inquiry. In addition, the use of nonliterary evidence and scholarship to support the analysis of Rowlandson's narrative and the broad symbolic motifs of her religious imagery also exemplifies the aim of Humanities Core to provide students with the full range of knowledge and skills that will enable them to use historical information, logical argument, and the great works of world culture as a window on themselves and the world they share with the scholars and artists who came before them.

Assessment: How Calls for Standards and Diversity Don't Necessarily Conflict

Assessing the success of these curricular reforms is an important objective for the ongoing research agenda associated with the Humanities Core course. Assessment is overseen by the writing director, Elizabeth Losh, and supported by intramural and extramural funding.[16] That agenda includes the regular monitoring of broad programmatic goals and more specific outcome measures related to student writing in various sample groups, within individual sections, and across the course as a whole. This research utilizes tools ranging from traditional surveys of student attitudes in course evaluations and more specific polls of research practices and language usage to analyses of quantifiable data from the writing sample and verbal reasoning portions of the MCAT examination and from blind readings of essays by multiple readers using holistic or primary-trait scoring. Additionally, since UCI is a leader in student informatics readiness and electronic educational environments and has an extraordinarily diverse campus of language communities, the entire student body is polled in surveys that focus on two areas of particular campuswide interest: the use in the freshman year of digital and conventional library research resources and prefreshman language and literacy experiences.

The multimodal study of information literacy practices among students in Humanities Core has been complemented by information about Web traffic on particular library and course Web sites and through the systematic review of results from the various online exercises in research methodology. Other measures include written evaluations from students and instructors, Web traffic logs, transcripts and reports from focus groups, collection of exceptional student writing samples through essay contests, data from the campus library about the number of queries from students in the course, surveys on pilot projects, and, of course, grades. Findings from this research are often counterintuitive to those who assume that electronic research inevitably undermines traditional library research skills. For example, among a rarefied group of twenty-two nominees for research prizes, the number of students who said that their use of the campus library was increased by the availability of digital resources was actually nine percent higher than the number of those who said that the virtual archive had decreased their conventional library use.

The centralized structure and common curriculum of Humanities Core is particularly conducive to large-scale composition research and assessment projects. The enrolled student body is markedly heterogeneous and includes a full spectrum of entering competencies, from basic writers who fail the UC placement examination in composition to honors students whose prose is already fluent and mature. Quantitative measurements derived from data about high school preparation, undergraduate major, ethnicity, language background, and family income level provide a valuable context for the writing program administrator-researcher. And because the assignments and instruction are standardized, specific at-risk (or successful) student populations can be targeted for study, and the effectiveness of specific strategies for intervention can be evaluated against a more general norm or control group. In addition, the longitudinal assessment of student progress is supported by a major research project with a six-year history in which approximately ten percent of students are chosen at random to participate in a year-long comprehensive study. Students submit their writing portfolios electronically, so that a full sequence of finished essays can be linked to the student's digital profile of demographic and academic information. This process maintains the anonymity of students and preserves the integrity of periodic blind assessments of typical patterns of writing development by specialists from outside the program and future longitudinal study over the four-year experience. Furthermore, because the database consists of searchable electronic copy, essays that cite the same passages or sources can easily be grouped together for comparative purposes, and even the structural morphology of sentence-level and paragraph-level constructions can be analyzed more efficiently according to schema like those envisioned by Richard Haswell (see his "Documenting Improvement").

Results of this research have been presented at national and international conferences,[17] and they are applied in the continual revision of the assignments as well as incorporated into more general administrative decisions regarding academic planning and the allocation of resources across the campus. These results vary among these different foci and methods, but this research consistently confirms the pedagogical efficacy of integrating the teaching of critical reading and analytic writing within a large, highly centralized interdisciplinary course utilizing extensive Web-based instruction and research. Qualitative analyses by external reviewers in 2001 and 2004 praised the Humanities Core course for fostering a "culture of writing" and for presenting a "model of collaborative academic planning." Based on personal interviews with students and instructors as well as comprehensive review of course materials and evaluations, these peer assessments by faculty members from other universities have encouraged the continued commitment of institutional capital for what is admittedly an expensive and labor-intensive enterprise compared with many composition programs and more conventional first-year English courses.[18] More recently, these qualitative judgments about the success of the course have been corroborated by quantitative data that reinforce the intuitive conclusions and, at times, have surprised even supporters of the course. For example, for many years the conventional wisdom at UCI had been that students who take a stand-alone conventional composition course performed better on the writing sample and verbal reasoning portions of the MCAT examination than those who took Humanities Core. However, when this assumption was tested in 2003 with data from 153 students from the August 2002 MCAT testing session, it was proved false: Humanities Core students outperformed their single-track peers on the verbal reasoning section and did equally well as their single-track peers on the writing sample. Far from being distracted from the task of learning basic expository writing skills by the reading assignments, lectures, and discussions—a common concern about such courses—Humanities Core students were shown to perform as well on quantitative indexes of writing competence as their peers enrolled in a conventional stand-alone composition course.[19]

Other parts of the research agenda have addressed other common questions about such intellectually ambitious, interdisciplinary courses that integrate the teaching of reading and writing. Students whose writing skills are judged substandard by some measure have traditionally been excluded from core curricula and segregated into remedial courses defined by a focus on surface features like grammar and syntax or otherwise limited to direct instruction in writing. An experiment in the Humanities Core course suggests, however, that the benefits of writing instruction may be compounded when combined with the more complex conceptual analysis associated with the formal lectures and extensive reading assignments of an integrated curriculum. For the past four years, some students who underperformed in the first quarter of Humanities Core have been enrolled in the second quarter in a specially designed section that includes intensive intervention on writing and gives them the option of taking part in weekly one-on-one hourly consultations with a professional writing counselor from the university's Learning and Academic Resources Center. Data clearly demonstrate that students who participated in this pilot program not only were statistically more likely to earn higher writing grades that quarter than those in a similar low-performing control group; they also continued to outperform nonparticipating peers in the subsequent quarter of writing instruction in a regular section. In the 1999–2000 year, students in the experimental group had mean writing grades that were thirty-three percent higher than peers in the control group in the winter and maintained grades that were still sixteen percent higher in the spring without any supplemental assistance after having been mainstreamed. In the second year of the program in 2000–01, the long-term benefits were even more marked: the experimental group outperformed students in the control group by twenty-five percent in the winter and thirty-one percent in the spring.

Similar concerns are often expressed about other kinds of students in such courses: Does the current digital divide in access to computing and electronic resources privilege students with particular socioeconomic advantages? Do students with a home language other than English find multitasking in more than one discipline or channel of communication too demanding, given issues of linguistic interference that they bring to the situation of writing? This latter concern is especially apropos at UCI, where approximately sixty-four percent of students speak a home language other than English and many report more than one second language spoken in the increasingly complex and diverse southern California ethnic enclaves from which they come.[20] To address this issue, UCI has sponsored a three-year ongoing home-language survey that is currently composed of data from over 2,500 detailed questionnaires and supplemented by in-depth case studies with ethnographic interviews. The survey asks students to report on the genres in which they read and write in their home languages, to provide information about their prior academic experiences with learning a second language in a school setting, and to assess their personal sense of competence in using the conventions of Standard English. The significance of this work cannot be overemphasized, given the large number of highly successful biliterate and sometimes triliterate students in the study, from whom we can gain more information about strategies deployed by high-achieving students who defy stereotypes predicated on a failure model.[21] In the first preliminary findings, researchers discovered that students were substantially underreporting their home-language experiences, perhaps from fear of the stigma associated with the ESL label. This effect was particularly marked among the highest achieving students. For example, in response to a general administrative survey used as an intake tool by the campus, only thirty percent of students from the Humanities Core course who won prestigious prizes from the UCI's nationally recognized Undergraduate Research Opportunity Program (UROP) in 2002 initially reported a home language other than English; however, a review of their detailed questionnaires in the Humanities Core research project indicated that the actual number of UROP winners with second-language backgrounds was seventy percent.

These large-scale studies reinforce what for many instructors has been a long-standing intuitive faith in the connection between teaching reading and teaching writing, and they also provide an important evidentiary correlative for the more abstract theoretical arguments associated with the debate over first-year English. In addition, they point to the potential for translating the Humanities Core course to campuses that increasingly rely on hybrid instruction that combines traditional and virtual learning environments and to institutions that draw students from multilingual communities created by patterns of global immigration. Since the Boyer Commission recommended the development of more courses like Humanities Core—research-oriented, writing intensive sequences organized around a common first-year experience—the forces of technology and globalization have only increased the need for these curricular reforms. With such high stakes, it is all the more imperative that we apply the highest standards of research and evidence to the evaluation of these courses if we are to justify the time, energy, and resources required to meet that need.

The Humanities Core course described in this essay differs significantly from traditional first-year English, both in its content and in its relation to the whole university. The most significant differences are a multidisciplinary approach to the humanities that spans different historical periods and national cultures and that builds on connections among various media and disciplinary perspectives; the complete integration of reading, writing, and research throughout the course in all assignments; an emphasis on the technological as well as the discursive dimensions of literacy as the basis of intellectual community and intercultural communication; and its function as a forum for collaborative teaching that spans not only disciplinary boundaries but also professional divisions among students, postdoctoral lecturers, and faculty members. Some of these features are products of the particular institutional history of the course and the present relation of Humanities Core to the rest of our university; other differences reflect a distinction between English courses and introductory humanities courses that is customary at most universities. As these features work together in the curriculum of the Humanities Core course, however, they constitute a coherent and purposeful response to the current trend in first-year education toward discrete, heterogeneous courses with specific cultural and methodological foci that enforce misleading barriers between reading and writing, between research and expression, and between the content of texts and the discursive and technological practices by which those texts exist and function in the university and in contemporary society. These barriers are intellectually indefensible, and they are socially and institutionally ineffectual. Just as it is anachronistic to treat the English language today as coterminous with any single national culture, so, too, is it misleading to interpret, analyze, or compose written texts without recognizing their inevitable and profound continuity with aural and visual experience in today's world. It is equally imperative to understand the dependence of these media on the technologies of production and transmission that join them together in a global network that defies compartmentalization along traditional disciplinary or national lines. That comprehensive perspective on the cultural significance and social function of any single text, medium, or methodology is the primary pedagogical objective of Humanities Core. It also constitutes the principle of coherence that unites the multifarious approaches, forms of instruction, and pedagogical activities in which students participate throughout the year, and it serves as the foundation for intellectual community among students across our campus and among tenure-track faculty members, postdoctoral lecturers, and graduate students throughout the humanities.

That said, it would be equally misleading to imagine that such a perspective radically departs from the traditional objectives of first-year English or that Humanities Core displaces courses focused more exclusively on the conventional objects of literary study, that is, literary texts in the English language and the teaching of writing. The sequence of nine writing assignments described above addresses all twelve learning objectives outlined in the former MLA President Elaine Showalter's book *Teaching Literature*, where she argues for a closer connection between teaching and the scholarly practices of literary study.[22] More specifically, over the course of the academic year, Humanities Core also aims to connect writing explicitly to many of the aspects of contemporary literary theory that Showalter claims are essential to connecting literary scholarship to literary pedagogy, including "performance, authorship, genre, intertextuality, hybridity, subjectivity, structure, agency, chronology, canon formation, and narrative" ("Teaching").

In fact, what Showalter identifies as major trends in contemporary literary discourse are precisely those that benefit most from the presentation of literary works in the context of other disciplines in the humanities, and the converse is true for methodologies based on other humanist disciplines: the practices and values of any discipline are most visible when studied in dialogue with those from other fields. The operating assumption of the Humanities Core course is that discipline-specific instruction is essential to postsecondary education and that the particular objects of knowledge inherent to disciplinary training—in this case, literature (English or American or anglophone), culture, expository writing, and so on—are appropriate foci for undergraduate and graduate programs. What is not appropriate is to introduce students to those objects and the disciplines in courses that isolate those topics from the more general cultural, intellectual, and institutional contexts from which they have emerged and in which they continue to function.

There are, of course, benefits to be gained from exposing students at all levels to great works of literature, and the teaching of writing certainly deserves a central role in all undergraduate education. But the conceptual depth of literary study, the full complexity of written discourse, and the social and historical weight of the English language as part of our experience within and beyond the university will be visible to students only if they are equipped to understand how those disciplinary topoi are situated in relation to the other kinds of knowledge, media, and technologies of communication that surround us. Those relations, and the social practices that support them today and in the past, are therefore the most effective focus for first-year instruction, and they must be embodied fully in pedagogical objectives, the conceptual content of the curriculum, and the reading and writing of the students. Such a focus avoids superficial gestures toward breadth and the empty rhetoric of interdisciplinarity—respectively the past and present banes of first-year education in the humanities. It also establishes a clear purpose for first-year English that is different in kind from the academic programs students will encounter in the rest of their educational careers, but no less rigorous and respectable in its content and pedagogical practice.

Notes

1. David Laurence has also commented on this "intellectual fragmentation" and claims it is leading to the "organizational atomization" of departments of English throughout the country (15).

2. This shift has already started. The institutional functions served by freshman English in the past, understood apart from academic objectives, have become the focus of a new attention to the first-year experience at many colleges and

universities across the United States (for an overview of twenty-five such programs see Cutright). Much of this attention has been directed to the development of learning communities, residential academies, freshman seminars, and other programs designed to identify effective practices and survival strategies and impart them directly to students at the beginning of their college careers. *The 2000 National Survey of First-Year Seminar Programs* found that many such programs pay some attention to the content and methodologies of various disciplines, but usually with respect to developing academic skills rather than intensive intellectual engagement with a particular discipline or body of material. Most tend to emphasize advising, counseling, and other support services associated with what might be termed academic socialization, with "ease of transition/adjustment to college" the second most commonly stated objective of first-year seminars after "develop[ing] academic skills" (Natl. Resource Center 16). Tellingly, even at four-year institutions, fewer than half of these seminars are housed in an academic college, division, or academic affairs office (as opposed to an administrative unit or support center), and well under ten percent of the courses have a home in an academic department (60–64). Questions of programmatic self-interest aside, separating the practices and ends of academic socialization from rigorous engagement with the content and issues of intellectual inquiry raises serious questions about what we can—and should—expect from courses taken by students during their first year.

3. UCI has a diverse student population in which most students report a home language other than English. Large numbers of students from Chinese, Korean, Vietnamese, Spanish, and Filipino linguistic minorities are represented in the course, although no single second-language paradigm predominates. Even within the same language group, students report varying levels of literacy, spoken fluency, and cultural immersion. In addition, these students manifest problems typical among all developing writers who are still acquiring knowledge of the conventions of academic English. To serve this population, the year-long curriculum regularly addresses sentence-level writing pedagogy along with the conceptual topics of the assignments. Sentence-level instruction in Humanities Core emphasizes the connections between grammar and logic and aims to avoid the pitfalls of writing instruction for second-language students that Barbara Kroll describes in "The Rhetoric/Syntax Split." Furthermore, in the Exploration and Discovery cycle of the course, a faculty member with a second-language background lectures each quarter, thereby giving students an opportunity to see models for success in academic culture from persons with biliterate backgrounds.

4. Although the Humanities Core course acknowledges the complexity of developmental patterns for individual writers and the need for four-year curricular planning, this sequence is aimed at substantive outcomes by the end of the freshman year. Humanities Core also incorporates the "WPA Outcomes Statement for First-Year Composition" for the current professional consensus on reasonable exit goals for rhetorical knowledge, critical thinking, use of writing processes, and familiarity with conventions of written discourse.

5. This account of the early years of the course is based on McCulloch 229–30.

6. Brook Thomas, a former director of the course, described this principle as "teaching the conflicts." The phrase is based on Gerald Graff's *Beyond the Culture Wars: How Teaching the Conflicts Can Revitalize American Education*, but generally this pedagogical strategy reflects a form of American liberalism that Lionel Trilling expressed over fifty years ago: "A culture is not a flow, nor even a confluence. The form of its existence is a struggle, or at least a debate — it is nothing if not a dialectic" (qtd. in Thomas 121).

7. Course topics from 1970–95 are described in Thomas.

8. As Michel Foucault points out, such power struggles between disciplines are perhaps inevitable because any disciplinary organization will seek to appropriate specific forms of knowledge and exclude competing parties from access and dissemination (*L'ordre*).

9. In the postmodern university these interdisciplinary teams can also imagine new moves or new games in discourse like those described by Jean-François Lyotard (51–52). One measure of success in this area is the frequency with which lecturing faculty members cite the importance of their interdisciplinary collaborative experiences in Humanities Core in written acknowledgments for their own scholarly books or articles.

10. The archived Web site for 1998–2001 is accessible at www.humanities.uci .edu/mclark/HumCore2001/Core2000Archive/index.html. The authors of this essay were the director (Clark) and writing director (Losh) for that cycle. (The Web site for the current cycle of the Humanities Core course can be viewed at http://eee.uci.edu/programs/humcore/. The director is Gail Hart; Elizabeth Losh continues as writing director.) Model examples of Web-based lectures on the archived site are those by Robert Moeller (winter quarter) and Michael P. Clark (spring quarter); the spring quarter as a whole best exemplifies how Web-based instruction can be integrated consistently throughout all the lectures and assignments, including the capstone research project. The sequence of assignments connected to the curriculum in composition is available under Assignments for each quarter. The year-long online sequence of research assignments is available under Discovery Tasks for each quarter.

11. For the actual assignments, see the links to Essay Assignments on the fall quarter Web site at www.humanities.uci.edu/mclark/HumCore2001/Core2000Archive/Fall.html.

12. See the clips at www.humanities.uci.edu/mclark/HumCore2001/Core2000Archive/Films.html.

13. See Assignments at www.humanities.uci.edu/mclark/HumCore2001/Core2000Archive/Winter.html.

14. Although challenged by many recent scholars, Bloom's hierarchy and the vocabulary of certain aspects of older preprocess modes of writing pedagogy, such as the Toulmin model mentioned earlier, can be useful as a common interdisciplinary

language for composition instruction by nonspecialist instructors if those terms are adapted within more contemporary pedagogical systems.

15. See the updated version of the Millersville site at http://muWeb.millersville .edu/~columbus/.

16. Funding for research was provided by the Teaching and Learning with Technology grant program for the University of California system and by UCI's International Center for Writing and Translation and by local grants from the Humanities Center, the Instructional Resource Center, the Division of Undergraduate Education, the Office of the Campus Writing Coordinator, and Network and Academic Computing.

17. E.g., Digital Resources in the Humanities, National Resource Center on the First-Year Experience, Conference on College Communication and Composition, Computers and Writing.

18. For a criticism of the "core" paradigm from a purported cost-benefit perspective, see Lee Ann Carroll. This essay obviously takes issue with Carroll's claim that the genre of the "Great Books paper" is "not directly transferable to other writing situations" and, by way of counterargument, points to her observation that students in her own longitudinal study found this type of course to be "a high-light of their college experience" (81).

19. It could be counterargued that a portion of this MCAT statistical effect is attributable to the disproportionate number of high-performing students who are self-selected by their choosing to take what is perceived by students as the more difficult or challenging interdisciplinary curricular option. However, the authors of this essay would reply that qualitative data and the enthusiastic expressions of approval for the stated course objectives from administrators and faculty members in both the School of Biological Sciences and the campuswide honors program support our interpretation of these data.

20. In 2002, the top ten second language groups were as follows: Chinese (12%), Tagalog (10%), Vietnamese (8%), Korean (8%), Spanish (5%), East Indian languages and dialects (5%), Farsi (2%), Arabic (2%), Armenian (1%), and Japanese (1%).

21. This research was conducted in conjunction with the campus writing coordinator Susan Jarratt and will be part of a forthcoming essay on biliterate writers and transnational identification.

22. Showalter's objectives include greater subtlety and sophistication in the student's awareness of textual features such as tropes and other complex uses of language; increased understanding of connections between the text and the biographical, historical, and cultural contexts in which it was written and is read; and a heightened sense of how texts can be used to think creatively about one's own experiences and relations with other people.

Reinventing Literary History at Barnard College

*A*t first glance, Reinventing Literary History at Barnard College looks suspiciously like a survey of English and comparative literature rather than a composition course. This new first-year English program also features an evening lecture series designed to provide portraits of literary genres and movements ranging from classical epic to modernism. Initially, students sometimes wonder how reading Milton's dense poetry and convoluted theology will teach them to write straightforward, logical essays. A dose of Ernest Hemingway's "clean, well-lighted" prose might seem more to the point. But the vast majority of Barnard students can already compose disembodied versions of Hemingway's miraculously simple declarative sentences. They can even produce competent five-paragraph essays. Nevertheless, the distinction between description and analysis eludes them. Technically, they can write their way from here to there, but, as Gertrude Stein would lament, there's no there there. At Barnard, we invoke literary history to fill the magnitude of this contemporary void. Since our institutional raison d'être as a women's college challenges exclusionary pedagogical and aesthetic pretensions, we offer courses in three parallel traditions: Legacy of the Mediterranean, The Americas, and Women and Culture. Our goal is to teach students to engage in written dialogue with literary history, to employ revisionist critical methodologies that give voice to Eve's paradigmatic defiance of Milton's canonical muse.

Form and content are as inextricably linked as chickens and eggs, despite academic quarrels over which came first. Often, this fundamental expository fact has been lost on first-year Barnard students who have been admitted into a Seven Sisters college on the strength of purely formal proficiency. Their superficial mastery of form exacerbates a profound failure of content. To compensate for this imbalance, the pedagogical pendulum between form and content swings dangerously close to the latter of the

Margaret Vandenburg

two extremes in Reinventing Literary History. Larger institutional considerations have also propelled us in this direction. Five years ago, when Barnard's
Committee on Instruction embarked on a review of the college's extensive
general education requirements, they heeded the English department's plea
to abolish AP exemption for First-Year English.[1] We enhanced the literary
component of the new First-Year English: Reinventing Literary History
program to accommodate the influx of students who, though proficient on
paper, might need to be convinced that learning to write intelligently about
challenging texts is an ongoing process.

For all its attention to content, Reinventing Literary History is still a
composition course. We encourage our instructors to conduct seminar
discussions as though they were workshops on the construction of individual paragraphs in an essay written, each day, by the collaborative efforts
of the entire class. In this way, composition transcends formal proficiency
to become an integral part of our critical methodology. Student comments
are interpreted in the context of a larger series of arguments formulated
in response to interpretive approaches implicit in each literary work. To
this extent, our methodology is informed by structuralism's emphasis on
inherent formal properties that help to elucidate meaning and content.[2] At
the same time, we place each work securely in its historical moment, thus
balancing more formalist approaches with the new historicism. Our students learn to explicate rather than explain, writing less as external observers than as translators fluent in the language of the works. Ideally, their
arguments develop organically, not unlike Michelangelo's statues emerging from within the stone's essential core rather than being carved, however artfully, from without. Composition courses featuring more purely
rhetorical instruction have been lauded for teaching students to use various modes of exposition and analysis. Though performing this work less
directly, Reinventing Literary History students benefit from the theoretical premise that content is embedded in form. I would venture to say that
at Barnard the idea that engagement with formally complex and nuanced
literature produces more layered and sophisticated writing has ceased to
be merely theoretical. Since the inauguration of this new first-year English
program, colleagues throughout the college have remarked that our stu-

dents are more analytically circumspect than those previously trained more exclusively in rhetorical and research skills.

The great virtue of teaching writing through the lens of literature is that this model prepares students to write effectively across the curriculum. There are, of course, many valuable approaches to teaching the art of exposition. Though biology departments are not clamoring to sponsor composition programs, one might assign nothing but scientific treatises without jeopardizing the process of learning to write well. But the literary model advances students' analytic abilities, which are brought to bear less directly when reading more descriptive writing examples. Writers from diverse disciplines often agree that moving from analytic to descriptive writing is more easily accomplished than moving in the opposite direction, not because one is necessarily superior to the other but because analysis involves more conceptual mobility than description. To ensure that analytic expertise is sufficiently integrated into more purely expository skills, literature must remain the lens rather than the subject of writing courses. In this way, programs like Reinventing Literary History prove flexible enough to accommodate students of all proficiency levels. Less accomplished writers can practice more straightforward composition while more advanced writers hone their interpretive and argumentative prowess. Interdisciplinary methodologies, including the new historicism, feminism, Marxism, and postcolonial and psychoanalytic criticism, deflect the danger of concentrating too exclusively on skills related to literary criticism.

Hence, despite the ambitious curricular goals implicit in its imposing title, the central text of Reinventing Literary History is student writing. The pedagogical premise of the first-year English programs represented in this volume is that teaching students to appreciate well-wrought literature enhances their ability to write well. To this end, we engage in close reading of literary works that are surrounded by primary sources and images assembled on the elaborate Web site attached to the course. In addition to improving writing across the curriculum, this interdisciplinary framework fosters independent research and interpretive originality. The evening lecture series, featuring distinguished professors from the larger Columbia academic community, facilitates moving from one historical period to the next without disrupting the seminar format of biweekly classes. In an effort to demonstrate that none of the three traditions represented in the curriculum is really as dead (and white) as naysayers claim, we schedule excursions to Metropolitan Opera productions, Shakespeare plays, and museums, most notably the Schomburg, the Guggenheim, and the Museum of Modern Art. Writing assignments include explications de texte, thematic structural analyses, and interdisciplinary research essays that demand not only facility negotiating the Web site but also familiarity with Columbia University's vast library system. Writing the final research paper trains students to cite sources and balance multiple analytic voices without sacrificing the primacy of their own arguments.

Each of Reinventing Literary History's three rubrics—Legacy of the Mediterranean, Women and Culture, and The Americas—features a chronological progression of literature that concomitantly constitutes and critiques seminal aesthetic and cultural traditions. The Legacy of the Mediterranean explicitly pays homage to the great-books tradition, while the other two rubrics call attention to the constraints of canonicity:

Legacy of the Mediterranean

Autumn: *Hymn to Demeter*; *The Bacchae*; *Aeneid*; *Inferno*; *Canterbury Tales*; Shakespeare play, New York City production; *The Princesse of Clèves*

Spring: *Paradise Lost*; *Candide*; *The Prelude*; *Frankenstein*; Darwin, Marx, and Freud essays; *Heart of Darkness*; *The Waste Land*; *To the Lighthouse*; *Their Eyes Were Watching God*

Women and Culture

Autumn: *Hymn to Demeter*; *Oresteia*; *The Metamorphoses*; *The Pillow Book of Sei Shonagon*; *Lais*, Marie de France; fairy tales; *Cymbeline*; Sor Juana Inés de la Cruz; *Oroonoko*; *The Memoirs of Lady Hyegyong*

Spring: *Paradise Lost*; *The Princesse of Clèves*; *A Vindication of the Rights of Woman*; *Wuthering Heights*; Emily Dickinson; Gilman, Engels, and Freud essays; *Mrs. Dalloway*; *Doctor Faustus Lights the Lights*; *When Rain Clouds Gather*

The Americas

Autumn: *Popul Vuh*; *Royal Chronicles*; *The Tempest*; *Tears of the Indians*; Edwards and Mather; *Hope Leslie*; *The Interesting Narrative of the Life of Olaudah Equiano*; Anne Bradstreet, Phillis Wheatley, and Andrés Bello; "Benito Cereno"; Jefferson and Toussaint L'Ouverture; *A Son of the Forest*

Spring: "Nuestra América"; *Song of Myself*; *The Blithedale Romance*; *Incidents in the Life of a Slave Girl*; "The Slaughterhouse"; *Dom Casmurro*; José Martí, Langston Hughes, Helene Johnson, and Jean Toomer; "The Bear"; Borges and García Márquez short stories; *Miguel Street*

Though Barnard is one of the five colleges in a university whose dedication to the Western canon is almost unrivaled in American education, we are a women's college well aware of the dangers of aesthetic elitism and political exclusion. Inviting students to choose one of the three rubrics implicitly topples the tower of monolithic canonicity. In addition, the overarching title of Reinventing Literary History underscores the virtue of presenting each tradition through the prism of revisionist critical methodologies, especially the new historicism and feminism. The gerund construction transforms the noun phrase *literary history* into a verb phrase whose activity is writing itself.[3] The name of Barnard's new course is intended to inspire both students and faculty members to engage actively in reinventing a literary history that is constantly in danger of becoming a static, tyrannical entity. The iconoclastic power of Audre Lorde's critique of political and aesthetic elitism notwithstanding, "the master's tools" can "dismantle the master's house" through the activity of student writing.

Whether educators blame the Internet or MTV, students in the new millennium find it difficult to focus on the meaning of what they read and write. Even students who love ideas have seldom been expected to think critically, let alone philosophically. Collectively, they firmly believe in the existence of virtual reality and can claim with Cartesian certitude: I e-mail; therefore I am. When used deliberately, the Internet can be a valuable resource for scholarly communication and research. But to the extent that computers foster mental and physical passivity, their screens bear an uncanny resemblance to "boob tubes." Though our students are capable of reading the *Hymn to Demeter*, the actual meaning of the words on the page is often lost somewhere in the black hole of cyberspace. If some colleges do indeed grapple with what the media describe as a national crisis of literacy, Barnard professors confront the rarefied but potentially more insidious problem of intellectual complacency. Our students' first essays on the *Hymn* are often competently written, demonstrating proficiency in form. But with very few exceptions, they possess little or no real content. Students who have never received a grade lower than an A– gasp when they flip to the last pages of their essays, routinely skipping the foregoing comments in their haste to confirm the belief that college will mimic high school in its indulgent confirmation of their right to excel without thinking. The first task of First-Year English faculty members is to disabuse their students of this primal error. The honeymoon phase of the semester — the first two weeks when lively class discussions really do approximate the exalted Ivy League experience described in orientation brochures — is over the instant that first grade hits them like a ton of grammar books. In days of yore, when formal composition infractions met with draconian censure, red marks in the margins of student essays constituted the apotheosis of instruction. Our most formidable contemporary challenge is to transform punitive marginal monologues into seminar dialogues that will ultimately foster a more successful marriage of form and content.

This compositional dialogue swings the pedagogical pendulum back toward form. For all its nominal devotion to content, the architectural framework of Reinventing Literary History is composition. At its best, architecture provides an organic union of form and function not unlike the expository complementarity of form and content. Ideally, the structure of buildings is so well planned and executed that this union, so difficult to achieve on the drawing board, appears effortless in the actual buildings. But of course nothing about drafting or writing is effortless.[4] Though the seminar component of the course creates the artful Socratic illusion that wisdom springs Athena-like from the minds of students, faculty members must still be willing to work fiendishly at home, marking essays in preparation for the endless round of student conferences that have been the mainstay of composition programs since time immemorial. We in the trenches know that workshopping essay after essay not only year after year but decade after decade is far less arduous when student arguments are inspired and engaged. In the interests of pedagogical reciprocity, first-year English programs should both awaken young minds and sustain the intellectual interest of faculty members whose passion for what they teach invigorates the compositional process.

The great myth about English professors is that they know how to teach writing. We are not the authors of this myth. Admittedly, we take pride in knowing how to write well, and this hubris makes us the easy prey of faculty members from other disciplines who shirk their intrinsic responsibility to teach writing by foisting the job on us. This collegewide pedagogical displacement ostensibly justifies scapegoating English departments for poorly written senior theses in psychology and philosophy, no matter how flagrant the fallacy of infinite regress. Reinventing Literary History gestures in the direction of teaching writing across the curriculum with interdisciplinary Web sites and research paper assignments. But an infinite number of links to new-historicist Web sites cannot remedy this failure to share the responsibility of teaching writing. No matter how brilliantly conceived, first-year English programs will ultimately fail unless writing-intensive courses are interspersed throughout a student's undergraduate career, in chemistry no less than anthropology. At the very least, each department should provide an introduction to the major, a required course that navigates the critical and methodological landscape of the discipline. Periodically, curricular committees might revisit the question of whether first-year writing programs are housed in English departments by design or by default.

Graduate English programs often provide pedagogical support for PhD candidates working as adjunct instructors in their own colleges, but until recently these training programs were administered by academics who had never been taught to teach writing themselves. Veteran English professors passed on successful teaching techniques they had discovered during the course of their careers. Composition theory need not replace this guild approach to pedagogical instruction; Chartres was, after all, built by artisans who never went to school to learn their trades. But the influx of professionals actually trained in writing as directors of composition programs introduces a wider variety of teaching models, complementing the timeworn wisdom of research scholars who are often especially good at teaching exceptional students but somewhat at a loss with struggling stragglers.[5] Skeptics may say a little bit of theory goes a long way, but the way is well worth going. One need not espouse portfolios and metacognition to appreciate the power of process writing. At Barnard, old and new approaches to teaching writing have proved anything but incompatible, inspiring faculty workshops in which pedagogy itself is revised and improved.

Though revision is a generally accepted pedagogical practice, freewriting and peer editing often provoke particularly vexed debates in faculty forums about the writing process. Even I harbor a nagging suspicion that the purported value of freewriting has been eclipsed by its approximation to the activity of e-mailing, especially when the problem is not so much that students cannot write as that what they write lacks substance. But when a well-trained advocate of freewriting documents how journal entries enable her students to escape the deadening effects of the kind of prefabricated language George Orwell laments in "Politics and the English Language," I begin to change my mind. What a revelation to compare several peer-editing styles, complete with elaborate or ingeniously simple guidelines that add rigor to the exercise without sacrificing freedom from premature authoritarian intervention. Perhaps my dogged devotion to formal exposition inhibits analytic exploration. Invariably these faculty forums disrupt my pedagogical equilibrium. And just as I believe students learn more when we upset their complacency, I find that I teach writing best when I am slightly off-balance and more receptive to how different writing problems demand different solutions.

In keeping with the philosophy that successful writing is tantamount to revision, Reinventing Literary History students write each of their essays in at least two versions. Instructors meet with students to workshop the first version, and another stage is often implemented with peer editing. Ideally, each revision initiates the kind of radical re-vision originally championed by Adrienne Rich: "Re-vision — the act of looking back, of seeing with fresh eyes, of entering an old text from a new critical direction" ("When" 35). Rich's manifesto epitomizes Reinventing Literary History's curriculum as well as its writing pedagogy. Re-vision is an activity whose mobility outdistances the static limitations of product and canonicity. Having long since become a mainstay in feminist and composition discourse, this methodology still seems revolutionary to students accustomed to writing essays once and for all, usually in the wee hours of the morning the essay is due. Remarkably, stronger writers who have mastered the superficial art of reducing complex texts into neatly contained essays often resist the way process disrupts their formally accomplished, albeit simplistic products. They are encouraged temporarily to countenance what seems like compositional chaos in order to transform flat form into layered content. If a student persists in producing merely technical rather than conceptual re-visions, I ask her to cut everything but an essay's central paragraph before writing the next version. I remember one student in particular whose mutinous glare in the face of this directive finally vanished during her last required conference, when she summarily altered her thesis in the light of new evidence, thus internalizing the methodology of revision. At that moment, much to our mutual satisfaction, we ceased to be adversaries, and she subsequently confessed that she had begun to equate writing with thinking.

Institutional support for peer editing at Barnard is provided by the Writing Fellows Program, staffed by students trained in the three-credit course The Writer's Process. Routinely attached to writing-intensive courses across the curriculum, as well as on call at the Writing Center, fellows initiate strategic critical dialogues to help students hone preliminary versions of their essays. Though this program is in no way remedial, first-year students constitute roughly fifty percent of the center's walk-in population, in part because of the challenges of the Reinventing Literary History program. Admittedly, a danger of our curriculum is that the content of the course at first intimidates rather than inspires some students. Second-semester students in both Women and Culture and Legacy of the Mediterranean write their first essay on Milton's *Paradise Lost*, at which point one or two students in each class experience firsthand the terrible sensation of being expelled from the garden. Without compromising the integrity of the program, which should be as useful a resource to students writing their senior theses on florescent chromatography as it is to first-years wrestling with Milton's angels, writing fellows accommodate floundering students who wish to schedule weekly meetings. Up to three sections of students also enroll in a prerequisite to First-Year English: Reinventing Literary History, a course called Studies in Writing, staffed by faculty members trained in ESL and other specialized pedagogies. This configuration of courses, along with an energetic adjunct staff working side by side with seasoned tenured faculty members, enables us to address a wide range of compositional deficiencies in weaker writers while motivating our strongest writers with rigorous curricula and revisionist critical methodologies.

Though I recommend that instructors pitch seminar discussions and essay topics as high as possible, we must also provide special prompts for students who need more help with writing. One particularly effective strategy is the microcosmic approach, which, in the spirit of explications de texte, encourages students to concentrate their interpretive energies on emblematic passages. In addition to cutting the textual task down to size, this technique demystifies rather than compromises the critical process. Though far from an isolated example, one student stands out as having implemented this strategy to great advantage. Repeated visits to my office hours failed to relieve a crippling writer's block that dissolved the minute she realized that, if nothing else, she could intuitively grasp the theme of obfuscation in the *Inferno*. She simply needed permission to focus on what she understood rather than fret over every line in every canto. This student, who had all but wept when we first met to discuss her incomplete essay, ultimately chose to write her research paper on spiritual enlightenment in Dante. The satisfaction of having successfully navigated these forbidding regions of literary history more than compensated for the intimidating nature of the journey. Even our least accomplished students are often relieved to escape the condescension implicit in less challenging curricular choices, thus justifying our refusal to track them according to AP scores or entrance examinations. Even if measuring aptitude were possible, quantifying academic potential implies that education is a product rather than a process, precisely the pedagogical trap we intend to avoid at Barnard.

In addition to First-Year English, Barnard students are required to fulfill a complementary requirement, First-Year Seminar; half of the incoming class takes one course in the autumn and the other course in the spring, and vice versa. Whereas First-Year English is a writing course taught under the auspices of the English department, First-Year Seminar is a writing-intensive course taught by faculty members from departments across the curriculum. One-third of the First-Year Seminars feature the shared-text curricula of Reinventing Literary History, so students can choose to complete any of the three traditions. Since all three rubrics — The Americas, Women and Culture, and Legacy of the Mediterranean — span origins through the Enlightenment in the first semester and then cover works from the Reformation to modernism in the second, students can also switch from one curriculum to another without sacrificing the full historical sweep. The remainder of the First-Year Seminars offer an eclectic array of courses with tantalizing titles, such as Love; Death; and Slavery to Wages: Labor, Coercion, and Freedom. This range of courses characterizes Barnard's curricular philosophy. General education requirements are extensive, but students always enjoy a modicum of choice. The First-Year English / First-Year Seminar sequence also exemplifies the college's commitment to sustained writing instruction in seminars with limited enrollments of sixteen students. When the Studies in Writing / First-Year English / First-Year Seminar sequence insufficiently prepares students to meet the challenges of their chosen majors, we ask them to enroll in a special section of Essay Writing, a course taught by the director of the Writing Center. In effect, students for whom writing proves particularly difficult have access to a full two years of intensive expository instruction, all under the supervision of the director of First-Year English.

Teaching writing as revision potentially demonstrates to students what their professors know all too well — that beautiful prose was once the ugliest of ducklings. Some instructors bring in copies of their own ruthlessly edited works in progress or facsimile pages of Ezra Pound's editorial interventions on early drafts of *The Waste Land*. In the lexicon of writing-as-revision pedagogy, the word *draft* is anathema because it implies a half-baked piece of writing. Students must submit their best work in each version of their essays or the potential of the process is squandered. And there can never be too many cooks in the kitchen. We try to teach our students to sift through the responses of various readers so that conferences with professors and peers and writing fellows might all be incorporated into revisions. Assigning two or three versions of each essay preempts the possibility that the final product is nothing more than a last-minute effort. Many instructors contend that the process of revision results in significantly higher final grades. To the extent that this contention is true, we have cause to celebrate, but often it masks the more insidious culprit of rewarding students for merely fixing the flaws marked in the margins of their essays, an exercise in the transcription of marginalia that does not constitute true revision. Regrettably, the problem of grade inflation is much larger than this local example. The consumer culture mentality of American education has spawned inflation on a national scale, undermining the tremendous pedagogical function of grading. We need not wield grades like so many gloating tyrants plying whips, but when used constructively they can serve as valuable navigational devices, charting progress toward the destination of successful writing.

Though I obviously do not view education as a bitter pill to be forced down students' throats, the pedagogical balance that facilitates intellectual growth should not preclude all vestiges of academic authority.[6] The seminar format of First-Year English is invaluable when it fosters student participation in the production of meaning in the classroom. But the art of listening is in danger of extinction. The optimum attention span of many contemporary students is somewhere between three minutes and three seconds, depending on the speed of their Internet connection. For this reason alone, I favor reviving old-fashioned, not to say anachronistic, program components like the distinguished lecture series in Reinventing Literary History. Few academic experiences are more gratifying than the spectacle of two hundred first-year students seated in an auditorium, listening dutifully, if not attentively, to Helene Foley's lecture on ancient Greek cults. Since the students have read the *Hymn to Demeter* in Foley's annotated scholarly edition, their appreciation of celebrity culture sustains them for the first five minutes, whereupon the astonishing insights of this chair of their own classics department begin to captivate their attention. At the beginning of the semester, historical information from lectures often appears undistilled in the introductions of student papers, giving faculty members the opportunity to conduct workshops on transforming blocked paragraphing into point-by-point argumentation. Rather than isolate research and close reading in discrete paragraphs, this more sophisticated structure enables writers to integrate sources more effectively into interdisciplinary essays. In this way, virtually all the supplementary components of the Reinventing Literary History program—its museum tours, theater and opera excursions, and lecture series—can be channeled into the program's central goal of preparing students to write effectively in courses across the curriculum. Larger institutional benefits include the fact that history, philosophy, Spanish, religion, classics, art history, and American and women's studies departments have the opportunity to showcase their most distinguished and scintillating professors and begin recruiting majors. The lecture series promotes academic community by breaking down the disciplinary barrier erected by the name First-Year English.

In an attempt to value the old yet ring in the new, we have constructed a state-of-the-art Web site to enhance the interdisciplinary breadth of the Reinventing Literary History curriculum.[7] So, for example, the site devoted to the *Aeneid* provides several translations of this and other works by Vergil, as well as comparative versions of the story of Dido, including Chaucer's tale from *The Legend of Good Women*; Marlowe's play *Dido, Queen of Carthage*; and Henry Purcell's opera *Dido and Aeneas*. Secondary sources on generic conventions help students place Vergil's work in the epic tradition as a whole. An image collection features Roman frescoes, Carthaginian coins, and vivid digital reproductions of early illustrated manuscripts of the *Aeneid*. Links include a multimedia history of the hero's journey in classical literature and culture. But for all this Internet splendor, we limit the extent to which students can rely on our Web sites when writing their research essays. These technological bells and whistles are meant not to replace hands-on research but to provide models of responsible Internet usage, islands of valuable Web information in a sea of barely critical dross. Nothing can compare with an afternoon spent in Columbia University's gorgeous libraries. Love of learning has long been inspired by the hushed mystique of the stacks, the tangible texture of thought on the printed page. If I sound like a romantic, I have books to thank, not their pale digital shadows. Recent innovations such as CourseWorks and bulletin boards, where students exchange ideas electronically, are particularly suited to large lectures. They might complement but will never replace the dynamic, collaborative discovery of meaning in seminars. The communal setting of the evening lecture series, peer-editing sessions scheduled outside class time, and the seminars themselves provide ideal opportunities to revive the endangered art of intellectual conversation.

Another invaluably old-fashioned, which is to say classic, component of the Reinventing Literary History program is its great-works curriculum. No amount of revisionist critical methodology can disguise the fact that the Legacy of the Mediterranean is unapologetically canonical. But this methodology does help safeguard against blind faith in what might be called canonical propaganda, expressed both overtly in the particular case of Vergil's celebration of Augustan empire and more covertly in general assumptions of aesthetic and geographic ethnocentrism. The flip side of this cultural hubris is the narcissistic kind of pedagogy that has recently allowed students to indulge their craving to read about those closer in time to themselves.[8] First-year students may prefer to read Kate Chopin's *The Awakening* and Alice Walker's *The Color Purple* rather than Mme de Lafayette's *The Princesse of Clèves* and Harriet Jacobs's *Incidents in the Life of a Slave Girl*. But on completion of courses like Women and Culture, most students would agree that their appreciation of contemporary literature has been greatly enhanced by the study of literary history. Prefiguring the threat of oedipal prerogative in Walker's novel, Persephone's abduction in the *Hymn* adds archetypal and historical breadth to modern experience, exemplifying how the personal is political. Ideally, what theorists call the other will seem less and less distant to new-millennial students. And to the extent that the other is within, reading about Dante's epic journey into the nether regions of collective guilt can counteract the impulse to scapegoat. The Reinventing Literary History curriculum is designed to cure the pathology of intellectual and cultural narcissism, thus embodying the expansive spirit of the liberal arts.

The history of the great works tradition at Columbia University is thus felicitously ironic. The core curriculum at Columbia College was originally designed to promote patriotism in the face of World War I. Ostensibly, young men needed to be taught the value of the cultural traditions the war was meant to defend. In addition, immigration seemed to threaten the precarious canonicity of American culture, and the creators of the core curriculum felt that educating one and all in the same Western tradition would bolster a common national identity.[9] At Barnard, we are studying great works to achieve radically different results. We are attempting to wrench students out of the comfortable confines of their limited points of view, reintroducing the notion that though personal experience per se may not be universal, humanity most certainly is. And if humanism seems a vague and rather elusive concept,[10] surely Chaucer and Shakespeare can still remind us of what William Faulkner, in his Nobel Prize speech, called "the old verities and truths of the heart, the universal truths lacking which any story is ephemeral and doomed" (*Essays* 120). We are reinventing literary history because it has become inappropriately exclusionary, but we need not reinvent the wheel. For all modernity's solipsistic belief in progress, a doctrine that masks a multitude of sins, we are all still players on the same stage.

Hence Reinventing Literary History at Barnard negotiates between the profane and the sacred,[11] addressing lowly sentence fragments one minute and transcendent masterpieces the next. No matter how lofty our goals, students still know full well that the course fulfills the most dreaded general education requirement, with the possible exception of lab science. They are seldom if ever deceived by the fancy names we fabricate to dress up college composition. Nevertheless, though they can read between the lines of the course description even before we teach them the art of explication, their initial resistance begins to wane as the seemingly distant past comes to life. Admittedly, some students manage to remain impervious to the collective aesthetic achievements of Homer, Ovid, and Dante, but I have yet to meet the young woman who can resist the bawdy charms of the Wife of Bath. Ultimately, the seductions of textual content begin to mitigate the onerous task of attending to matters of compositional form. Inspired by the Wife's rhetorical audacity, formerly complacent students abjure the passive voice. The grammatical perils of dangling participles seem more imminent in sentences depicting Puritans suspended like spiders over the pit of hell. Such compositional epiphanies do not necessarily convert physicists into

English majors. But at their best, first-year English courses like Reinventing Literary History convince students that reading and thinking and writing are as inextricably wed as form and content, thus providing the foundation of the liberal arts education.

Notes

1. During the past few decades, the Barnard registrar assigned no fewer than six new names to the course, including Freshman Studies in English, Reading and Writing, Freshman English Seminar, and Language and Literature. Far from suggesting that the Barnard first-year English program is more confused than that of other colleges, this proliferation of names reflects the widespread pedagogical crisis documented in Maxine Hairston's seminal article "The Winds of Change: Thomas Kuhn and the Revolution in the Teaching of Writing." Focusing in particular on the influx of composition theorists into a profession heretofore dominated by literary critics, Hairston detects "enough evidence of insecurity and instability to suggest that the traditional prescriptive and product-centered paradigm that underlies writing instruction is beginning to crumble" (80). Ideally, having incorporated composition theory into the practice of teaching writing for the past few decades, contemporary first-year English programs are now in a position to combine process and product-centered paradigms.

2. Just as we balance the formalist, text-centered critical apparatus of structuralism with the new historicism, we endeavor to transcend the limitations of structural binary oppositions by incorporating the theories of Hélène Cixous and Jacques Derrida into our critical methodologies. Cixous's "other bisexuality" and Derrida's *"différance"* prove particularly relevant to liberal studies at women's colleges devoted to defying the "dual, hierarchical oppositions" that render "all conceptual organization subject to man" (Cixous and Clément 63–64).

3. Erika Lindemann rejects the recent rediscovery of literature in first-year English programs, arguing that the writing process should "focus not on nouns but on verbs: planning, drafting, revising" and that effective writing instruction is thwarted by sustained attention to "consuming texts, not producing them" ("Freshman Composition" 313). Reinventing Literary History's revisionist approach to nouns (to the literary texts themselves) is meant to transform reading and literary analysis into a much more active process, a form of interpretive production indistinguishable from the act of writing itself.

4. For a particularly useful as well as entertaining article on the universal woes of the writing process, see Alex Johnson's "Why Isaac Bashevis Singer, Truman Capote, Joseph Conrad, and Virginia Woolf (among Others) Were Having a Bad Morning." Students often exhibit remarkable relief when they realize they are not the only ones trapped in the eleventh circle of the authorial inferno.

5. Historically, this ideal complementarity has often been thwarted by allegedly incompatible theoretical approaches to teaching writing. Gary Tate bemoans the

gradual disappearance of literature as the "text" of first-year English courses in "A Place for Literature in Freshman Composition." Columbia College's long-standing composition requirement, Logic and Rhetoric, supported Tate's contention that "rhetoric replaced literature in the freshman composition course," favoring "Aristotelian devices" over literary analysis without engaging in the kind of "sustained debate" this volume attempts to foster (318). Significantly, even Columbia has inaugurated a new course, University Writing, in which texts figure much more prominently than they have since the inception of the Logic and Rhetoric program in the mid-1980s. The Reinventing Literary History program seeks to balance compositional form with literary content.

6. According to David Bartholomae's logic, this bid for the redistribution of power is really just an acknowledgment of the implicit authority of knowledge and its institutional accoutrements: "At worst, the 'democratic' classroom becomes the sleight of hand we perfect in order to divert attention for the unequal distribution of power that is inherent in our position as teachers, as figures of institutional/disciplinary authority" ("Writing" 66). Where Peter Elbow wants to "appeal to what students can learn 'in the absence of instruction'" (Bartholomae, "Response" 87), Bartholomae supports the pedagogical premise that teaching writing through the lens of great works enhances rather than undermines students' intellectual and authorial autonomy: "There is no better way to investigate the transmission of power, tradition and authority than by asking students to do what academics do: work with the past, with key texts" ("Writing" 66).

7. To access the Reinventing Literary History Web sites, use the link on the Barnard College English Department Web page or proceed directly to www.barnard.edu/english/reinventingliteraryhistory.

8. Don H. Bialostosky's "Romantic Resonances" implicitly contextualizes this concept of pedagogical narcissism in the so-called Romantic debates about the extent to which the pleasure principle—what Wordsworth calls "the grand elementary principle of pleasure" ("Prefaces" 252)—motivates readers and writers. Wordsworth contends that poets provide the kind of instant gratification students seek in more contemporary curricula, where "the man of science" (252) or, as Bialostosky asserts, the academic insists on delayed and ultimately more profound aesthetic pleasures. In addition to clarifying how the urge for instant gratification undermines the ultimate pleasures of less immediately accessible texts, Bialostosky historicizes Elbow and Bartholomae's ongoing conversation about how best to teach students to become writing subjects: "The Bartholomae-Elbow exchange may thus be read as part of the two-hundred-year debate opened by romanticism over writing, education, selfhood, pleasure, power, and knowledge" (93).

9. Histories of the creation of Columbia's core curriculum include Cross, Bell, Belknap, McCaughey, and Rosenberg.

10. In an argument in favor of reintroducing literary curricula into composition courses, Tate recounts the resistance of a "well-known rhetorician" who scoffed, "Oh, that old humanist thing!" ("Place" 321). Such an insult passes for high praise

in my book, let alone the great-books tradition. Bartholomae emphatically cor-
roborates the humanist philosophy of Reinventing Literary History: "I think the
composition course should be part of the general critique of traditional humanism" ("Writing" 71). In his vocabulary, "critique" refers to the practice of critical
and academic writing within the tradition of humanism, rather than the impulse
to reject it.

11. Reinventing Literary History's revisionist critical methodology supports
Elbow's reaction against the "tradition of treating [key texts] as monuments
in a museum, pieces under glass" ("Being" 74). Nevertheless, I beg to differ with
his contention that "no matter how good or hallowed they may be," we should
"not treat them as sacred" (74). Aesthetic reverence need not undermine readers'
ability to appreciate the common humanity that constitutes the very sanctity of
masterpieces.

The First-Year Humanities Program
at Earlham College

*E*arlham College is a Quaker school for undergraduates in Richmond, Indiana, a gray industrial town with about forty thousand inhabitants. There are eleven hundred students, about ten percent of whom study off campus. Earlham operates by Quaker business procedures, recruits Quaker students and faculty members, and seeks to make education part of a quest for peace and social justice. The college prides itself on a commitment to excellence in teaching; as one cliché has it, Earlham is a "teach or perish" institution. (Your groundbreaking book on the poetry of empire will draw the attention of only a few students and colleagues, but everyone knows how your Keats seminar is going.) Admission to Earlham is selective but not as selective as the faculty would like. Because of its peculiar mission and its reputation for good teaching, Earlham attracts far more than its share of bright, well-prepared, and idealistic students. Because of its social mission, it recruits significant numbers of foreign students, racial minorities, and economically needy students. Because of its relative obscurity and its location, the college admits some students who are far behind their classmates in preparation. Teaching students with this range of abilities is a challenge, one especially daunting in a required first-year humanities course that emphasizes sophisticated reading, writing, and discussion. I came to Earlham in 1966, my first job after graduate school. I fell in love with the place and have never seriously considered leaving. One source of my happiness was the Humanities Program.

First-Year Humanities, 2002–03

The Earlham College Humanities Program has existed for almost fifty years.[1] It requires all students to read and write about the same texts in two

Gordon W. Thompson

first-year courses, Humanities A and Humanities B. Humanities A sections never exceed twenty students and average eighteen students. Humanities B sections never exceed thirty and average twenty-five. Almost all sections are taught by full-time faculty members from the English, history, and classics departments.

The goal of the Earlham Humanities Program is passionate, thoughtful, and articulate engagement with challenging texts. We push our students to read accurately, interpret creatively, test ideas responsibly, and write persuasively. Our main vehicle is the dialogic paper, in which students first demonstrate that they have understood a text, such as Plato's *Republic*, Louise Erdrich's *Love Medicine*, Patricia Nelson Limerick's *The Legacy of Conquest*, or Niccolo Machiavelli's *The Prince*, and then reflect on the implications of that text for the world they inhabit. In other words, we try to persuade our students that mastering an author's argument or deducing an author's weltanschauung is not enough, impressive as that achievement is. They must also engage in a written conversation with each author in which they present their judgment of a text's value. They may write about the validity of an argument, the power of a vision, or the beauty of a composition. They must put their own minds up against the writers' minds.

The showdowns between authors and students are rarely equal contests. It is dispiriting to read students' lame refutations of John Stuart Mill, irony-free interpretations of Jane Austen (just like a soap opera), and allergic reactions to almost any religious document. ("What I really hate about God," one student wrote about the book of Job, "is his holier-than-thou attitude.") Even excellent readers are overmatched by the authors they read. Students' responses usually improve rapidly, however, when they learn that their task is not simply to agree or disagree with a text or to state their approval or disapproval of it but to reflect on its implications for their lives. *Implications* is a lovely word, really, and a paper about the importance — or lack of importance — of Job in the twenty-first century is likely to be more interesting than a paper about how annoying God is. What matters to us most is the habit of active reading. We want our students talking back to texts from the beginning of their careers and in all their courses. We tell them that their minds are every bit as important as William Shakespeare's,

Edward Gibbon's, and Toni Morrison's. The authors of our texts get to choose the topic under consideration, but each student gets the last word.

The Humanities Program emphasizes participation in class discussions; participation is twenty percent of the final grade. I rather think Earlham is unusual in its determination to develop participation skills. Some years ago, I spoke at a Great Lakes College Association workshop on teaching freshman English, and other attendees were appalled that Earlham graded on participation. Earlham's Quaker identity is partly responsible for this practice. We make something of a fetish of collaboration over competition, so we feel an obligation to teach students how to work together. We try to get them to become good listeners, forceful speakers, constructive critics, and cheerful recipients of criticism. We point out to them that almost all requests for letters of recommendation that we receive ask how well an applicant works in groups; solo performances are increasingly rare in the world our students will be entering. We suspend classes for a week in the middle of Humanities A to meet individually with each student and chat about how he or she is doing in the course. We usually spend as much time reviewing students' progress in class participation as we do on their writing.

I am proud of Earlham's attention to participation. I have seen too many meetings and too many careers ruined by rudeness, poor listening, self-absorption, petty squabbling, and long-windedness to believe constructive participation is unimportant. In addition, effective discussion groups are wonderful arenas in which students can test ideas for papers. They can trot out crude interpretations and, if their classmates push them hard, refine those ideas until they become interesting and compelling. Finally, group readings are often richer than individual ones. Perceptive and hardworking groups experience texts in distinctive ways, and that is why we, as teachers, can enjoy teaching certain works again and again.

The most controversial feature of the Earlham Humanities Program is the common reading list. The reading list for the first year is the same for all sections of Humanities A and Humanities B. Readings for Humanities A are provocative texts from a range of disciplines—literature, history, philosophy, religion, and politics. In fall 2002, we taught Adrienne Rich's

"As If Your Life Depended on It," Nawal El Saadawi's *God Dies by the Nile,*
Yusef Komunyakaa's *Thieves of Paradise,* Marion Kaplan's *Between Dignity
and Despair: Jewish Life in Nazi Germany,* Jhumpa Lahiri's *The Interpreter of
Maladies,* Plato's *Symposium,* and Gabriel García Márquez's *Love in the Time
of Cholera.* We try to select texts that challenge the students — that make
them think and move them to respond. We also try to choose texts that
speak to one another; and invariably they do, although usually not in ways
that we anticipate. We constantly remind ourselves that we must assign
works that are excellent, but I doubt if we have much of an idea what that
description means, or at least not an idea that we could all agree on. After
spouting a few platitudes like "consummately well-written," "cogently
argued," and "widely influential," we invariably fall to quarreling about
whether particular works are really excellent. The Humanities A list
changes every year.

Humanities B juxtaposes works of history and literature. It is here that
the shared custodianship of the Humanities Program by the English, classics, and history departments is most evident. Instead of solely mining texts
for ideas, which is the main focus of Humanities A, we start to study texts in
their historical and social contexts. Students are asked to write comparison
papers and to do some minimal research into the backgrounds of the works
they read. They are still expected to respond to the works, but more emphasis is placed on interpretation than in Humanities A. We want our students
to become capable of sophisticated readings that operate on different levels.
We want them to learn to offer sound historical assessments, sensitive aesthetic responses, close stylistic analyses, and defensible ethical judgments.
We usually create two or three clusters of texts in Humanities B. In spring
2002, we used an Arab cluster and a New York City cluster. The Arab unit
included Albert Hourani's *History of the Arab Peoples,* Leila Ahmed's *A Border
Passage: From Cairo to New York — a Woman's Journey,* and Tayeb Salih's novel
A Season of Migration to the North. The New York City unit focused on the
first half of the twentieth century and included Edith Wharton's *The House
of Mirth,* George Chauncey's *Gay New York,* Ralph Ellison's *Invisible Man,*
Ann Douglas's *Terrible Honesty: Mongrel Manhattan in the 1920s,* and several
of Bernard Malamud's stories from *The Magic Barrel.*

Although the texts and assignments are the same for every section, instructors are free to do several things in their own ways. I am obsessed with the need to master textual details, so I afflict my students with a steady barrage of quizzes—at least one a week. Some Humanities program instructors give quizzes, some do not. I usually teach what we call a living-learning section of the program, which means that all my students live on the same hall in one of the dormitories. Usually three or four sections (out of eighteen) are living-learning sections. I like teaching these sections because the students become a more cohesive group (which makes participation less intimidating), they are more likely to talk about books and papers outside class, and they can often relate the texts they are reading to the experiences they are having in college. Teachers also go about writing instruction differently. I require drafts of papers on Mondays, return those drafts on Wednesdays, and get the final copies from students on Fridays. During the first half of Humanities A, I have students make copies of their drafts for one of their classmates as well as for me. During the second half, I divide the class into tutorial groups and require that they write for four of their classmates as well as for me. I believe this helps students develop a sense of audience.

Teaching in the Earlham Humanities Program is exhausting work and requires playing quite a different role than I do in my literature classes. I am constantly grading various stages of papers. (Late at night I often recall the words of a composition instructor I once met, who said that he feared student prose destroyed brain cells.) In class, I work hard to create a productive reading group, one that draws on the intelligence and imagination of all the students. I also try to model the educated amateur who loves to read history and philosophy and religion, even though those are not my areas of scholarly expertise. Most draining is the psychological wear and tear of the program—for both the students and for me. Learning to read and write well requires a willingness to take chances, to make oneself vulnerable, to receive criticism. Few students come to college with such willingness. They are more likely to be angry, frustrated, or depressed. It is my job to keep their spirits up, to offer them encouragement as well as criticism, to remind them of the importance of our enterprise, and, above all, to help them think through their interpretations and plan their papers. I set aside five hours a week when they can come visit with me in my office.

The Humanities Program burden is made easier for me by interactions with colleagues. We talk about our classes constantly in hallways and offices, but the key event is the weekly staff meeting. Every Friday afternoon at four o'clock, all Humanities Program teachers (and a few interested librarians and counselors) gather at one of our houses. Whoever is hosting provides fruit juice and vegetables for the wholesome members of the staff, wine and brie for the sophisticates, and beer and pretzels for me. After half an hour of relaxed conversation about the week's highs and lows, we settle down for some serious discussion of assignments and teaching strategies. During the last hour, one of us gives a presentation about the next book we will be teaching—its beauties, its flaws, and its potential problems. We end with a book chat of our own, almost as if we were students in a Humanities Program class. I usually leave Friday meetings impressed by my colleagues, eager to teach the next book, and grateful once again to be teaching in this program.

A Brief History of the Earlham Humanities Program

The principles and practices of the Humanities Program evolved over time, usually in response to crises. A few essential features of the Humanities Program were first put in place in the 1950s by two members of the English department, Wayne Booth and Helen Hole. Instead of a freshman composition course, which they found deadly, they proposed a common reading list of varied humanistic texts; dialogic papers in which students talked back to authors; and small, discussion-centered classes. The most original feature of the program that Booth and Hole created was the tutorial. Each class of roughly twenty students met once a week in tutorials of five students each, in addition to the three weekly plenary class sessions. (Since teachers met with each tutorial, they were required to devote seven hours a week to Humanities Program class sessions.) Students made copies of each paper for everyone in their tutorials, including the teacher. Tutorials were devoted to critical discussions of the papers—the persuasiveness of the arguments, the validity of the interpretations, and the clarity and power of the writing. Students learned to write for an audience of fellow readers, and they learned how vulnerable writing could make them feel. Teachers learned to bring plenty of tissues to tutorial meetings.

The one-semester program requirement survived the 1960s, when, nationwide, general education requirements were under fire for being authoritarian and spirit killing. As a Quaker school, Earlham fancied itself in the vanguard of the civil rights and antiwar movements, and activism on campus was high, albeit peaceful. We were sticks-in-the-mud when it came to curricular change, and the Humanities Program, generally regarded as a successful, rigorous introduction to college-level thinking and writing, was never under serious threat of elimination or diminution.

By the 1970s, the Humanities Program was something of an institution. We were proud of how we prepared students to read and write, and we enjoyed a little low-level admiration in academic circles for what we were doing. The writing tutorials, in particular, were considered unique. Other factors at the college, however, made changes in general education requirements imperative. The faculty had added requirements without removing any, and too large a portion of student class work was devoted to general education courses. Some of the requirements did not make much sense. Two English literature requirements were indefensible. One, English 10, was a grab bag of seminars on whimsical topics selected by instructors. All English 10 classes included a research project, library instruction, and "creative" presentations that were sometimes embarrassing — crudely daubed paintings, ear-splitting musical compositions, and galumphing interpretive dances. The other requirement was a rather dull and mechanical introduction to the study of literature by genres. At the same time, Earlham's historians were stuck with a requirement that neither they nor their students liked: a two-semester overview of Western civilization. The course was provincial and obsolete.

On the positive side, in the 1970s Earlham indulged itself in a creative frenzy of interdisciplinary education, a frenzy that continues to this day. In the 1960s, several faculty members had transformed their interdisciplinary enthusiasms into programs, most notably in Japanese studies, but in the

1970s, we all caught the fever. The greatest generator of interdisciplinary activity was a large grant that three young professors, two in philosophy and one in religion, received from the National Endowment for the Humanities. Suddenly, all were free to develop team-taught, interdisciplinary courses as part of what came to be called PIE—the Program in Integral Education. A philosopher and physicist developed a course on cosmology that included original research at Indian burial mounds in Ohio. A historian and economist created a course on the transformation of the American West. I participated in the grandest experiment of them all: a year-long class for fifty students, Personal Identity and Social Role. The six of us teaching the course came from the biology, psychology, sociology, philosophy, religion, and English departments. It was a thrilling teaching experience (though I still resent the sociologist who told our students not to take *Nostromo* seriously).

The NEH grant had its intended effect. After the money ran out, we continued to teach together and experiment with interdisciplinary courses. In the ensuing years, the Earlham faculty created numerous interdisciplinary programs that are still flourishing. Among the most successful are Peace and Global Studies, Women's Studies, African and African American Studies, Human Development and Social Relations, Jewish Studies, Legal Studies, Environmental Studies, and Museum Studies. The most remarkable spin-off of the NEH grant, to my mind, was the revised Humanities Program.

Five men—two historians and three English teachers (including me)—began talking in the mid-1970s about ways to merge the general education courses in our disciplines into a unified humanities program that concentrated on effective reading, writing, and discussion. We were inspired by our interdisciplinary teaching under PIE, but we were also under severe pressure from the academic dean to cut the general education requirements in our departments from five to four and to get rid of English 10 and the two-semester overview of Western civilization. In a surprisingly short time, we designed the framework of the Humanities Program and its division into Humanities A and B, as described in the first part of this essay.

In 1976, the Earlham Humanities Program was launched. It still takes my breath away that my colleagues—all those scientists and social scientists—agreed to turn approximately one-fourth of every first-year student's schedule over to the English and history departments. (Within a year, the classics department had joined us.) Despite the need for premed students to start biology and chemistry and physics right away, Earlham's science faculty members said intensive reading and writing had to come at the beginning. In spite of the desire of language students to start year-long language study and in spite of the disinclination of some social science students to take literature and history seriously, the teachers in those divisions embraced our proposal to claim a huge chunk of every freshman schedule. When the Humanities Program became somewhat famous and its founders traveled to other colleges to advise them on creating first-year writing and reading programs, our hosts were always stunned that our colleagues put so much trust in us. They often said, "That could never happen here."

As soon as the program was up and running, we found ourselves making adjustments, mostly by adding to the program. We soon recognized that we needed frequent staff meetings, and that's when the Friday afternoon meeting was born. It began as merely an exchange of information, but we quickly added the book presentation and the discussion of teaching strategies. Over the years, the book presentations became more and more ambitious, sometimes including an original interpretation of the text, a review of relevant scholarship, a celebration of the work's importance or beauty, and a criticism of its faults. Several presentations led to publications. I still use some of the insights I gained from listening to brilliant reports on Thucydides, Gibbon, Cervantes, Morrison, Jacob Burckhardt, John Woolman, Dante, Sigmund Freud, Saint Augustine, W. E. B. DuBois, and Ssu-ma Chien. The beer and pretzels were good too.

After two or three years, it was clear that we needed a Humanities Program handbook for students and new teachers. I spent part of a sabbatical writing such a handbook. I described the program courses and outlined their assignments. I also wrote a two-part introduction, "What Are the Humanities?" and "Why Do We Study the Humanities?" Relying partly on my old favorites, Aristotle, Matthew Arnold, and Ernst Cassirer, I wrote many lovely words about language and forms and "our common humanity," "overcoming provinciality," and "ultimate concerns." We put the handbook to use right away and added to it as we felt the need. We added a note on plagiarism. Peter Suber, a philosopher who frequently taught in the program, wrote a brilliant little essay on argumentation, the best piece of its kind that I know. Before long we had the handbook copyrighted and made students buy it along with their Humanities A texts.

By the 1980s, the Humanities Program was a fixture at Earlham College. Over the years, as older faculty members retired and younger faculty members were hired, the solid consensus on which the program was built softened and the program became less monolithic. New teachers fought to make the reading lists more inclusive and less dedicated to so-called great books in the Western tradition. Some members of the staff considered the dialogic paper too prescriptive or too limiting for students' imaginations. They succeeded in making the writing assignments less formulaic, and they relegated Suber's essay on argumentation to an appendix of the handbook. Younger faculty members also objected (correctly) that my introductory pieces were based on an essentialist, traditional, European conception of the humanities and their value in a liberal arts education. A committee of three was dispatched to write a new introduction, but they were unable to do so. There was no shared vision to take the place of the old one, so the committee merely inserted caveats throughout the document. They told students that there is no longer any scholarly agreement on what the humanities are and why we should study them. We all felt better about destabilizing a little the goals and assignments of the program.

I think we succeeded, for a while anyway, in embracing more divergent worldviews and more diverse texts. The problem we could not conquer was the amount of work teaching the program entailed. The English professor Paul Lacey spoke for everyone when he said that teaching the Humanities Program required as much work as teaching two upper-class literature or history courses. There were the steady preparation of new texts, the incessant paper grading, the weekly staff meetings, the book reports, and the administrative obligations. Most troublesome, however, was the psychic toll of challenging eighteen-year-olds to read, write, and think. Maybe today's students are ruder than their parents were, but it has always been only the rarest student who really likes being criticized for bad writing. The dialogic paper can be an especially humbling experience. Humanities Program teachers spent hours in one-on-one sessions with students, not only tutoring them on their particular writing problems but also administering pep talks, tongue-lashings, or avuncular advice. We reduced the number of texts and the number of papers, got rid of the writing tutorials, gave increasingly perfunctory book reports, abandoned staff grading sessions, and opened a writing support center staffed by capable upper-class student tutors. These measures helped—but not enough. Teaching the Humanities Program remained a heavy burden. Most staff members, almost all of them tenured or tenure-track professors, sacrificed courses in their disciplines and deferred scholarly projects to do this frontline kind of teaching—heroic teaching, in my view.

Assessment of first-year writing and literature programs is notoriously difficult, but by every measuring system that we could devise, the Humanities Program was successful. We kept dossiers for students and persuaded colleagues outside the program to read through them for signs of writing improvement. The readers were impressed by the progress student writers made (although they were also impressed by how often advice from instructors was ignored). For years, the college has interviewed all graduating seniors, and, overwhelmingly, they look back in gratitude to their experience in the program. When alumni are polled, they are even more grateful. As a literature teacher who prefers stories to data, I am more impressed by the anecdotal evidence of students who contact us after graduation to say that they are doing the writing for their medical research team, their political action group, or their academic department. I am moved most of all by letters, visits, and e-mails from graduates who started far behind their classmates and are now enjoying jobs where they write all the time. One young man had to leave college for a week during his first year because his brother in Fort Wayne was shot dead on the street; he now has a promising business career. A young woman from Gary was admitted to the college conditionally because of her poor verbal skills; she received honors on her comprehensive exams in English and has just finished her master's degree. Both say that they learned to do serious thinking and writing in their humanities courses. And finally, to be utterly impressionistic, I love it in my advanced literature courses when I listen to students energetically but politely debate competing interpretations of difficult texts and think to myself, They could not analyze with this precision or discuss with this passion and considerateness without their preparation in the Humanities Program.

Teaching Writing

In my thirty-seven years in the Earlham Humanities Program, I learned the contradictory lessons that each student's writing problems are unique and that all student papers fall into ten (or so) basic types. I rarely finish the first page of a student paper without recognizing the kind of paper it is. There is the generic "good student" paper, lacking in personality as it discusses themes or symbols in error-free prose. There is the folksy essay, which compares a one-sentence summation of Aristotle's "message" in *Nichomachean Ethics* with some advice handed down from the author's Uncle Bob. There is the "I become a different person when I write" essay, in which a student mangles interesting ideas in pretentious, incoherent, out-of-control prose. There is the quotation-bloated essay, in which a trivial thesis (Elizabeth Bennet is an independent young woman) is illustrated with lengthy textual citations connected by single sentences by the student author, usually beginning, "Another example of my thesis is…" There is the "I prefer the sciences" essay, which lays out a not very imaginative interpretation in a highly schematic way, often including sentences like "In this paper I will show" and "In this paper I have shown." And so on.

It does not annoy or depress me that student papers are so easily classifiable. I know that there are interesting, thoughtful people on the other side of those pages. They cannot write good arguments because, as Gerald Graff maintains in *Clueless in Academe*, they have never experienced the pleasures of argumentation. They do not write clear, simple prose because they have a ridiculously inflated notion of what college-level writing is. They do not reveal their personalities in their papers because they do not feel invited to do so. The joy in teaching writing is meeting the unique students struggling to write good papers and helping them find a real voice, inviting them into conversation with skilled writers and perceptive readers.

The inconvenient truth is that writing is best taught one-on-one — that is, one teacher working with one student. Anything else is a compromise. I learned this truth most powerfully when, for several years, I taught in Earlham's August Academic Term — a three-week intensive writing program for the thirty or so entering students most at risk because of their writing. All students had been admitted to the college on the condition that they pass the August term. I was responsible for nine students. I had three student tutors (excellent upper-class students well trained in composition instruction), each of whom had three tutees. The students had three hours of class in the mornings; they met individually with me for half an hour each afternoon; they wrote papers under the watchful eyes of their tutors every night. I never felt more like a writing teacher than I did during those daily half-hour conferences. I could concentrate on each student's misreadings, bad arguments, and stylistic horrors. One of the most useful exercises was grading their papers together. We sat side by side, and, as they read their papers out loud to me, I praised and criticized their work. They got to see how their writing came across to a sympathetic reader, sentence by sentence, word by word. It was not my great teaching that led to dramatic improvement in writing; other instructors were every bit as successful. It was the concentrated attention to the individual student's writing difficulties.

I replicate the August Academic Term experience as much as possible in my Humanities Program teaching. I urge students to come to my office during the five hours a week I make available to them (roughly an hour a day). Sometimes I demand that they visit me. Most students spend a lot of time hunched over computers writing papers, but they spend little time planning and revising those papers. Planning and revising are exactly what goes on in my office. (I prefer several short visits of about fifteen minutes to lengthy sessions during which the student and I both lose our focus.) I like to have students come in right after they have finished reading a text, or even while they are still reading it. As soon as a student sits down, I say, "You talk; I'll write." I ask questions about the text, usually starting with the student's reaction to it and pushing on from there to interpretive claims. I write down any comments about a work's meaning. After a few minutes of this, I show the student the list of interpretive assertions made, and together we construct an argument out of those claims. The student then goes off and provides evidence and explanations for this interpretation. At a later meeting, I ask the student about his or her own thinking on the ideas found in the text, and I again write down the student's assertions, thoughts, and feelings. When shown what has been said, the student usually finds a line of argument in defense of his or her response to the text. Then we look for a structure that combines the student's interpretive argument and response argument.

Ideally, the student stops by with a rough draft after several planning sessions. We read through it together and then the student goes off to make the paper as clear, efficient, and persuasive as possible. When the student returns with a finished copy, we proofread together. (Earlham's Academic Support Center also provides student tutors who will proofread with Humanities Program students at hours long past my bedtime.) Collaborating with students during the prewriting and postwriting stages helps me discover each student's special character and cast of mind, which should come through in their papers. It also helps students identify their strengths and weaknesses. During individual conferences I try very hard to communicate excitement about ideas, books, and papers — and the minds of students.

Of course, no school can afford to staff writing programs so that all students can work one-on-one with their professors; that would require classes of eight or nine students. It would also require professors to abandon much of their scholarship to meet individually with students. I can give personal attention to those of my students who come to my office, but most of them do not. If more students did, I would not be able to accommodate them all. So, out of necessity, most students do not receive the best kind of writing instruction.

Earlham's Humanities Program tries to approximate the experience of one-on-one writing instruction in the classroom. While all sections have the same writing assignments — usually seven dialogic papers — instructors are free to use different techniques to teach effective writing. Our weekly staff meetings keep us in constant conversation about exercises that work and exercises that fail, and most of us end up using the same strategies. We use a lot of freewriting. For example, we might encourage students to write frantically for fifteen minutes about Gibbon's tone in a passage on early Christians and then plan an imaginary paper based on what they have written. We take into class excerpts from papers written the week before — five opening paragraphs, five closing paragraphs, or several paragraphs dealing with textual evidence. Many teachers (but not I) use overhead projectors and spend a class hour criticizing a classmate's paper. As I said above, in the early years of the Humanities Program we used writing tutorials and required students to make copies of their papers for four or five classmates and meet with the instructor for an hour a week to discuss those papers. All these exercises are effective, but none of them is nearly as effective as the one-on-one meeting.

In recent years, we have moved toward shorter, less demanding texts so that we can devote more time to teaching writing. Once we made our students read and respond to eight or nine challenging texts in a semester — Tolstoy, Morrison, Samuel Johnson, DuBois, Dickinson, Rich, Thucydides, Mill, Natalie Zemon Davis. Now we seek out brief essays, short poems, and three or four books, some of them by authors we consider more accessible — Dylan Thomas, Stephen Jay Gould, Annie Dillard. We made this adjustment because too many students have too many writing problems that demand concentrated attention. Too many still cannot write a good dialogic paper by the end of the semester and have trouble keeping up with reading assignments in long and difficult texts. Whereas we once never stopped reading and writing, nowadays we regularly take breaks of a week or two from our reading to concentrate on writing in a systematic way.

I am troubled by these changes, but I see no alternative. There is no point in complaining about declining standards and weaker students. In my view, today's students are brighter and work harder than ever before, although many of them have not read much or written many papers. I am not lamenting the shrinking number of golden oldies from our class lists. What I worry about is the partial abandonment of huge ideas cast in compelling language. Most students recognize a text of vast importance, and they know when they are being assigned "softballs." To me a great book is one that brings out a kind of crude greatness in students, a book that makes them think hard about their world, their lives, their values, their prose. We are assigning fewer such books.

Afterword

The Humanities Program at Earlham College is dead. In November 2002, faculty members officially adopted a revised general education program that reduced requirements across the curriculum and reassigned the goals of the Humanities Program to two bundles of separate seminars. The first bundle, Interpretive Practices, consists of about twenty separate seminars on twenty different topics, and students select one during either the first or second semester of their first year at Earlham. The second bundle, Comparative Practices, consists of about fifteen separate seminars, and students select one sometime during their sophomore year. Gone — for the foreseeable future if not forever — are the shared reading and writing experiences of all first-year students, the common reading lists, and the weekly staff meetings with their discussion of texts, assignments, and teaching strategies.

The official and unofficial celebrators of Earlham College (and I am usually one of the latter) say that nothing essential has been lost. Our first-year students still read challenging works of literature, history, religion, and philosophy in small classes. They still write dialogic papers, cultivate discussion skills as they pursue shared insights with other students, and receive affectionate support and rigorous criticism from full professors in a variety of disciplines. There are significant new benefits. Teachers assign more texts that they love, and students select the seminars that interest them instead of having to study an assigned array of works. Perhaps morale is soaring as teachers and students place themselves where they most want to be. I do not worry about a decline in attention to writing in the new system. We have agreed on paper assignments and the amount of time to be devoted to writing in all seminars. We have imported writing experts to talk with us about the writing process and how it can best be taught. As a college we are more determined than ever to teach writing well. Many Earlham professors think we teach writing more effectively using different texts in every section.

Even as we congratulate ourselves on these changes, however, we recognize that a few precious things have been lost. Staff solidarity is gone; it is now not exactly *sauve qui peut*, but we are more on our own than ever before. We confer with two or three of our friends as we design and teach our seminars, but we no longer have a sense of shared mission. The common first-year experience is gone as well. Three hundred first-year students no longer argue with one another about books they are all reading; they no longer pack an auditorium to listen to an author of a book they have all read. The interdisciplinary integrity that was part of the Humanities Program is gone too. For twenty-five years, I taught works of history that were selected by historians and shared with me by historians, religious texts selected by theologians, and philosophical essays selected by philosophers. Those of us in the English department chose novels and poems to share with teachers in other disciplines. The education I received from my colleagues and the support they gave me in my teaching fill me with gratitude. I'm sorry it is over.

The end of the Humanities Program at Earlham was inevitable and right. Only two of us who revised the program in the 1970s are still at Earlham, and one of them—not me—has gone a-deaning. As younger faculty members replaced retiring teachers, they felt less and less ownership of the program. They have ideological commitments that did not square comfortably with the goals of the Humanities Program. They are, in my view, less adventuresome about teaching outside their disciplines. They have expertise that they want to share with students. They resented the workload that the Humanities Program imposed, and, because they were not fully committed to the program, they resented having to deal with the student complaints, tears, and anger that are part of serious writing instruction. More and more instructors tried to wiggle out of the program's obligations. The academic dean found it increasingly difficult to staff the program. New faculty members outside the humanities also gave the program less support than did their predecessors. Younger faculty members in these areas are largely indifferent to writing instruction and mildly resentful of the large chunk of the freshman year given over to reading and writing. A program as ambitious as ours needed the generous support that the entire Earlham faculty once accorded it. Clearly, it was time to end it.

The Earlham Humanities Program contributed hugely to my happiness as a college teacher. Now, thousands of student papers later and a few years away from retirement, I feel the satisfaction of having spent my time doing useful work. I also think I have learned a few things about teaching first-year English courses. I have learned that hardworking students with a wide range of abilities and diverse cultural backgrounds can interpret and respond to challenging texts in remarkably sophisticated ways. I have learned that teaching first-year students how to read, write, and discuss at the college level requires from the teacher an ever-shifting balance of supportiveness and pressure. I have learned that teaching writing inevitably requires some one-on-one instruction. Finally, I have learned that it is most rewarding to teach first-year students when one is a member of a congenial staff with shared goals and a commitment to talking through its differences. There is no better preparation for teaching a text than arguing with colleagues about it beforehand. There is no better way to put one's own teaching difficulties into perspective than listening to war stories from colleagues engaged in the same enterprise. And, if an entire faculty, from the president to the most recent appointment in the physics department, embraces a program and offers encouragement, well, that is heaven indeed.

Note

1. The program I describe was laid down in 2004. I wrote this essay in 2002, when it was fully operative.

Connecting with the Humanities at Centre College

*T*he six of us are members of the English faculty at Centre College, a selective liberal arts college in Danville, Kentucky. Founded in 1819, the school currently enrolls about eleven hundred students. Like most schools of its kind, Centre has strong philosophical and institutional commitments to writing instruction. Faculty members here, whatever their discipline, regard the ability to write well as both an important practical skill and the hallmark of an educated mind. Unlike many other institutions, however, Centre no longer offers traditional writing classes, whether taught by an English department or a composition program. Instead, all our writing instruction has been integrated into subject-oriented courses, with especially close attention paid to writing in Humanities 110 and 120, a two-term interdisciplinary humanities sequence that all first-year students must take and that the six of us teach regularly.

The process by which this change came about was gradual, driven less by an overarching theory than by evolving curricular concerns, but the strikingly positive results have strengthened our belief in the benefits of integrating writing instruction with subject work. While all of us have years of experience teaching standard composition courses at Centre and elsewhere, we've come to feel increasingly uneasy with the free-standing, somewhat contrived nature of the enterprise. Because the composition course is not linked to the exploration of a particular subject, it tends to create an artificial writing situation that exacerbates one of the most troublesome aspects of college writing: the tendency of students to write to impress the teacher or to jump through imaginary hoops rather than to pursue a thoughtful engagement with the subject at hand. If writing is, as we believe, integral—not just secondary—to that process of intellectual inquiry, it makes sense to us that we teach it where and when the inquiry occurs. All

Helen Emmitt, Daniel Manheim, Mark Rasmussen, Milton Reigelman, Maryanne Ward, and Philip White

general education courses at Centre are now required to have a strong writing component, but the first-year humanities sequence is an especially good place to make sure that students get careful attention paid to their writing early on. Humanities 110 and 120 is in many ways Centre's signature course, the common starting place for our students' intellectual life at college, a shared point of reference throughout their four years. Moreover, our experience with the course has showed us that the subject of interdisciplinary humanities is particularly well suited to the teaching of first-year writing, and in this essay we explain why, sharing some of our ideas and approaches as we go along.

The Humanities Sequence

On the surface, Centre's humanities sequence may look like a garden-variety survey of Western Civ. The first term examines the literature, drama, philosophy, and art of the classical world, while the second term turns to European literature, drama, art, and music from the Middle Ages to the nineteenth century. What sets the course apart is how it's taught. Faculty members are drawn from academic programs in art, classics, drama, English, music, philosophy, religion, and modern languages, but instead of relying on group lectures or team teaching, each instructor is responsible for teaching all areas within his or her section of the course. (Sections are capped at around twenty.) So, an English faculty member teaching Humanities 120 may cover works by Shakespeare and Austen but will also present Giotto's fresco program for the Arena Chapel and Rembrandt's self-portraits, as well as Bach's Little Fugue in G-minor and Mozart's fortieth symphony. Musicologists teach Plato, drama professors teach Michelangelo, philosophers teach Dante.

At Centre, faculty members in humanities-related fields are usually hired with the expectation that they will teach this course regularly. For all of us, venturing outside our disciplines is at once exhilarating and terrifying, in roughly equal parts. (The first day teaching music can be especially traumatic for some—like childbirth and combat, a story to be often retold.) Fortunately, in the years since 1980, when the course was first offered, an extensive support network has been developed to assist those teaching the course. During the school year, there are group briefings on particular topics — on Aristotle's philosophy, say, or on Renaissance art — led by experts in those fields from among the humanities staff. Some valuable written materials have grown out of those briefings and are passed down from year to year as instructor's guides. Faculty members new to the course are closely mentored, both by the chair of the humanities program and, less formally, by more seasoned teachers of the course, and there's much chatting in the halls about whatever we may be teaching that week — the Francesca episode in Dante, the Parthenon sculptures, or Plato's divided line. The college has also funded some memorable summer workshops for instructors, including one on teaching music and a hands-on sculpture class.

For faculty enrichment, though, it would be hard to top our two trips abroad to study on-site the art covered in the course. The first trip, in 1990 to Florence, Padua, and Rome, was cosponsored by the National Endowment for the Humanities and Centre College. The second, in 1997 to Athens and the Peloponnese, was entirely financed by Centre. We've recently added a unit on northern Baroque art to the course, and plans for a trip to Holland and Belgium are well under way.

Often we're asked by colleagues at other schools what it's like to teach material so far outside our fields. For the six of us, there have been few drawbacks and many satisfactions. One pitfall, not immediately obvious, is a common tendency to over-prepare, especially early on. One of us remembers the first time he taught a Mozart symphony. The night before class, he made an emergency visit to the home of a colleague in music, who patiently went over the symphony with him, score in hand. The next morning, this teacher photocopied extensive excerpts from the score and brought them to class to support his points. That day's meeting, as he recalls it, was a "mild disaster," as the students, many of them unable to read music, were presented with far more material than they could handle. In subsequent years, this instructor learned to cover less and accomplish more.

In fact, first-time teachers of the course tend to stick closely to the material and approaches covered during the group briefings, and classes during that first year can have a rather heuristic feel, since instructors learn about the material from how their students respond to it. So, an instructor may present a comparison of two works by Duccio and Giotto, well schooled by an art history briefing to point out Giotto's many advances in technique, only to find that the students like Duccio better. Well, of course: Duccio comes at the end of a long artistic tradition, whereas Giotto is starting something new. Which artist is likely to be more adept, more pleasing? In encountering the student response, the instructor learns something about the material and teaches it better the second time around. The normal progression is for faculty members in the course to get freer and more improvisatory in their teaching as they go along and as they develop their own sense of the arc of the course. In the end, we all come to feel that teaching material outside our disciplines also enhances our teaching within them; certainly all of us are far more comfortable bringing art and music into our literature classes than if we'd never taken up the challenges of the humanities sequence.

Few courses can match this one in the way it spurs cooperative learning and collegiality among its teachers. The real point, though, is to show students who take the course that a love of art, drama, literature, philosophy, and music is not merely a matter of professional specialization but an essential part of a well-rounded life. As enthusiasts for material outside our disciplines, we as teachers serve as models to our students for what it means to care for, and connect with, the humanities. Indeed, many of us feel that our best teaching in the course comes in the very fields where we are least expert and thus least haunted by anxieties about scholarly rigor.

This approach to teaching interdisciplinary humanities is particularly well suited both to Centre's student body and to the school's generaleducation curriculum. Most Centre students come from Kentucky and the surrounding states, and as a group they are exceptionally high achievers: valedictorians, class presidents, captains of athletic teams. They are students who could have gone anywhere to college, but they've chosen to stay close to home and to attend a college that promises a caring, supportive environment. For the most part, they do not have an especially broad experience of the world, a characteristic that the college has begun to address over the last fifteen years with an extensive program of study abroad. (At present, about 75% of our graduating seniors have spent time studying in one of our foreign programs.) Many entering students have had rich experiences with the performing arts through local theater or music groups, but going to museums or professional theater or concerts is not a regular part of their lives—very few of them have seen an opera or listened carefully to a symphony or lost track of time while looking at a painting.

In short, what many of Centre's students lack is the experience of an unforced, unpretentious engagement with the humanities as a natural part of their lives, the sort of experience that is much more readily available to students from big cities in other parts of the world. It's this experience that the humanities sequence tries to offer to them. An invaluable resource in this effort is the college's Norton Center for the Arts, which hosts an extensive performance series that students may attend for free. All of us include events from this series on our syllabus and require attendance. During one recent year, students attended performances by the Philadelphia Orchestra, the London City Opera, Wynton Marsalis, the Emerson String Quartet, and Shenandoah Shakespeare Express as part of their work for the course. Often, visiting artists offer special workshops for the first-year humanities class: especially memorable in recent years have been those presented by the Kronos Quartet, Anonymous Four, the Academy of Ancient Music, and the Aquila Theatre Company.

Finally, in keeping with our nonspecialist approach, some faculty members have begun to build more practical experiences into the course, notably through a vase-painting workshop and exhibition associated with the unit on classical art and through the Hallelujah Project, a group performance of excerpts from Handel's *Messiah* that was part of a unit on baroque style. There's no reason why such participatory experiences shouldn't continue to flourish and multiply, just as there is no reason why the course shouldn't expand to include non-Western material, especially as new instructors come in. By its very nature, the course is fluid and open to change. It is what we make of it.

Humanities and the Writing Requirement

All Centre students must meet basic skills requirements in three areas: math, foreign language, and writing. For many years, students met the writing requirement in one of two ways. Students who had scored above a certain level on their English ACT or verbal SAT received credit for basic skills in writing at entrance, whereas students with lower scores were placed in a traditional composition course taught by English faculty members during the fall. These three-credit courses, designed by the instructors, typically focused on such genres of writing as personal narrative, argument, analysis, and the research paper; class work emphasized the writing process and the mechanics of grammar and documentation. Roughly a quarter of each entering class had to take this course to meet the basic skills requirement in writing.

Over the years, we found that students required to take the composition course fell into two distinct groups. One group consisted of students with basic writing problems, due to weak abilities or weak high school preparation or both. Students in the second group were certainly not mature writers, but they mainly needed help with such higher-level skills as organization, paragraph writing, and developing ideas. In 1990 we decided to try to meet the needs of this second group through writing-intensive sections of Humanities 110. Numbered Humanities 111, these were designed as four-credit courses, rather than the usual three, and included a weekly sixty-minute lab devoted to writing. The experiment worked well; most students in the sections seemed to acquire the skills they needed to make the transition to college work. But we still were not sure that the college's basic skills requirement in writing operated as well as it should. The fall term writing courses, whether in composition or in writing-intensive humanities courses, amounted to a one-shot inoculation that didn't always take and that wasn't always given to everyone who needed it. Some students who tested out of both courses turned out to be surprisingly weak writers once they encountered the challenges of college writing, but there was no course designed to meet their needs. Nor was there a required course for students who passed one of the fall term classes but were still weak writers.

Our next step was a radical change in the writing requirement, a change that we think has been a remarkable success. Rather than allow first-year students to meet the requirement through test scores, we decided to use those scores as the basis for initial placement in the composition course, in Humanities 111, or in Humanities 110. Then at the end of the fall term the writing of all first-year students was subjected to a review administered by a subcommittee of the English program. This review examined the performance of each student as a writer during the fall term, based on feedback from instructors and a required writing sample. Those students whose writing was judged to be competent were given credit for having met the basic skills requirement and qualified for Humanities 120 in the spring. Those students whose writing fell short of competency, whether or not they had been required to take composition or Humanities 111 in the fall, were then required to enroll in Humanities 121, a writing-intensive section of Humanities 120. Again, this was a four-credit class, with a weekly sixty-minute writing lab. Students who passed this course automatically met the college's basic skills requirement in writing.

In fall 2000 we took the final step and dispensed with our traditional composition course entirely. At that time, the college was in the midst of a top-to-bottom curriculum review and reform, and as part of that process the English program moved all first-year writing instruction into writing-intensive humanities sections. Our success with these sections had convinced us that they could be used to address the needs of even our weakest student writers. Under our writing requirement as it now stands, students are placed at entrance in fall term sections of humanities on the basis of their test scores. Roughly one-fifth of each year's entering class is required to take Humanities 111 in the fall, in sections with a maximum enrollment of fifteen students apiece. After the midyear review, about a tenth of the class is placed in Humanities 121 to meet the writing requirement.

In short, all students needing additional coursework to meet the basic skills requirement in writing now do so through writing-intensive sections of the first-year humanities course. It is important to emphasize, though, that these sections are not the only places at Centre College where writing gets taught. All general education courses must include a writing component, so student writers are mentored by instructors in subject courses throughout their four years. Some of our best and most dedicated teachers of writing are colleagues in history and government, in anthropology, biology, and math. We believe that this shift away from the traditional composition course has had several practical benefits. Students now receive instruction on writing assignments that have immediate relevance to their coursework, rather than in a separate context designed to provide exercises for the real thing that happens elsewhere. The inveterate impression that writing is somehow separate from learning and thinking is not reinforced by symbolic and institutional division between writing teachers and subject teachers, since students who need special help get it through writing-intensive sections of classes already required as part of their general education work. And students' writing proficiency is assessed not by the completion of a single writing class (or by test scores) but by the students' written work in class. As a result, we are doing a better job of monitoring our students' performance, as well as giving them help with their writing when and where they need it most.

What have these changes meant for the first-year humanities sequence? We believe that the heightened emphasis on writing has invigorated the course, enabling our students to become both better writers and better learners. The overarching goal of the course remains what it has always been: to help students connect with the humanities—with literature, art, philosophy, drama, and music—in ways that enhance their lives. Writing about the material is an especially vivid way for students to make this connection. And the benefit is reciprocal: as students find their connection to the humanities through writing, they also find themselves more connected to what they write and thus likely to become better writers. In the process, we as teachers (indeed, often as nonspecialist colearners) can use our own enthusiasm for the material to energize our students' linked experience of humanities and writing.

Teaching Writing: Some Approaches and Assignments

Even before the writing-intensive sections were introduced, the first-year humanities sequence was a natural place in Centre's curriculum to address student writing. Other general education requirements at the college—in social sciences, life and physical sciences, and religion and philosophy — may be met with different combinations of courses over different years, but the humanities sequence is a requirement for all entering students. Accordingly, shared topics for formal papers have always been designed by the humanities staff as introductions both to the discipline and to college writing, with particular emphasis on the first paper in the fall, usually on a topic from Homer's *Odyssey* and almost always a student's first major writing assignment in college. All instructors hold individual conferences before this paper is due, and most require a graded revision. The first paper is also an opportunity to introduce some expectations and protocols of college writing, including proper use and documentation of sources; as part of the preparation for writing it, students complete an exercise on avoiding plagiarism and discuss the exercise in class. Other shared paper topics in the two-term sequence may include analyses of sculpture and paintings from the college's collections, dissections of philosophical arguments in Plato or Aristotle, close readings of passages in Dante or Shakespeare, and written responses to concerts or plays.

Since the advent of the writing-intensive sections in 1990, new writing assignments have been developed for use in class and in the weekly writing labs, and many of these assignments, in turn, have been adapted for use in the regular sections. This cross-fertilization has integrated writing more fully into the course content, and some of the assignments that have resulted from it offer particularly striking examples of how writing can help students connect with the humanities and how connecting with the humanities can help students become better writers.

Each faculty member who teaches the course adopts different approaches and strategies, though we also pool ideas. Since one goal of the sequence is to encourage our students to be slower, more leisurely readers, observers, and listeners (no small challenge in our information-drunk age), the agenda for a class or writing lab session might be something as simple as choosing an episode in Dante or a passage in Shakespeare and asking students to read it over carefully during class and jot down their ideas, perhaps in response to a particular question. (For instance, how does Dante contrast Farinata and Cavalcante in canto 10 of the *Inferno*? Which details make that contrast vivid? What might be Dante's purpose in making it?) Spending a block of time reading and rereading a passage with such questions in mind, continually jotting down notes — for many of our students, this activity is something entirely new. The in-class writing can then be used as a basis for class discussion, or it can be collected and responded to by the teacher and perhaps used as prewriting for a more formal paper due later on.

Other exercises might be similarly directed toward slowing down the gazing eye or attuning the listening ear. Students writing about sculpture and painting tend naturally to drift into some form of narrative, especially if the piece is representational. One instructor encourages his students to consider works in formal terms by having them describe a piece of nonrepresentational art — an abstract glass sculpture from his collection or a slide of an abstract expressionist painting. From here, they may go on to consider the formal features of more representational pieces from the college's collection of nineteenth-century bronzes. Similarly, in studying music, students taught some basic musical terms may apply them by listening to an aria from Mozart's *Marriage of Figaro* and writing about how the orchestration supports the vocal line. Assignments like these mirror the exercises in prewriting and developing ideas that are often performed in a regular composition class, but here the assignment is closely tied to the course content, as students learn to experience the works more fully by writing about them.

Many instructors ask students to connect the works studied in Humanities 110 and 120 with their own experiences, self-image, or understanding of the world. One of us, an Americanist, puts his rationale this way:

> The students who take the writing-intensive sections of the course tend to be those who were least engaged by their humanities classes in high school: most of them simply don't define themselves as artsy types. I hope to convince them that the arts, even ancient ones, can be connected to all sorts of things that they think about in their daily lives. Art and philosophy are not simply about some romantically inspired notion of creativity but, rather, things that involve us every day, whether we like it or not. I am not a specialist in any of the fields we study, but I can admire and respond to all of them, and I try to devise assignments that will encourage my students' capacity for such response.

Like the personal narrative unit in a composition course, such assignments prompt students to invest themselves in their writing, but here that investment is applied to a more thorough engagement with the course material. In an essay on the *Odyssey*, students may be asked to recount some experience of recognition and reunion of their own. They must then briefly discuss one of the recognition scenes in the epic and consider similar and dissimilar elements in the two events. Students may also be asked to map some of their own educational experiences onto categories of thought in Plato's divided line or, in an essay on Euripides's *Medea*, to compare Medea with a modern mother who killed her children. They see the discontinuities between Euripides's antihero and Susan Smith right away; but those who think about it also surprise themselves by finding some unexpected similarities, as when one student observed that both women wanted to kill their children in order to be able to go on thinking of themselves in the same way, to go on being who they wanted to be.

Several instructors take students out of the classroom to observe classical elements in local architecture — the college's administration building, for instance, or a downtown bank — and write about what they see. To study landscape, one instructor hands each student a small cardboard viewfinder and sends them out on campus to find their own perspectives. After they have attempted to describe in writing what they have seen — and determined which elements made their landscape a worthy view — they are ready to discuss in class how landscape artists have organized their own vistas.

Back in the classroom, students stage mock trials wherein Creon and Antigone — or the Athenian Assembly and Socrates or God and Ugolino — become the prosecution and defense in a courtroom setting; both sides submit written briefs before the trial. Creative responses help the students connect with the works they encounter. What sorts of structures can you imagine reflecting our world the way that Chartres Cathedral or the Arena Chapel reflect theirs? What might you include in a commemorative portrait of Odysseus, Henry V, or yourself? What happens if Romeo and Juliet don't die or if Bottom can't remove his ass's head? One instructor first asks students to write about how they might design an image of some classical or biblical story (Apollo's pursuit of Daphne, say, or Abraham's sacrifice of Isaac) and then shows them in class how artists have depicted the same episode. All these assignments encourage students to engage the works from their own experience, helping them reckon more directly with the choices that authors and artists face.

One of us finds assigned writing in journals especially effective in fostering this ongoing response. After completing each day's reading assignment, students write down two or three points that strike them as important, and class discussion begins with these "preparation points." These discussions in turn are the basis for a more formal journal entry about each work, due on the last day the work is discussed. The journal entries must focus at least one carefully developed paragraph on how that work addresses key concepts studied in the course, such as human nature, moral and cultural values, and the purpose of education and the arts. Students take into consideration both the works themselves and what has been said about them in class. This journal writing supplements, but does not replace, the longer required papers. As this teacher remarks:

> It has been said that writers are merely readers inspired to emulation, and I always try to encourage a writerly approach to reading and a readerly approach to writing. Taking a writing-intensive course in a student's first year of college is a great way to encourage habits of reading actively early on; that is, it's a great way to inaugurate an adulthood of inquiry and thought.

As in any writing course, assignments are carefully sequenced to build students' abilities. Again, however, the assignments are designed to help forge the initial connection with the humanities that's essential to the course, and the need to make that connection feeds back into the writing. Because most students come out of high school with only the haziest notion of the distinction between summary and analysis, many instructors begin the term by asking students to confront that distinction head-on. The first writing assignment may be a brief plot summary of an early book of the *Odyssey*, followed by a longer paper analyzing the same book in relation to a particular question or in support of a particular argument. These paired assignments allow instructors to assess the level of each student's writing and to mark clearly for students the difference between summarizing what a text says and analyzing how an author says it. A similar pair of assignments works well with an early canto of Dante's *Inferno*.

One instructor's assignment focuses vividly on the summary-analysis distinction. Students in his class are given Cliffs Notes summaries of several passages from a literary work—selected books from Homer or Vergil, say, or scenes from a Greek or Elizabethan play or cantos from Dante's *Inferno*—and are asked to pick one example and discuss the differences between the summary and the actual work. The assignment allows students to teach themselves some important aspects of a work, and because they have to choose from among four or five passages, they have already reconnoitered some important territory before they begin to write. The assignment may even inculcate a healthy scorn for such prepackaged study aids. And it is endlessly recyclable.

From assignments focusing on the distinction between summary and analysis, instructors, particularly in the writing-intensive sections, may move on to comparison and contrast. The art we study lends itself to this activity. Giotto's and Duccio's enthroned Madonnas, for instance, offer a minicourse in hieratic scale, the beginnings of perspective, the legacy of the Byzantine approach, and so on. At first these distinctions may seem too subtle for beginning students. So in preliminary writing assignments an instructor may find a modern painting that is startlingly different from the works covered in class and compare an earlier painting with it. (Works by Klimt, Modigliani, or Picasso have served especially well for this purpose, as might works from non-Western artistic traditions.) This approach hones the students' sense of what to look for when comparing and contrasting and thus trains them for writing examination essays, as well as more complex papers. Just as important, it prepares them for subsequent engagement with the arts wherever they go. Not only do upper-class students studying abroad send us postcards proving they went to see a particular work of art studied in humanities, they also insist that seeing the original changed some part of the work for them and write about technical aspects of the works with confidence and clarity. When one student spending a semester in France made herself an impromptu museum guide for a group of British tourists, she conceded she was only using abilities she had begun to develop two years earlier in Humanities 120.

As well as encouraging clarity of description and introducing analytic approaches to particular disciplines, writing assignments may emphasize the connections between disciplines that students might otherwise miss. A class that considers various theories about why the Parthenon is curved and what ratio was used to plan the building may then profitably consider why Homer structures the *Odyssey* using flashback. Students made familiar with the Hegelian dialectic of thesis-antithesis-synthesis through their study of the *Oresteia* may then be asked to look at Polykleitus's *Doryphorus* ("The Spear Bearer") and write on the following topic: "The *Doryphorus* is a synthesis of earlier sculptural styles. Agree or disagree." Or a paper assignment may ask students to compare the narrative structure of *Pride and Prejudice* to sonata form. Such translations across disciplines require especially careful planning on the students' part before they begin to write.

However much our approaches and assignments may differ, all of us who teach first-year humanities try to help students build a repertoire of writing skills throughout the course. All students receive guidance in developing their ideas, finding a thesis, and planning what they have to say. After an assignment is completed, sample papers are reviewed in class, and student examples are used to teach points about sentence writing, paragraphing, and grammar. Again, this approach mirrors what might happen in a regular composition course, but when a paper topic on, say, stylistic differences between Homer and Vergil is crucial to understanding course content, students tend to use the best papers to study for the final exam. Student writing suddenly takes on a new importance.

Besides building skills, first-year students need to get a feel for what is expected of them in college writing and how these expectations differ from those in high school. What kinds of thinking does this assignment ask of them? How should they go about doing it? Given the range of disciplines it covers, Centre's first-year humanities course seems well placed to address this crucial aspect of the writing situation. As one of us notes:

> I try to be transparent in all my assignments. I explain to the students why I
> have structured the essay assignment in a particular way and what skills I hope
> they will develop. I want them to learn to be flexible, to modify the paper form
> to fit the assignment.

In this sense, an interdisciplinary humanities course is an ideal introduction to college writing. It shows students how and why expectations shift among academic disciplines, perhaps reassuring them that these shifts are not merely attempts by mean-spirited teachers to hide the pea under a different shell but reflect real and interesting distinctions in the kinds of thinking required in different fields. By thinking and writing across the humanities, our first-year students may become more adept at thinking and writing across Centre's curriculum as a whole.

By now it should be clear why we think that the fuller integration of writing into the humanities sequence has enriched our students' experience of the material and helped them to become better learners. But what about the other half of the equation? Can we really be sure that this course is better for our students as writers than our old composition course was? To some degree, our answer must be subjective: we sense that the students who come out of the course now are more confident and capable in their approach to college writing than our students were a decade ago. One significant bit of empirical evidence backs this impression up. Since the writing-intensive sections were first introduced, the rate of student retention at Centre has gradually but steadily increased. By far the most likely students to leave early are those with the weakest skills and preparation, those who find the academic expectations here particularly daunting. Both the faculty and the administration feel certain that the careful nurturing of those students in the writing-intensive sections of first-year humanities has influenced their decision to stay.

Finally, there is anecdotal evidence for the success of our approach. A few years ago, for instance, a student who had been in a writing-intensive section went on to win the college's award for the best upper-class paper in history. Asked about his accomplishment, he was unashamed to give credit to his work in the writing-intensive course. As he put it, "I always knew what I wanted to say, but I never had to look so closely at my words." For this student, at least, the course had provided the training to help him succeed as a college writer and beyond. In the process, like other students in the course, he had made a connection with the humanities that might stay with him for the rest of his life. For a single course, that's not a bad combination of results.

Group II

Literature as Source and Focus

Crawling before Writing

*T*wenty-seven years into my teaching career, old ways finally seem new again. Two other senior colleagues and I gave a workshop three summers ago meant to introduce a welcome influx of young faculty members to our department's quirky first-year course, Critical Reading and Writing: Literature. Though all else in the Holy Cross English curriculum has at least been buffeted by the transformative changes of the last twenty years, this course has remained remarkably stable. We do not require either a composition course or an introduction to literature course for students at Holy Cross. We know that other forces — our college distribution requirements, the expectations of our highly regarded premed and prelaw programs, and the nature of a liberal arts college — will bring approximately ninety percent of our 2,700 undergraduates to the English department before graduation. And though we offer a few small sections of basic composition, Critical Reading and Writing introduces analytic writing to at least two-thirds of each incoming class. In fall 2002, 295 students from a class of 701 enrolled in Critical Reading and Writing: Poetry, the first course in the literature series; in the spring, 251 registered for Critical Reading and Writing: Fiction. Students may enroll in both semesters of the course, and quite a few do, but they need not. Of the two, faculty members immediately and students eventually agree that the poetry part of the course provides the most effective writing instruction for those who may take only one.

For the last decade, however, new faculty members joining the department, well-trained in newer critical methods, have questioned the restrictive aspects of a course rooted in formalist approaches to literature. Senior faculty members often pronounce the name of the course as "craw" (invoking those circling black birds that never leave New England), but it might be wiser to add the "l" and speak more truly of "crawl," since our first-year writing course, designed for all students, requires tremendous patience of

Helen M. Whall

its teachers and students. At Holy Cross, all members of the English department, regardless of rank, teach at least one section of Critical Reading and
Writing each academic year. As a result, new faculty members must teach
the course, despite varying degrees of discomfort with its premises and
methods. In general, over several years of teaching, new faculty members
find ways to adapt or modify the course—or, conversely, to adapt themselves to it.

In 2000, however, when the distinguished professor of rhetoric Patricia
Bizzell became chair of the Holy Cross English department, she decided a
more direct approach would be helpful. Bizzell's life-long commitment to
basic skills and writing across the curriculum led her to conclude, by the end
of her first year at the helm, that new faculty members would benefit from
specific training in teaching Critical Reading and Writing. She called for a
summer seminar in which seasoned teachers of the course would teach its
basic elements to those new to the department. Our young colleagues, she
argued, had no reason to recognize the course's particular premises. For
most recently trained scholars, formalist skills had not been separated from
more advanced theoretical transactions, as they are in our first-year course.
Bizzell knew the time had come for teachers to teach one another and to
review the origins of their craft. She was right.

Our summer workshop for new faculty members reviewed the art
of close reading, as exemplified by the New Critics and such theorists as
I. A. Richards before them. Three of us who had been teaching Critical
Reading and Writing introduced our colleagues to the pedagogical exercises
we have used for years in the optional course we offer all first-year students.
It is a course I myself teach, a class that embodies the principles of close
reading, a class that applies applied criticism. And in the process of teaching
teachers, I finally came to understand the true strengths of a course I have
seen empower hundreds of independent first-year readers.

I speak of the course "I myself teach" rather than "my course" because
Critical Reading and Writing now belongs to everyone who teaches it. But it
does have a progenitor. Robert Cording introduced the principles and core
exercises of the course when he joined the Holy Cross English department
more than twenty-five years ago. Cording not only shaped the course, he

shepherded it through the early days of resistance. (The course is taught by faculty members from all ranks and is writing-intensive; there was resistance.) More important, as an established poet, Cording has argued authoritatively against the pernicious belief that analysis undoes creativity, that criticism destroys beauty. His work as critic and poet more than convinces our upper-level students to shun that belief. At the same time, the essential strengths of the Critical Reading and Writing program have been borne out by the many good critical readers and writers we send to other departments.

Given the freedom even our untenured faculty members enjoy, yet another strength is that in a department of twenty-four full-time faculty members and many visiting instructors, the course remains on the books. That does not, finally, reflect the heavy-handed imposition of authority. Rather, all who adhere to the course's principles of first making sense, then moving to close reading, and always maintaining a light reading load, inevitably imprint the course and make it their own. We almost all agree that sonnets best suit the first weeks of the course and lyrics the latter part, but we also agree that we need not use the same sonnets and lyrics. Even the essay assignments may vary, as long as there are a minimum of four and they are analytic and argumentative. As new players catch on to the purpose of the first exercises — and it is these exercises that most set the course apart from other traditional courses introducing literature to students — they contribute new ones designed for their favorite sonnets and lyrics and place them in our communal exercise file.

The last third of the course has always offered more flexibility for both teachers and students. Some teachers pursue comparative exercises centered on like poems; others use poems read in a set context or poems written by contemporary poets. Discussions of how best to close the course have invited an abundance of ways to challenge the success of Critical Reading and Writing. How far can we take students in one semester? If we hand them a poem from this week's *New Yorker*, will they be able to read it — and then write a coherent essay about it? More than any other required course, the poetry segment provokes corridor conversation; it is perfect for collaborative work and faculty development — of the aging as well as of the young. Yet we could not fully grasp this potential of the course until we had a sufficiently large cohort of the young to make such collaboration comfortable. Now I can walk into our department workroom and flip through file folders that hold new exercises each week. In fact, I do not think I have taught the same class twice in the last five years. Since I am by specialization a Shakespearean, I take delight in the magpie principle and gratefully lift anyone's exercise if I think it will help me help my students. Unlike the playwright, I do give attribution when I can, and so I am constantly introducing colleagues to students who have as yet met only one English professor: me. Most of my colleagues do likewise, refreshing their own version of Critical Reading and Writing each time they offer it and introducing the concept of fellowship to the impressionable first-year student as early as September. For each of us, then, the course is both stable and constantly changing, both "ours" and "mine." That is as it should be, for we agree that above all we must, even as Richards insisted in 1929, meet our students where they are — and they are in a world that is constantly changing. That world is also one that, within the same entering class, has prepared some and failed others in the arts of critical reading and writing. Our opening exercises serve both as leveling field and new beginning for all students in the class. They address what Richards identified as the first of the "chief difficulties of criticism," what he called, "the difficulty of *making out the plain sense* of poetry." He writes early in *Practical Criticism*:

> [A] large proportion of average-to-good (and in some cases, certainly devoted) readers of poetry frequently and repeatedly *fail to understand it*, both as a statement and as an expression. They fail to make out its prose sense, its plain overt meaning, as a set of ordinary, intelligible, English sentences, taken quite apart from any further poetic significance. And equally, they misapprehend its feeling, its tone, and its intention. (12)

I suppose the truth of 1929 cannot grow any truer, but Richards's observations about a population's inability to make a sensible sentence, let alone make sense of a poetic one, certainly seem truer than ever. And that is why we begin Critical Reading and Writing with a series of tedious, labor-intensive, ultimately addictive exercises called literalizations. I have kept the term *literalization*, introduced by Cording in 1977, though he and others in my department now refer to the same exercises as paraphrases. I, too, had begun calling the exercises paraphrases but have lately abandoned that more familiar term. I have discovered the hard way that *paraphrase* means too many things to too many high school teachers (and, of course, to those later New Critics who inveighed against the "heresy of paraphrase" [Brooks]), the most dangerous of which is, Put the poem in your own words. So I have returned to the more idiosyncratic neologism, literalization, which is, in effect, what I ask students to do for the first nine classes, one poem for each class: make literal the poem, make literal sense of what is happening in the poem. Here is a typical first assignment, one that I have adapted slightly since its first appearance in the departmental files:

Shakespeare: Sonnet 65

1	Since brass, nor stone, nor earth, nor boundless sea,
2	But sad mortality o'ersways their power,
3	How with this rage shall beauty hold a plea,
4	Whose action is no stronger than a flower?
5	O how shall summer's honey breath hold out
6	Against the wreckful siege of batt'ring days,
7	When rocks impregnable are not so stout,
8	Nor gates of steel so strong, but Time decays?
9	O fearful meditation! Where, alack,
10	Shall Time's best jewel from Time's chest lie hid?
11	Or what strong hand can hold his swift foot back?
12	Or who his spoil [of] beauty can forbid?
13	O none, unless this miracle have might,
14	That in black ink my love may still shine bright.

Assignment

Mark the beginning and ending of each sentence. Pay particular attention to lines 9–10: are these one or two sentences? Be ready to justify your choice.

Identify the subject and central verb in every sentence, particularly in the first sentence. Write this sentence out in prose that makes its grammatical structure clear before you answer any other questions.

Identify all pronouns and the words to which they refer. (For example, to whom does "their" in line 2 refer? "this" in line 3?)

Without looking outside the poem, answer the following: To what does "this rage" (line 3) refer? "fearful meditation" (line 9)? "Time's best jewel" (line 10)? "Time's chest" (line 10)? "this miracle" (line 11)?

Identify any words you do not know or which you sense may have changed with the passage of time; consider, too, if any words have a special meaning in this particular context. Look these words up in a good dictionary. (For example, how would you gloss "action" in line 4? What about "wreckful" in line 6? What does *gloss* mean?)

Consider the literal meaning of phrases such as: "How with this rage shall beauty hold a plea / Whose action is no stronger than a flower?"; "summer's honey-breath"; "wreckful siege of battering days"; "strong hand"; "swift foot"; "spoil of beauty"; "my love may still shine bright."

Though we will not go into this area, do you notice a pattern behind the language in lines 1–4? in lines 5–8?

Divide the poem into structural units. How does the rhyme scheme suggest the shape of these units?

What is the logical relation between the structural units you found? (Answer these questions in full sentences!)

Literalize this poem, using grammatical prose. Try not to increase the number of sentences but make sure you clearly show the logical movement of the poem. You may use parenthetical phrases to assist in literalizing metaphors and making clear complex figures of speech. Do not worry about the beauty of your prose, just the logic.

When handing out both my syllabus and this first assignment, I try to be as transparent with my students as possible. I tell them why I am doing what I am doing and that they are always free to ask me why if, along the way, some small torture does not seem to have an obvious pedagogical goal. Such transparency helps the eighteen-year-old enter a more cooperative mode with exercises that might otherwise crush the ego. I often draw on the work of Robert Scholes, who has lucidly commented on the craft of poetry and the art of "writing *through* literature" in numerous books (Preface iii). In the preface to a volume on that practice, Scholes writes directly to the teacher:

Most obviously — and most importantly — we mean something different from "writing *about* literature." It is our belief, based on a lot of years in classrooms all over the country, that we teachers make a mistake when we separate the writing done by students from the texts they write about. What literature has to offer us — teachers and students alike — is pleasure, information and something else: the most powerful and creative ways to use language — those things that make our literature literary. (Preface iii)

I make a similar appeal to my students, promising a reward if they participate in the rigors of training. Since over eighty-five percent of our students are involved in some intramural sport, using the analogy of practice and games works well — as do finger exercises and repetitive mastery of the scales for pianists, barre exercises for dancers, and so on. By beginning with a real life analogy for the rewards of mastering the craft of critical writing, I can reassure my students and use an active example of a literary device as a vital tool in everyday persuasive argument. I even make this trick transparent before introducing the first assignment. I tell my students that their sense of control is about to be challenged; this knowledge does not circumvent their experience, but it does preserve a certain degree of trust early in the semester. The sports-music-dance analogy also makes a promise of reward, of pleasure ahead, which we explicitly discuss.

Even very good students find the first nine questions in the above exercise difficult to answer. Our schools now de-emphasize grammar drills; most Americans want to read poetry by line rather than by sentence; and few older, let alone young, readers have a clear grasp that familiar metaphors are still metaphors. I ask students to record in their notebooks their answers to the first nine questions, which we discuss in class (I only collect their literalizations). A good deal of rubble gets cleared away in those first fifty minutes of class discussion, the most important item being the notion that all opinions are equal when talking about a poem. There are six sentences in the poem: not eight because some of the sentences have dependent clauses, not seven because of the exclamation point, not ten because of poetic license. There are six sentences because of Shakespeare's use (in this edition of the sonnet) of terminal punctuation and appropriate capitalization. Fights break out. And I get to explain to my students the rules and how there got to be rules. I usually pause here to suggest to them that there are better and worse opinions and that for the time being they should take comfort in rules. (One small violation of the transparency principle: only after students have grasped that there are such things as grammatical rules will I introduce poetry that gleefully breaks them. Then I can say, Ah, but now you know that breaking a rule communicates meaning, and if you didn't know the rule, you couldn't argue that "opinion.")

Like most of my colleagues, I prefer to begin the course with Shakespearean sonnets, though my motives for doing so may differ from theirs and have nothing to do with my work as a Shakespearean. I find that late-sixteenth-century language and syntax stress the need for literalization because, though the words and sentiments seem familiar, their expression is alien to twenty-first-century readers. (By contrast, modern poetry initially seems accessible and so actually sets students up for a harder fall.) Students need to resolve the conflict between the familiar and the alien. Once they do so, they quickly see the benefits of literalizing.

I use the nine opening classes for multiple ends, making clear that human beings are capable of simultaneous mental activities. That point is best demonstrated with lower-level functions. I therefore, in some sense, establish a foundation for critical writing from day one not only by taking on the bête noir of opinion but also by anticipating the beasties of academic discourse attempted by the young. It is much easier to conduct a small grammar review while analyzing a complex compound sentence than it is to teach first-year students complex compound sentences. I can ask them to look for the main subject and verb in a Shakespearean sentence to make sense of it, and then can explain to them why they are lost; I can show them on the board that contemporary American prose is predominantly back loaded, that is, it opens with a strong subject and verb and is followed by clauses and other subordinate material. Sixteenth-century prose — and the poetic sentences they are lost in — is more frequently front loaded. Students need to dig through the clauses to find the main subject and verb. What is the application to their own writing? They learn to write back-loaded sentences with active verbs if they want to be clear. Better yet, I can target the *it* and *this* phenomena, as in the assignment's third question. Students almost always get lost in the labyrinth of Shakespeare's deliberately cryptic "this" and "it" references, and so it becomes clear to them that using the same tactic in what should be the clarifying prose of argument would be wrong. They might still use the elusive *it* and *this*, but my feedback will connect with something.

This exercise, typical of all that follow, also emphasizes logical thought, starting with the logic of grammar and extending to the logic of word choice. As with grammar, mistakes can be made in selecting what a word means, especially in early chosen poems. Students must eliminate glosses that entered the language after the composition of the poem; they must also recognize words they initially misidentify as the wrong part of speech. After a few lost points, they quickly develop a better eye for the italics of a dictionary. Is that word an adverb or a noun? transitive or intransitive? And what do those terms mean? Look them up. I assure my classes that I have an unnatural attachment to dictionaries but that good ones can be like the best of hypertexts. (As a side note: at the end of my last Critical Reading and Writing class, I asked the students to be a simulated search engine, but by then they had grown used to my ways and enjoyed the project.) The ongoing simultaneity of the literalizing exercises stresses good reading habits even as it focuses on the logic of context as the basis for meaning.

Logic, I explain, must dictate the translation of metaphors into similes and of symbols into what they represent. In the first exercise, students see that "beauty" has been personified even though there is no capital letter. Beauty "hold[s] a plea." What could that mean? The dictionary will help to some extent, and the better the dictionary, the closer the student will come to something like the phrase "make a case." Locating that judicial metaphor should lead the student to a parallel dictionary selection for "action" in line 4. I am, at this stage of the game, willing to accept a consistent pattern in which "hold a plea" becomes "defend itself" (as if in court) and then "action" can become "power," another meaning available in most dictionaries. The point is, students learn to let sentences themselves provide a context of meaning that will ultimately be the basis for discerning larger contexts. But the finishing touch at this early stage of preanalysis, a stage that Shakespeare accommodates well, is asking students to observe and describe all organizational structures in the sonnet. Completing this task shows why it makes sense to identify the legal metaphor of the first sentence, which is also the first interlocking rhyming unit and the first of a series of questions. Having made those observations, also discoveries, students champ at the bit of interpretation, which is good. I want them to know the desire to interpret but keep it unfilled until they have the tools with which to do so successfully.

I grade the literalizations on a ten-point scale, assuring the class that I will drop their lowest mark, combine the other eight, and translate those grades into one letter grade. I also tell my students that those who do not catch on to the literalizing process quickly or those who are unhappy with their grades are free to continue submitting literalizations until they are satisfied. Year after year, students have become determined to master this foundational skill. For many, including some very good students, it is not easy. Here is an example (my own) of what I consider a good literalization of sonnet 65:

> Since death already overcomes the power even of such seemingly enduring things as brass, stone, and the limitless sea, how can beauty make a case (as if in a court of law) against the force of mortality when beauty's own argument is no stronger than that of a flower? O, how shall the fleeting fragrance of summer flowers (representatives of summer itself and therefore of beauty) survive the destructive attack of winter, when time already erodes seemingly indestructible rocks (like those in a castle) and strong steel gates. What an awful thought: where shall the best thing time ever provided — beauty — hide from time itself, time which also brings decay? What or who can stop the advance of time? Who can forbid time's destruction of beauty? No one and nothing — unless this miracle of a poem has the power to let my love (both my beloved and my love for that person) endure forever in ink on the printed page.

I return a possible literalization with the first three exercises, always emphasizing the word *possible*, because there is much room for diversity. As students in the class grow skilled at literalizing, I use their own examples. Cheating has never been a problem. I actually encourage collaborative work on the questions; when it comes to the literalizations, pride and pragmatism tend to take over. The work is too idiosyncratic, too individualized to survive mass reproduction. It is also true that I teach in ideal circumstances: my classes are capped at twenty-five. Still, there is something so intensely personal about the first three weeks of interaction that the method of the course seems to draw out the best in students. Those who were the jumping-jack students in AP high school English class—the ones who always had their hands up, always knew what something stood for in a poem but had no real notion of why they knew what they knew—are quieted down for a bit, though usually they are more intrigued than humiliated. Those who thought they hated poetry realize they just never understood it and begin to breathe more easily. My favorite moment came almost four years ago when a woman, who later became an English major and a fairly accomplished poet, beamed and announced, "I love this; it's just like geometry." Indeed, the proof must be correct, not just the answer.

I stay with Shakespearean sonnets for the first three to four classes, letting the exercises increase in metaphoric difficulty until they reach something as complex as sonnet 73, "Thou see'st in me that time of year," a poem that incorporates similes within metaphors as well as metaphors within metaphors. Then, just to keep us on our toes, I usually bring in another Renaissance author's sonnet, often one by Philip Sidney, something like "Loving in truth," a sonnet so like and unlike Shakespeare's work that even first-year students grasp the point of structural and thematic differences. The pressure to interpret builds like steam. Since this Sidney sonnet, like so many of Shakespeare's, closes with a reflection on the poet's own powers, questions about the nature of poetry also arise, as does my favorite, Aren't we killing the beauty? I let these questions surface. For now we can have a serious discussion about what poetry is, a discussion that goes well beyond earlier ones that focused on rhyme scheme, capital letters, and writing conventions or floated into the overly warm air of cliché.

Arguing the case for argument is much easier after the first few weeks of literalizing than on day one of class, when students do not yet know how to analyze literature. Having eliminated the real effort literal comprehension requires, students know in their gut that some other effort must now be extended. Dispelling the pent-up energy of "but doesn't that mean ..." (which I blocked them from during class discussion) is a good place to look for a thesis. I do not dictate thesis statements, but I will vet a thesis for any student who wants to try one out on me or on the class and encourage sharing thesis points, assuring the class that no two students will carry out an argument the same way. In Critical Reading and Writing, I have found it especially helpful to keep emphasizing the words, *what, how,* and *why*. These words become our writing mantra. We know the what, we ask the how of the what, the why of the how, the how of the why, round and round. (Graduates have teased me with promises of embroidered pillows with these words circling a favorite poem.) The point is, the "why of the how of the what" technique keeps students focused on the evidence of the poem and on poetic technique. First-year students can manage such an argument; they can master the evidence of a poem. English majors must and will go well beyond these limits, but I unapologetically admit that for nonmajors who might never take another English course, I here use poetry to teach critical thinking and critical writing as much as I use it to introduce them to literature.

Depending on the class and its skills, even as students are writing their first essay, I vary the challenges of the remaining literalizing exercises. I usually make an abrupt shift after five or so Renaissance sonnets to something like William Wordsworth's "Nuns fret not," another poem about poetry but also a sonnet whose language is deceptively accessible. I warn them. It doesn't matter. Most students need the experience of falling back into bad habits to remember how dangerous those habits are. Students forget their mistake with Shakespeare's exclamation point in sonnet 65 and deny Wordsworth the ability to write a one-sentence sonnet. The easily distracted ignore the date of composition, neglect the dictionary, and come up with quite amazing images for such constructions as "maids at their wheels." The students groan when we run the exercise sheet in class, aware that it was they and not the maids who were caught sleeping at the wheel. I usually relent and let them rewrite the literalizations before handing them in, knowing that the lesson has been learned.

The next lesson is more important, and here I am even more inclined not to disclose to students ahead of time the mistakes students of the past have made. I do warn my students that they are about to encounter a new challenge to the literalization process—determining the tone of the poem. But that is the only warning I issue because now, sufficient trust having been established so that even the meek are willing to provoke unintended laughter, students must experience how wrong they can be if they do not listen for the nuances of language and forego assumptions about who can say what in a poem. Edna St. Vincent Millay works well in this regard, for her very name, unknown, it seems, to American high school students, already misleads them. One of my favorite exercises uses her 1923 work "I, being born a woman." Even the date seems to confuse the young, who, as did the young of my youth, work from a few biases. These biases include the notion that sexuality is a fairly recent discovery, that poets speak of love not lust and ladies, poets or not, never admit to experiences of lust, except to their friends.

1	I, being born a woman and distressed
2	By all the need and notions and my kind,
3	Am urged by your propinquity to find
4	Your person fair, and feel a certain zest
5	To bear your body's weight upon my breast:
6	So subtly is the fume of life designed,
7	To clarify the pulse and cloud the mind,
8	And leave me once again undone, possessed.
9	Think not for this, however, the poor treason
10	Of my stout blood against my staggering brain,
11	I shall remember you with love, or season
12	My scorn with pity, —let me make it plain:
13	I find this frenzy insufficient reason
14	For conversation when we meet again.

Assignment

Mark the end of each sentence. Now mark the beginning and end of each
   independent clause.
What is the subject and verb in each independent clause? (Pay attention to
   which verbs are passive and which are active. Note, too, which verbs take
   objects and what those objects are.)
Why does the poet use a colon to end line five? Is the colon used differently in
   line twelve?
Look up all unfamiliar words and select meanings that suit the context of the
   poem.
What is the organizational structure of this sonnet?
What one word most noticeably marks the turning point in the sonnet?
Literalize the poem.
Say what the poem is about in one sentence.

At this point in the semester, any student in the class should be able to make up
the exercise questions; I often have them do so. But here, the attention drawn to
Millay's colons should serve as a special buoy marking some interpretive crux,
as should the query about a one-word turning point. Advised for weeks now to
attend to logic words, students must identify what Millay's "however" reverses.
They needlessly torture themselves trying to turn "bear your weight upon my
breast" into a metaphor while staring blindly at "the fume of life" as if it were not
one. Only the rare student whose parents have warned her about the dangers
of "propinquity" seems to have an inkling of the game Millay might be playing.

   Now that each student has been allowed the opportunity of making
a fool of him- or herself by being a college student incapable of locating
a sentence, class discussion of answers to the above questions is usually
uproarious and serious at the same time. Controlling the tone of a class
about tone is crucial to success. In this course that provides for so much
simultaneous learning experience, with wit and good will a teacher can also
explain why and how it is that even readers who have begun to understand
the importance of seeing the text project their own values or preconceived
views onto the screen of literature, especially poetry. Because a clean literalization of Millay's poem, or one of John Donne's Holy Sonnets, which
provokes much the same response, leaves students convinced that they were
wrong, that their misreading was not a matter of opinion, the lesson tends

to stick and, like so much else, can be drawn on later. And by now, because there is no alternative, we have entered the realm of argumentation. Their first essay is due in a few days.

Though I stop collecting literalizations, turning our attention after nine classes to a different kind of work sheet and more fully to the next three essays, I advise students always to literalize whenever they sense themselves confused by or in a poem. If I sense in a class discussion that we as a class are lost, we will stop and make literal sense together. But for a few weeks, new question sheets will focus on longer lyric poems, works like Robert Lowell's "Skunk Hour," Sylvia Plath's "Black Rook in Rainy Weather," and Li-Young Lee's "Persimmons." In each of these poems, structural problems arise that force students to watch verb tense closely and locate the speaker with care. We talk about the relationship of speaker to poet and, as we prepare the second and third essays, discuss writing strategies, including ways of making the line, image, or metaphor do things, so that we don't get constantly caught up in tiresome references to "then the speaker says." Because these poems and their kin are highly personal lyrics, students are tempted to enter into them. We talk about the myth and necessity of objectivity.

From this point on, we analyze one poem in each class, often stopping to prepare for or review the upcoming or just-returned five-page analytic essays. There are four of these essays, and each allows students greater freedom and demands more responsibility of them. Always, I assume that students have literalized the poem before writing on it — or at least developed the instinct for knowing when to do so. And they know that all that work, the work they might once have known as paraphrase or once wrote of as "Webster says," is prewriting. Literalizing and then feeling the burning need to analyze helps students understand the difference between summary and argument. Literalizing and then yearning to speak of beauty helps students locate, not obliterate, the artistry of art. Classroom discussions begin to introduce the necessary language of assonance, alliteration, and enjambment because now such words seem needed and are not just part of a vocabulary drill. In one semester of Critical Reading and Writing: Poetry, I have watched students undergo an intellectual growth spurt akin to the physical one of adolescence.

In the later stages of the course, I like to move the students beyond formalism by widening the nature of what they must look up to literalize a poem. Perhaps one of the most interesting poetic triptychs I have asked them to work with begins with John Keats's "Ode on a Grecian Urn," moves to Wallace Steven's "Anecdote of a Jar," and closes with Ishmael Reed's "I am a Cowboy in the Boat of Ra." I am not sure who is more stunned, they or I, to learn that the British Museum that inspired Keats is still more familiar to students than is the contemporary jazz musician Sonny Rollins, referenced by Reed. But when I am lucky, at least one student knows how to sing scat, and we improvise as we discuss the complexity of the world today's students have inherited. At this point I show them how to become a search engine; we call it "doing the Google."

Ultimately, Critical Reading and Writing is more than simply learning how to read and write analytically about poetry. It is a course that uses poetry to teach the discipline of critical thought and conscious information retrieval. It is a system that harnesses the intelligence of individual students so that they might best know how to be in charge of where to lead that force. I have lately come to see that this most old-fashioned of pedagogies can also lead to the most wonderful of collaborative moments in a class and between students and teacher.

That collaboration, moreover, is not limited to gifted students only in need of polishing already acquired skills. We are lucky at Holy Cross. The middle fifty percent of SAT scores are 1270–1330. But I have often had in my mix of "crawlers" students for whom English is a second language, students for whom reading and especially writing have always been an immense challenge, and students who fall well below the median. These students often demonstrate the most immediate progress. There are no limits, finally, as to where a teacher can take a class in the last two weeks. Other than loading on sheer volume, a truly counterproductive strategy, there are few mistakes to be made. Students come to enjoy their own power, their ability to convince one another, to make sense.

We know as a department that students need constant reinforcement in the art of making sense, and so we offer Critical Reading and Writing: Fiction in the second semester not only for those who were unable to take the poetry segment in the fall but also for those who would like to expand on that segment and continue polishing their skills while learning about narrative form. In 1998, however, the department conducted a study of upper-level writing and reached a consensus. All of us conceded that we could immediately determine, when reading junior and senior essays written by English majors, which of them had taken Critical Reading and Writing: Poetry. For the first time, we agreed on a requirement for English majors—the basic course we offer to all incoming students, the one that, ironically, prospective majors would often try to place out of, using their English AP scores of 4 or higher.

Few students enter Holy Cross declaring English as a major—perhaps as few as eighteen or as many as twenty-five. Most students interested in the major will almost naturally take an English course in their first semester, but last term, I had a junior English major sitting among my first-semester first-year students. She was somewhat resentful at first. By week 3 and her third 6 on a literalization, she was angry. By week 5 she was amazed at how much better she was doing. By the end of the term, she had risen a full letter grade in her two upper-level English courses. More important, she had become a committed liberal arts student; her grades had risen in all her courses. She had learned that work mattered, that work had its rewards.

I like to prove that the poetry segment also has a different kind of reward, something that outlasts a transcript and has nothing at all to do with an academic major. In the last few years, I have helped my Critical Reading and Writing students, especially nonmajors, see for themselves that they can pick up a copy of the *New Yorker* or *Atlantic Monthly* and make sense of the poems they find there. The fourth essay, an analytic essay on a contemporary poem, brings them to where they are now, to their world. It's slightly brighter, perhaps, than it was in September, a bit more burnished than when they entered it four months before.

The outcome of that summer workshop with colleagues has considerably burnished our departmental morale as well. Two colleagues who have since achieved tenure continue to use literalization in their Critical Reading and Writing courses because, they tell me, they now feel they can adapt those exercises well to their own theoretical orientation. Perhaps of even greater interest is that three adjunct professors who took positions at other institutions, which varied from a community college to neighboring Clark University, have taken their course folders with them as valued pedagogical tools. That, it seems to me, is the ultimate proof of a good pudding, one whose basic recipe has remained constant even though the tastes of those who crave dessert have changed.

The Detail versus the Debate:
Literature, Argument, and First-Year Writing

"**B**ut what does it mean?" my first-year writing teacher asked me, referring to a John Updike short story I had just written about. I don't remember
many specific questions put to me by my undergraduate instructors, but
I remember that one. "It doesn't *mean* anything," I said. "It's a short story."
She probably thought I was being a typically resistant first-year student,
someone who thinks that as soon as you try to analyze a piece of literature,
you're reading too much into it. But that wasn't it. My complaint arose out
of my sense of literature's ineffability, the impossibility of ever making it
mean something the way a line of ancient Greek would mean something
as soon as it was translated into English. It was the idea of a short story's
equivalence to a finite set of explanatory statements that irked me so much.
I loved short stories because they were balloons I could ingest, filling me up
with their plenitude. I didn't change my essay much. My teacher, thinking
I was full of hot air, gave it a well-deserved low grade.

It took me a long time to realize how good a question my first-year
writing teacher had asked me. It was driven home when I met my dop-
pelgänger, Maura.[1] I got to know her through my work on the Harvard
Study of Undergraduate Writing. From 2000 to 2004, I worked as a writing
instructor and as a research associate for the Expository Writing Program at
Harvard, which is trying to fill in some big holes in our knowledge of writ-
ting development. Composition specialists have an idea of what students
learn in their first-year writing classes, but what happens after they leave?
Funded by the Andrew W. Mellon Foundation and the Harvard President's
Office, this study examines how undergraduates develop as writers over
the course of their four years of college. The researchers surveyed 422 students, over a quarter of the class of 2001, and followed 65 of those students

Faye Halpern

intensively, interviewing them each semester and collecting everything they had written and instructors' comments and assignments. On the basis of this data, we wrote profiles of each of them.[2]

One student I profiled was Maura. She majored in religion, minored in English, and loved literature. A great close reader and an extremely fluent writer, she excelled at the details. She would follow the twists and turns of a literary text: one short line would generate a paragraph or more of analysis, rendered in lovely, complex sentences. Here she writes about a particular line in Salman Rushdie's novel *Shame*: "Shame, dear reader, is not the exclusive property of the East":

> It seems, then, that the fairy tale's universality is both a protection from the dangers of specificity and a means of broadening the collective understanding of the role, the gravity, and the relentlessness of shame. However, there is an irony, a sarcasm, in the narrator's voice when he speaks of the safety he finds in universality which complicates this simple understanding of the motivations for universality; by assuring his readers that nothing he says need be taken too seriously, the narrator seems almost to challenge his readers to take his tale seriously, to get upset, to take action: in short, he challenges his readers to read his story not as the fairy tale he claims it to be but as the realistic novel he denies he is writing.

This is terrific stuff, especially when we consider that Maura wrote it as a first-year student. But what we at the study noticed about Maura was something her instructors (with one huge exception) didn't seem to: even though her essays contained fabulous readings of literary texts, she had a hard time making a claim about their significance. Her thesis for the above essay was that the "coexistence of fantasy and reality pervades [*Shame*] and creates a problem of identification, challenging any simple classifications of real and make-believe." This might seem like a pretty strong thesis, especially since it lays out a clear path for her to follow: she must show that different passages in the text escape any simple classification. This novel is much more complex than we might initially take it to be.

Maura relied on what we at the study named the "complexity thesis," a thesis that announces that something (a short story, a historical event, a policy decision) is not as simple as it may first appear.[3] This kind of thesis is quite seductive since it promises to delve below the surface, what good academic essays do, and it must have held a special appeal for Maura. It set her up to do what she was so good at, develop a series of close readings that reveals the intricate workings of a text. Because this kind of thesis shares one characteristic of a strong academic thesis — it won't say the obvious about the object of study — and because it usually plays to a student's strengths, it can become a crutch for the student, a sign that the student has been stalled in her development as an academic writer.

For Maura a crutch is what it became. Here's a thesis from her junior year: "That authors as diverse as Teresa of Avila and T. S. Eliot would both concern themselves with such questions of prayer and knowledge speaks to their complexity." In her senior year she wrote, "[This essay will show] the complex ways in which religion, ethnicity, and the politics of national identity interact in Northern Ireland." Maura never experienced the pleasures of making a real argument, of saying something new in anything but an extremely local way. She could say something new about many particular passages but had a hard time using these passages to tell us something new about the text as a whole. She could not go further than making a claim for a thing's richness, its resistance to simple schemes of classification. I don't know if Maura would have gotten angry at a question about a story's meaning, but her writing exists as the logical endpoint of such irritation: her essays reveal the plenitude of any given text.

But what's wrong, really, with the complexity thesis? The comments Maura received on her senior thesis reveal its limitations. Here is what one of her senior thesis readers wrote:

> This thesis, written in smooth and admirably controlled prose, contains a number of vital insights into the complex of modernism, religion and Southern literature. Those insights arise mainly in the course of specific readings of individual texts, and their power does not much extend beyond these local confines.

Such comments as these were devastating, not least in their accuracy. The complexity thesis just doesn't add up to much; it enables the writer to focus on the detail rather than the debate. The details take over and cannot be summed up into a single, arguable position: saying something is complex isn't all that controversial, because, in the end, it isn't all that original.[4]

Most college essays—and I'm talking about essays across the disciplines—require more than the claim that something is complex. It's not enough in a history class to claim that the causes of World War II cannot be reduced to a single factor, nor is it enough in a psychology class to say that people's personalities result not from nature or nurture but from a melding of the two. Professors across the disciplines often try to ward off such theses in their writing guidelines. Here is an example from one of Harvard's most popular classes, Moral Reasoning 22: Justice. "[Y]our challenge is to craft a thesis that is defensible in 6 or 7 pages without being a statement of the obvious" (Ristroph). Harvard's Writing Center, which puts out a cross-disciplinary booklet on how to write academic essays, advises, "An essay has to have a purpose or motive; the mere existence of an assignment or deadline is not sufficient.... Instead, you should be trying to make the best possible case for an original idea you have arrived at after a period of research" (Duffin). These guidelines are all pleas for originality, for the students to arrive at their own controversial positions. Citing the complexity of a work places the student squarely in the herd since it resembles more an assumption academics make about the world than a position with which they would argue.

Harvard's Expository Writing Program aims to prepare students to write the kind of essay that will be expected of them in all their college classes, not just those that require them to write about literature. Since all first-year Harvard students, regardless of their AP scores, GPA, or preference, must take at least one semester of expository writing, only a small percentage of the students who take expository writing courses are latent English majors. The fifteen students who take my expository writing class Satire and Irony are no exception. I get a lot of future government and economics majors along with a smattering of science and history-oriented students (mostly male, for some reason). I suspect there's a high correlation between students who take my class and students who can recite large chunks of *The Simpsons* from memory. What a shock to them when they realize that nary a *Simpsons* episode will be viewed; instead, they have signed up for a highly literary class, which begins with Jonathan Swift's "A Modest Proposal," moves through Dave Eggers's memoir, *A Heartbreaking Work of Staggering Genius,* and culminates in Mark Twain's *Adventures of Huckleberry Finn.*

So why do I use literature in my first-year writing class, with its tendency to evoke hostile questions from two normally opposed camps, the nonreaders, who find literary criticism arbitrary, and those students who use literature as a supplemental form of sustenance and resist analyzing it? Why use literature, with its wealth of details and dearth of argument, in first-year writing classes? One simple answer is that I feel at home with literature and literary analysis, since I majored in English in college and became an Americanist in graduate school. But that's no justification, of course, just a fact of life (and a big one for schools where first-year English is taught solely by English graduate students). Actually, my own disciplinary training is embraced by the Harvard Expository Writing Program, which has decided that first-year writing is best taught through topic-based classes that rely on the expertise of the instructor. We at the program can justify these kinds of classes because we believe that different disciplines have something in common: their essays depend on having an arguable thesis and being able to support it using evidence.[5] For me, the idea is that one can use literary texts in a way that takes advantage of their wealth of details while still allowing them to mean something. One can use literary texts to teach students how to argue.

It is easy, though, to use literary texts to generate essays that do not support the use of literary texts in teaching first-year writing. To show how to generate essays made up of local bits of analysis with no unifying theme, no overarching thesis, I have only to dig up an assignment I used a few years ago:

> Pick an object in *Uncle Tom's Cabin*—living rooms or hats or babies or beds, anything you want—and trace it through the novel. How many different types of this object occur in the novel? What kinds of people does this object attach itself to? Does the representation of this object change in the course of this work? *The point of this topic is to use your object to illuminate a larger issue in the book.* (How does your object give us insight into what's going on with race in the novel, how does it reveal Stowe's techniques of persuasion, or how

does it add or detract from Stowe's argument with slavery, etc.?) Pick your object accordingly.

I was proud of this assignment when I wrote it: I thought it would force students to attend to the details and then make those details into something unified and important. Looking back, I find it remarkable how much my first-year writing teacher's question haunts this assignment: on the one hand, I ask students for plenitude, and, on the other hand, I want them to form that plenitude into something meaningful. As you can imagine, the assignment never worked that well: it asks students to notice a bunch of details and then tells them — in italics — to make those details significant. It does not, however, give them any clues about how to do that. It reminds me of a parody I once saw of a plan for a water purification plant: "Dirty water enters here," it read, showing a picture of a building; "clean water exits there."

The students who already knew how to answer the question, What do these details mean? could proceed by using my prompt. It wouldn't hinder them at all. The students who didn't — most of them — would receive no help. And assuming we want to pitch these first-year writing classes to students who don't know how to make details matter, it seems important that we let them in on the internal workings of the water purification plant.

One problem with my first-year writing teacher's comment (and my writing assignment) was its vagueness. What does it mean for a piece of literature to mean something? What does it look like when a cluster of details gains significance? Here is how I've translated what lay behind my teacher's comment: essays become meaningful when they argue for some position. This position is the student's thesis. To argue for a position, the writer must enter into a debate. There's no point in arguing for something everyone already agrees with: "Nathaniel Hawthorne was concerned about the evil he saw in men's souls," to take an example from my own high school oeuvre. On the other hand, the thesis doesn't have to come down on the reader's head like a sledgehammer: "Irony is a reprehensible mode in which to convey tragedy." It can be subtle. Yet even if it's subtle, a good thesis brings the writer out of hiding, the place where many writers, especially the ones who love to do close readings, have spent a lot of time. No one can find you—much less attack you—if you say something with which no one would disagree. "'A Modest Proposal' is not as simple as it first appears, as we can see through a close look at many of its passages." Without having to spend a moment to ponder, I know that I think so too.

Learning to use literature as a basis for essays with strong theses and arguments entailed shifting how I saw literature. It's not that I grew to see literature as offering overt arguments. How many bad essays (and book reviews) conclude that "X text teaches us we *can* go home again" or "X author shows us that without human connections we are lost." Who knew? Literary texts cannot be so easily summed up (and if this is what my first-year writing teacher was looking for, then I was right to get angry). But literary texts can provide an excellent forum for debate. Their wealth of details can offer students the means to argue for a particular position. These details assure readers that the text in question can be shaped into different readings. I am not saying that all readings are equal. Some are better than others, and that fact is crucial for making an argument about a literary text. What makes one reading better than another is often the way it handles the details: whether it can, for example, make sense of recalcitrant details rather than require the student author to bury them. It is because literary texts can sustain multiple readings and that some are better than others that they offer such a good means to launch an argumentative essay (and also why they provide good training for arguing in non-literature-based disciplines). They allow a student to show why one interpretation, despite another's seeming power, is better.

Some texts sustain multiple readings more obviously than others. I've found that it's easier for first-year students if I use literary texts that I think contain static and require the students to adjust the picture until it becomes clear. In the more introductory version of expository writing that about ten percent of the first-year class takes, a section of which I teach, I pick for my first unit short stories that contain an overt problem and beg for interpretation. I teach, among others, Susan Minot's "Lust," which requires the reader to reconcile the narrator's promiscuity with the unhappiness her behavior causes her. I've had students try to solve the problem by calling the narrator a slut (!), but this easy judgment can happen only if the student ignores many of the story's most provocative details, an omission that can easily be pointed out.[6] And believe me, I do. But when teaching Satire and Irony, not the introductory class, I feel compelled to center my first essay on "A Modest Proposal." Starting this way makes things more difficult: the carapace of cleverness surrounding Swift's essay makes it difficult for students to drive a wedge into it and open it up, to reveal to us something about it that we didn't already know.

Having written "to reveal to us something about it that we didn't already know," I realize how central that objective is to what good academic essays do. But how do students set themselves up to say something that will surprise the reader? They imagine what the reader might say that is a misconception and use their essays to offer a clearer picture of the text. Academic essays by beginners, who almost never know the positions that other people have taken with regard to the text in question, are fueled by acts of empathy. What might be a plausible misreading of the text?

I try to build this act of empathy into the assignment for the first essay, which gives students a number of options, two of which are these:

> How does "A Modest Proposal" deepen, complicate, or challenge a plausible idea about how satire works? Or, relatedly, how does a rigorous analysis of "A Modest Proposal" deepen, complicate, or challenge a plausible idea about how the piece itself works?
>
> Are there places where "A Modest Proposal" contradicts itself? Are there gaps in its logic? How should these self-contradictions or gaps change the way we think about the piece?

If all goes well, the student writer should first establish one way, a wrong but plausible way, to read the text. The writer needs to do that not only to set his or her own reading in relief but to make that reading reveal to us something new by disabusing us of a belief we probably held before reading the essay.

But perhaps one can see the problems in this assignment already. The more consummate the artistry of a piece, the harder it is to do more than confirm what readers already think about it. Students tend in this first essay to make the "plausible idea about how the piece works" rather too obvious. These plausible ideas are not quite as bad as, "Some may think that Jonathan Swift is counseling us to actually consume impoverished Irish babies, but I will argue he is not." But some come a little too close. As one of my students, Liz, wrote for her first essay, "Upon a closer inspection of the text, we can see that Swift's humor masks an underlying tone of anger and passion about the poverty ravaging Ireland." Few students, of course, would think it's worthwhile to suggest Swift does not want us to eat poor babies, but it's not unreasonable to think that noting Swift's anger is something worth doing. The problem with this first essay assignment—a problem that I've decided to live with for the moment—is that, in the absence of secondary criticism, students don't know what constitutes an obvious reading of "A Modest Proposal." Because it's a difficult text, it's hard to know whether one's reading is obvious or not. Irony requires one always to "close read"; you're a dupe if you read only the surface (which is one of the reasons it's so good to teach ironic texts to students). But an ironic piece's built-in complexity makes it hard for them to see what, once the reader has figured out the deeper meaning, is still obvious. It's hard for them, but not impossible—and the way out of this difficulty is, ironically enough, through the details.

My two examples of obvious theses about "A Modest Proposal" don't take advantage of the details. Even the less obvious thesis—that Swift is angry—could be figured out through common sense: doesn't it stand to reason that an author counseling his countrymen to eat Irish babies might be angry? It's not that one can't find details in the text to support this position; it's hard to find details that don't, details that would support an alternative reading. Yet there are students who are able to launch themselves into the realm of the counterintuitive, even in this first essay, and they do this precisely by noticing the odd details in "A Modest Proposal." And because I know that this attention to detail will help students succeed in their essay, I try to get them to notice the small, anomalous moments of Swift's piece in the assignment I have them do before they write the draft of their essay. They do what I call an annotation: they type out two or three passages from "A Modest Proposal" and mark them up, noting things like Swift's shifting tone, diction, humor, attitude, and so on. I emphasize that they probably won't get to use all the details they notice but that these details might prove helpful in formulating their counterintuitive thesis. I ask them in my comments on their annotations, What patterns can be found in these odd moments? I ask them in class discussion, Do they add up to something you didn't originally expect from this text?

There's a moment in Liz's not-quite-successful essay that shows how strong it could have been. The moment comes in the last line of her essay, when it's too late: "What we see, then, is that Swift's humor does not negate his angry tone, but that the two are in fact related." Now, here's a subtle and counterintuitive thesis, one that could not have been arrived at simply by knowing the general outlines of the text and the circumstances of its creation. It's not crazy to think people might, in general, think of humor and anger as opposed to each other and that "A Modest Proposal" in particular might work by oscillating between the two rather than relating them. In other words, this potential thesis has a plausible counterargument. Additionally, it captures a fineness of detail lacking in the claim that Swift is angry: to argue for this subtle thesis would require going to the details of the text both to register this relation and to explain it further (how exactly does this relation work?). It seems, then, that there are two ways to reveal to us something we don't already know. Students can come to counterintuitive readings by knowing what the common readings are, or they can come to them by noticing small details and using them to complicate their initial readings (with the assumption that their earlier readings are ones that most other people would have). This second means to a counterintuitive reading through noticing weird or recalcitrant details in the text is good news for those units where we do not want to give our students secondary reading, an actual record of someone else's plausible interpretation, which they can work against.

After the first essay assignment, I do have my students read secondary criticism. For their third essay, the students read both *Adventures of Huckleberry Finn* and criticism about Twain's novel. And I've found what Gerald Graff and James Phelan, the editors of the terrific Bedford edition of this novel, have found: it makes a lot of sense to group criticism around controversies. This is especially true in a first-year writing class since controversy is exactly what I'm trying to get them to generate and enter into in their own essays. *Huck Finn,* that wicked, problematic novel, offers many controversies to choose from. I choose two: the controversy over the ending—whether it's "cheating," as in Ernest Hemingway's famous characterization (*Green Hills*), or whether there are ways to justify it—and the controversy over Twain's depiction of race.

I've had students tell me that it's an odd, telling experience for them to read critics who are opposed to one another. "He's so right," they tell me they had thought after putting down Leo Marx's "Mr. Eliot, Mr. Trilling, and *Huckleberry Finn.*" "He's so right, too," they'll admit to having thought upon finishing James Cox's essay "Attacks on the Ending and Twain's Attack on Conscience," which takes Marx's essay as its foil.

Reading critics who offer different readings of a literary text literalizes for my students the idea of debate.[7] Seeing such a debate in action works much better than simply telling students that academic essays involve debate and that through debate we make progress toward the truth. My colleagues in expository writing who come from a philosophical background don't have this problem: all the assigned readings involve overt arguments, and they choose authors for each unit who overtly disagree with one another. But for those of us who use literature to teach first-year writing, debate doesn't come as easily.

Yet this lack of ease is why literary texts might work particularly well in first-year writing courses—and for students who do not go on to major in English. One of my colleagues who uses philosophical texts to teach argument worries that once his students leave the course they're only going to use counterargument in their essays when studying material that offers an explicit debate. They might be able to enter into a debate once it's been clearly established for them but might not know how to create one. Seeing that literature, which many of them view either as pure pleasure or pure distraction, can and should be made debatable helps students transfer the lessons they learn in my course to their other classes: it allows them to frame phenomena that might not seem overtly argumentative in terms of thesis and counterargument. They learn how even things that seem, initially, immune to interpretation can, in fact, be interpreted in various ways:

students learn to pick what they think is the best interpretation and support it using evidence. So what turns out to be my hardest assignment — writing about the consummately clever, hard-to-drive-a-wedge-into Swift — might be the best one for preparing them to recognize the possibility for debates, debates to which we, their teachers and fellow debaters, want them to add their own voice.[8]

In my first few years of using literature to teach writing, I didn't much emphasize debate and its sine qua non, counterargument. Consequently, I spent a lot of time wondering why the essays my students wrote didn't seem all that good. It's been a godsend, then, to be able to bring in not only literary criticism but also literary criticism that is self-consciously arranged into controversies. Students come to see that literature is something to argue about, just as political or religious issues are. Seeing these literary controversies lets them see what's left for them to do, what hasn't been done.

That students might have something to contribute to a live debate is a liberating idea; actually entering into the debate, they find, is not so easy. I think it presents a problem because so many of them are used to consulting critics only for affirmation. How many papers have we seen that contain statements like "Wayne Booth would agree with me that irony causes community. As he comments, 'I see that it [the reconstruction of irony] completes a more astonishing communal achievement than most accounts have recognized' (13)." How remarkable that beginners are so prescient in predicting the ideas of the critics we read. Many students find themselves disagreeing with Marx only to realize, after it's been pointed out to them, that they've disagreed with him exactly the way Cox does. But most of them eventually manage to add something to the debate, as long as I emphasize that that's what they're meant to do: to go from summarizing the critics to engaging with them. Students must give up their position of safety. I try to teach them that, rather than exist above the fray, they need to get down and dirty, to say something with which the reader might disagree (until, of course, the reader has finished the essay).

When I was a first-year student, I used my essays to demonstrate that a literary text could generate endless close readings, a claim that I realize now didn't need much proving. The unifying theme of these essays was my own ingenuity. I felt protective of literature in a way that made me set it in opposition to the academic essay. To pin a short story down would be to drain it of nuance, to leave it desiccated and lifeless. When I became a teacher of writing, I knew that this opposition between detail and argument was a false one. I also knew that close readings weren't enough. What I didn't know was how to make these close readings mean something (or how to make "mean something" meaningful). Bridge that gap, I told my students, over and over. Purify that water! The only thing I didn't tell them, because I didn't quite know the answer myself, was how. In my courses for the Expository Writing Program I try to reveal the inner working of the water purification plant: how to use details to generate alternative readings and have a thesis that argues why one is better than the other. I have learned a vocabulary to anatomize the academic essay, but more than that I have discovered a way to think about what successful academic essays do.

The academic essay, far from being antithetical to literature and its plenitude, might be particularly congenial to them. Academic essays hinge on debate, on the existence of many plausible but provably false positions. Literary texts, because they can be given more than one reading, seem well suited to teach students how to argue, how to claim and prove that one interpretation is better than another. Perhaps literature becomes less sacred when thought of in this way, but in making the sacred profane, students learn how to do more than write on faith.

Notes

1. The students' names have been changed. All the participants in the study have given us permission to use their materials.

2. For more information about the Expository Writing Program and the Harvard Study of Undergraduate Writing, see *Expository Writing*, www.fas.harvard.edu/~expos/. See also Sommers and Saltz.

3. The complexity thesis is not a problem simply for English majors. We at the study found another Maura in Jill, who used such a thesis in almost every essay she wrote for her sociology classes. Here's one of her theses from an essay she wrote her first year: "[A]lthough this model [that of 'ideological intermediary'] partially explains the role that Asian Americans have played in recent race negotiations, it is at the same time perhaps too limiting and generalizing an account of *an extremely ambiguous and complex situation*" (emphasis added). And here's the thesis

for an essay on a similar theme, which she wrote her senior year: "The story of Chinese-American Christianity is *a complex and dynamic narrative* that 'must be seen in relation both to the cultural past and to the changing cultures of the present' (Elwood 23)" (emphasis added). Note the similarity of the theses. They suggest, as does Maura's similar four-year reliance, how much some students depend on the complexity thesis.

4. Learning how to argue is important even beyond forestalling painful criticism like that above. The study found that the ability to argue, which allows a person to feel as if he or she is advancing a line of inquiry, is critical in sustaining an interest in academic writing. Despite a tremendously strong beginning, Maura became less interested in writing as her college career progressed.

5. Gordon Harvey, the associate director of the Harvard Expository Writing Program, has articulated the premises that are the basis for our topic-based writing program. One of his premises states, "There's a lot of common ground in academic writing, even though academic fields differ in their methods of analysis and style of presentation—enough common ground to justify speaking of 'the academic essay.'" Another premise advises, "The best introduction to academic writing isn't a seminar on that concept but rather one on a particular academic subject.... This kind of focus—on 'The Ethics of the Environment,' 'The World of George Orwell,' 'Imagining the Civil War,' 'Law and Psychology'—allows students to engage a subject in a sustained enough way to have something to argue and explain in their papers.... It also brings into play more immediately the academic energies and passions of the preceptor, who is after all the most immediate example of an academic thinker and writer."

6. Two other problematic stories I've used are John Updike's "A & P" and Gish Jen's "Who's Irish?" These stories work well for students who come to college better able to summarize than analyze. They contain mysteries that beg for an answer: Why does the narrator of "A & P" quit his job? Is the grandmother in "Who's Irish?" sympathetic? The stories thwart the impulse many basic writers have to dismiss academic essays, especially literary ones, as empty exercises of reading too much into things.

7. For David Bartholomae, first-year students learn how to write academic essays not by drawing on an internal storehouse of creativity but by "inventing the university," a phrase that might be glossed as "learning how to sound like an intellectual." The danger of such a model—and it's a model I find persuasive—is that it can sound as if teachers are simply trying to teach students how to play a game. That's not at all how I understand it, however (and I suspect Bartholomae agrees): learning how to sound like an intellectual does not mean inserting the appropriate jargon (ten points for every use of *problematic*); it means learning how to engage with other intellectuals, how to ask questions that other intellectuals will find interesting, and how to answer these questions in ways that they will find convincing.

8. Yet I have to admit that this last point is more evident to me than to my students (much as I try to make it to them). Most of them grasp the idea of a world

that is open to debate more with the third assignment, in which they see a debate in action, than with the first one, in which they have to generate a debate themselves. To be fair, it's only in high school and the first few years of college when we can honestly believe that we're the first person to come to any topic. Learning how to be more than an apprentice academic writer means not so much learning how to generate debates as learning what exactly the debates are that exist in our chosen field and how we can enter them with some authority.

"You May Find It a Different Story from the One You Learned in School": Teaching Writing in a First-Year Seminar on Historical Fiction

Storytelling about the past lies at the heart of my first-year seminar on historical fiction. Literature is the spine of my course, which consists of five units, devoted to the Battle of Gettysburg; the identity of the sixteenth-century Frenchman Martin Guerre; the turn of the twentieth century in America; the assassination of John F. Kennedy; and the life and times of Malcolm X. I pair a fictional account of the subject with either its historiography or secondary readings that enable the students to put it in a historical perspective. We screen related films and documentaries to broaden our aesthetic and critical appreciation of how the past may be rendered with sights, sounds, and moving images. We even study some material artifacts. Since historiography and historical novels are verbal—they are written—most of our seminar time is devoted to analyzing artful language rather than the historical events themselves. The primary questions we examine are what constitutes truth in historical fiction writing and fiction in history writing and what conventions, assumptions, and practices we invoke to guide our judgments in discriminating between these two genres of writing. I hope to show my students that narratives about the past are often competitive, even contradictory, and to explore with them how this can be so. Crucial to all our endeavors in this first-year seminar is student writing.

To showcase my writing pedagogy in the seminar, this essay focuses on the Battle of Gettysburg unit, the first unit. I team Michael Shaara's Pulitzer Prize–winning novel *The Killer Angels* with Ken Burns's documentary *The Civil War*. We watch the Battle of Gettysburg episodes in *The Civil War* and read the companion volume to the film, written by Geoffrey Ward with Ric Burns and Ken Burns. We analyze Burns's documentary and his view

Tamara A. Goeglein

of historical fiction with the help of Thomas Cripps ("Historical Truth: An Interview with Ken Burns") and Brian Henderson ("The Civil War: 'Did It Not Seem Real?'"). And, in preparation for a field trip to the Gettysburg National Military Park, the students read selections from *The U.S. Army War College Guide to the Battle of Gettysburg* (Luvaas and Nelson) and from Thomas A. Desjardin's *Stand Firm Ye Boys from Maine.*

My thinking on historical fiction is indebted to the scholarship of Hayden White, whose influential essay "The Value of Narrativity in the Representation of Reality" traces the history of historical discourse. For historiography to satisfy our conceptions of historical reality, past events must be narrated, "revealed as possessing a structure, an order of meaning, that they do not possess as mere sequence" (5). While past events have been recorded in annals and in chronicles, as White says, these nonnarrative representations strike us as less than true because their discursive discontinuities — their lack of integrity, fullness, closure — stymie our attempts to moralize history. What I find intriguing in White's essay is his suggestion that our perspective on history is shaped by our own aesthetic sensibilities. Unsettling for some of us perhaps is his notion that the past becomes more meaningful the more invisible the rhetoric, the more natural the conventions in history writing. Such provocations led me to assign White's essay in the first iteration of my seminar, which turned out to be a mistake. Rather than serve as a touchstone for the seminar, it became sacred doctrine for some students; for others, it remained a frustrating cipher. White assumes familiarity with a variety of history writing styles and, even more generally, familiarity with a variety of aesthetic styles, neither of which my students possessed. I now juxtapose fictional and historical texts, allowing their narrative, aesthetic, and rhetorical features to emerge as we compare them with one another and across time. From these experiences, my students increasingly gain the expertise necessary to make critical judgments about history in fiction writing and fiction in history writing.

As I look back to my own college education, I am struck that the current shape of my first-year seminar resembles in some measure the required humanities courses I took at Earlham College in 1980. In these courses, we read historical texts against literary texts against philosophical texts. In one course, we read a selection of Abelard and Héloïse's love letters next to Helen Waddell's historical novel *Peter Abelard*. This pairing gave rise not to discussions about historical fiction — as it would in my seminar — but to discussions about Abelard and Héloïse's spiritual commitments, their romantic love, and their intellectual compatibility. In this course, I also recall reading Jacob Burckhardt's *The Civilization of the Renaissance in Italy* next to Homer's *Odyssey* next to Thucydides's *The Peloponnesian War*. Such juxtapositions led us to ponder warfare and its motives, aftermaths, and leaders. In another course, we read Alexis de Tocqueville's *Democracy in America* next to Walt Whitman's *Democratic Vistas*. The humanities courses were not focused on a single topic, as is my historical fiction seminar, but rather they traced important themes across the readings. What I remember best about the courses is that literary texts caught fire when I read them beside historical texts. Their fictional truths were more real to me. I wanted to study literature because of these courses, and because of them I have tended to search for historical knowledge in literature. Once, after having written a humanities essay comparing Whitman's and de Tocqueville's views of democracy, I was drawn to Whitman's elegy "When Lilacs Last in the Dooryard Bloom'd." Its poignant lyrics and rhythms mesmerized me, pulled me into the sorrows inflicted by Abraham Lincoln's tragic death, and enabled me to empathize with the losses many Americans like Whitman endured. This juncture between history and fiction, this moment when the past seems palpable, human, and present before us in works of literature fascinates me and can account for my teaching this seminar on historical fiction.

I let my students gauge their own fascination in the Battle of Gettysburg unit, for which I have designed a series of three sequential writing assignments that encourages them to think deliberately, in and through critical writing, about what for them constitutes a real story about the past. While most of my students say history comes alive in historical fiction, they are likewise uneasy about this because fiction is often equated with falsehood. I hear, "Oh, I loved *The Red Badge of Courage*. I learned a lot about the Civil War from it, but I know a lot of the novel is made up." My initial set of writing assignments tackles this conundrum head-on since it dogs the study of historical fiction. Stated more generally, this conundrum dogs the study of all literature, for it asks how literature is related to our lives. How is the imaginary related to our actual existence? What truths can the imaginary tell us about ourselves and our past?

My first writing assignment asks the students to analyze narration in *The Killer Angels*, my second to analyze the devices used to create a sense of the real in *The Civil War*, and my third to analyze the basis for a historical critique of *The Killer Angels*. Typically, the first assignment draws the students into the battle and into the perspectives of the soldiers, the second disengages the students from an emotional attachment to the battle and the soldiers, and the third gets their hearts and minds working together as one interpretive engine. The writing assignments aspire to cultivate a historical imagination that is based in an understanding of fictional techniques, narrative styles, and rhetorical devices. They aspire to help students listen to past voices, determine what exactly they are saying, and evaluate them with a self-conscious regard for our own historical circumstances. Many of my students are already readers who enjoy reading but do not yet have the confidence to read literature written before yesterday. I hope my seminar builds this confidence, for it opens the door to most literary texts. While students do get a healthy dose of history, my pedagogy is literary and is designed to meet the needs of first-year students as they make the transition from high school to Franklin and Marshall College.

The Franklin and Marshall First-Year Residential Seminar Program began in 1989, when about a dozen seminars were offered as a pilot program. The faculty group that launched the pilot program expected the first-year seminars to

> develop critical thinking skills through the in-depth investigation of a theme or a topic;
> develop critical reading skills through careful class discussion of reading assignments;
> develop writing skills through techniques associated with process writing; and
> develop oral communication skills through class discussion and/or student reports. (Trachte 1)

All first-year seminars at Franklin and Marshall are classified as writing intensive, and ninety-five percent of our first-year students enroll in one.[1] The seminars are small—they are capped at sixteen students—and are generally composed of a self-selected group of students who preregistered the preceding spring.

Since 2000 Franklin and Marshall's writing requirement has evolved to acknowledge the success of the seminar program. Our writing requirement now consists of three phases: phase 1 is a first-year writing requirement that is fulfilled by completing a course designated writing intensive; phase 2 spans the first and second years and is fulfilled by completing a three-course, multidisciplinary general education sequence called Foundations; phase 3 spans the third and fourth years and is fulfilled by completing the specific disciplinary writing requirements of the major.[2]

The First-Year Residential Seminar Program was conceived as a way to integrate the academic and residential aspects of our students' lives: the sixteen seminarians live on the same floor of a residence hall, and they become the academic advisees of their seminar instructor. With help from a Pew Charitable Trusts grant in 1992, Franklin and Marshall reimagined the program slightly to include upper-level students, who serve as preceptors for the seminars. The hope is that this pod of sixteen first-year students, an upper-class preceptor, and the instructor will form a small learning community, which comes into being during the orientation week before classes begin in the fall. During orientation week, when our first-year students take placement exams, join clubs, set up their computers, and so on, they meet daily with their first-year seminar instructors to discuss a text their entire matriculating cohort has been asked to read over the summer. These meetings compose our Liberal Education Program, which is designed to model the liberal learning that Franklin and Marshall offers and that many faculty members see as the de facto beginning of the first-year seminar. Since 1989, our seminar program has grown nearly threefold—Franklin and Marshall now offers close to three dozen seminars whose instructors hail from all disciplines. Seminars taught in the 2002–03 academic year included Censorship and American Culture, The Environment and Human Values, Tuberculosis, The Atlantic World, Math and Sports, Two-Way Mirror: Germany and the

US, and The Personal Essay. Faculty members often remark that first-year seminars are the place "we teach our fancy." It is also the place where we form close and long-lasting bonds with students (many of whom remain our academic advisees for their entire career) because the seminars are intense, not the least because of the amount of writing required.

The Context for Writing

Shaara begins *The Killer Angels* with this statement ("To the Reader") about his historical fiction:

> *You may find it a different story from the one you learned in school.* There have been many versions of that battle and that war. I have therefore avoided histori- cal opinions and gone back primarily to the words of the men themselves, their letters and other documents. I have not consciously changed any fact. I have condensed some of the action, for the sake of clarity, and eliminated some minor characters, for brevity; but though I have often had to choose between conflicting viewpoints, I have not knowingly violated the action. I have changed some of the language. It was a naïve and sentimental time, and men spoke in windy phrases. I thought it necessary to update some of the words so that the religiosity and naïveté of the time, which were genuine, would not seem too quaint to the modern ear. I hope I will be forgiven that. (xiii; emphasis added)

I begin class discussion in the Battle of Gettysburg unit with an analysis of Shaara's apologia, which is both a justification and a plea for understand- ing. Much of the conceptual terrain we explore in the unit and in the course generally is conveniently packed into this excerpt.

I ask my students to consider Shaara's sentence, which articulates a dis- tinction between historical stories and fictional stories. What does he imply about the history of the Battle of Gettysburg by saying, rather innocuously, that his story is likely different "from the one you learned in school"? Does he mean that there is a single story that historians tell? How does Shaara distinguish himself from historians and their "many versions" of the Battle of Gettysburg? What does Shaara promise by his "avoid[ing] historical opin- ions and go[ing] back primarily to the words of the men themselves, their letters and other documents"? Is he promising a back-to-the-basics approach to history freed from those bothersome "historical opinions"? I pause in my string of rhetorical questions to settle into a couple questions I really do wish them to consider: Doesn't Shaara need to interpret those words that he updates? To what extent does the linguistic context contribute to the meaning of those words?

To illustrate the semantic pressure contexts are apt to apply, I distribute copies of Robert E. Lee's two reports on the battle known as Pickett's Charge. I see this as a quick reality check and a chance to sample some of what Shaara calls nineteenth-century "windy phrases." Lee's reports are excerpted in *The U.S. Army War College Guide to the Battle of Gettysburg*, which prints this preface to the documents:

> *Lee* never offered an explanation beyond that contained in his official papers, and his anxiety to avoid dissension among subordinates caused him to request *Pickett* and perhaps others to destroy the initial after-action reports. His own two reports on the campaign raise as many questions as they answer, beginning with his rationale for ordering *Longstreet's* attack on the 2nd. (Luvaas and Nelson 169)

Lee's first report is dated 31 July 1863, written twenty-eight days after the awful massacre of ten Confederate brigades on the third day of battle. The students note that Lee's tone is more optimistic, more confident in this sentence from the first report: "These partial successes [of the second day] determined me to continue the assault the next day [3 July]" (169). The second report is dated January 1864, written six months after the first one. I prod, Why might Lee have written a second report? How might six months of reflection and public criticism have prompted Lee to have at it again? The students are quick to pick up on Lee's attempt to distance himself from the responsibility for ordering the attack by pointing to this sentence:

> The result of this day's operation [2 July] induced the belief that, with proper concert of action, and with the increased support that the positions gained on the right would enable the artillery to render the assaulting columns, we should ultimately succeed, and it was accordingly determined to continue the attack. (170)

Compared with the directness of the first report, Lee's later rhetoric is evasive and passive. Who is determining what? Yes, Lee can be "windy," but here the wind seems to be blowing smoke. Fiction writers and historians alike must imagine what has been left unsaid in this second report and what Lee has apparently suppressed. We must listen carefully to the past. In this little exercise, I try to underscore the point that comprehending the words of Civil War soldiers requires our evaluating the sources and making informed decisions about what they can mean. The context's the thing, though we must be mindful that the historical record is not always complete, sometimes deliberately so. Neither the historian nor Shaara is a mere transcriber of words, a mere amanuensis of the past.

It is usually at this point in class discussion that an anxious student reminds us that there are in fact facts. Even Shaara knows this when he writes, "I have not consciously changed any fact." Later in the course, we read the opening chapter of Edward Hallett Carr's *What Is History?* ("The Historian and His Facts"), which bluntly claims that "the historian will get the kind of facts he wants" (26), but for now I ask my students to take a moment and think about where historians get their facts. Whence do they spring unbidden? The magnificent Gettysburg National Military Park is usually a candidate. The National Park Service has managed to preserve much of the environs and to showcase many of the famous battle sites. Gettysburg is about sixty miles from Franklin and Marshall, and since I always include a day trip to the battlefield, I encourage students to speculate what facts might come from the actual place. The museum features leftover bullets, records of troop positions, uniforms and gear, and rifles and cannons. And there is the landscape. For anyone with even a casual knowledge of the battle, the Peach Orchard, the Wheatfield, and the Round Tops are emblematic of the fierce, strategic warfare waged at Gettysburg. A student inevitably protests that the magnificent landscape spread out before us in all its concreteness cannot spread half-truths, as old musty documents can. And I respond that the landscape is indeed crucial to our understanding of the battle, but it does not lie because it does not speak to us. I have found that this claim — that material culture needs critical interpretation — is difficult for my students to grasp, though the "single-bullet theory" of the Warren Commission usually clinches it for most of them.

Many of my students call themselves history buffs, and they wear their factual knowledge of the past proudly — they have attended Civil War reen-actments, they haul in mementos from family vacations for show and tell, and they believe what they see. One bright buff mused that the roads through-out the Gettysburg National Military Park must have been convenient for the soldiers. "Oh, my," I thought. I am careful, however, not to squelch their enthusiasm: I concede that we can imagine what it might have been like on Little Round Top when Colonel Joshua Chamberlain and his men from the 20th Maine Infantry regiment repulsed Colonel William Oates's 15th Alabama. It is indeed thrilling to stand at the bottom of the fishhook battle line of the Army of the Potomac — the line that hooks around Culp's Hill to the north, traveled south along the shank of Cemetery Ridge until it curved around Little Round Top, forming the spur where Chamberlain was posi-tioned. For our speculations about landscape, or material culture in general, to be worthwhile — if we wish to cull facts from material culture — our his-torical imaginations must be educated. We must know that the geographi-cal contours of the battlefield are different from what they were in 1863: this knowledge is critical for retracing the rapidly shifting lines of fire in the Wheatfield, for example, where even slight rises or depressions in the field today can occlude from view what was visible in 1863 (or vice versa). I try to demonstrate this point with historical maps, field reports, and battlefield markers when we are standing in the battlefield, though these markers are often tentative and contestable. The truth is that the beautiful stone statu-ary lining the roads through the National Military Park, heavy and engraved with names, dates, and epitaphs, belies the slippery slopes of time, memory, and soil erosion.

Historical narratives are not photocopies of the past, depicting every material trace and expressing all known facts, but a self-consciously shaped collection of them. Shaara admits at the outset that he has "condensed some of the action, for the sake of clarity, and eliminated some minor char-acters, for brevity." Designing a narrative always involves condensation, expansion, compression, and elimination: it involves selectivity to tell the story you wish to tell, not the one you do not. I ask the students to compare the introductory comments that the historian Desjardin makes in *Stand Firm Ye Boys from Maine* with Shaara's introduction to see that both authors engage an apologetic rhetorical mode, one that seeks to palliate the inevitable failures of historical storytelling by explaining, even defending, its practical accomplishments. Desjardin writes, "Five minutes after the shooting stopped on Little Round Top in July 1863, it was already too late for anyone to entirely understand what had happened" (xiii). To understand the entirety of Little Round Top may be impossible, but to fashion a coherent story is not. Historians pick and choose, trying to get their stories right, as Desjardin remarks of his own: "it is my sincerest hope that this is the real story of the 20th Maine at Gettysburg" (xiii). At this point in our discussion, students are typically stumped how Shaara and Desjardin could both write the real story of the Battle of Gettysburg.

In this first unit of the seminar, history writing and fiction writing are closely aligned. A primary objective is to show how the novelist Shaara basically adopts the techniques of the vernacular historian exemplified here by Burns — both exhibit confidence in knowing and asserting truths about the past. The imaginary aspects of *The Killer Angels* are so sotto voce that students forget that the text is fiction, a feat nearly impossible with E. L. Doctorow's *Ragtime* or Don DeLillo's *Libra*. As we move through the course pairings, we explore how the relation between fiction and history, and between fiction writing and history writing, can shift and bend. In the second unit of the seminar, we read the historian Natalie Zemon Davis, who acknowledges forthrightly that her historical account of a sixteenth-century imposter entitled *The Return of Martin Guerre* "is an exploration of the problem of truth and doubt: of the difficulty in determining true identity in the sixteenth century and of the difficulty in the historian's quest for truth in the twentieth" (572). In *Libra*, DeLillo downright exploits the plight of the twentieth-century historian in the character of Nicholas Branch, who has been commissioned by the CIA to write a history of the J. F. K. assassination:

He [Branch] has abandoned his life to understanding that moment in Dallas, the seven seconds that broke the back of the American century. He has his forensic pathology rundown, his neutron activation analysis. There is also the Warren Report, of course, with its twenty-six accompanying volumes of testimony and exhibits, its millions of words. Branch thinks this is the megaton novel James Joyce would have written if he'd moved to Iowa City and lived to be a hundred. (181)

The postmodern historian, sardonic yet obsessive, is ultimately paralyzed by information overload and by the accompanying doubt that, whatever story he tells, it is necessarily incomplete. History is ever elusive, and the narratives that strive for the real story can only resemble the unreadability of Joycean fiction. For Branch (and DeLillo), the only possible history writing is fiction writing. But this is not so for Shaara, whose fiction writing mimics popular history writing.

The Killer Angels looks and feels like a history book, especially because there are graphic illustrations showing troop movements and shifting battle lines throughout the three-day campaign. I ask my students, When was the last time you read a novel with such accurate geographical maps? I continue, asking, Can we identify other big, obvious structuring devices Shaara uses to impose order on the battle? Students typically respond that the novel is divided into four chapters: "Monday, June 29, 1863"; "Wednesday, July 1, 1863"; "Thursday, July 2, 1863"; and "Friday, July 3, 1863." They note that the chapters in these sections are titled after the historical figures through whose perspectives the events of the days are then funneled. I ask them to think about how the pictures, section headings, and chapter titles orient and orchestrate our view of history. They sense immediately that "orient" and "orchestrate" are charged terms, and they usually ask me to gloss them. My students have radar for such unfamiliar phrasings, and they naturally launch their defense by demanding a reformulation of the question. I comply: How is our view of the events being manipulated to see the battle in a particular way? What I hope emerges from this question is that, in *The Killer Angels*, chronological time and the perspective of the soldiers are fundamental to comprehending the Battle of Gettysburg.

The First Writing Assignment

After we have discussed *The Killer Angels* for a day or two, I distribute the first writing assignment I call an exercise. For each unit, the students typically compose two exercises (500–600 words each). I do not give them much lead time to write the exercises — often I set up an exercise at the end of one class and collect it at the beginning of the next. The exercises tend to be local, circumscribed, and task-oriented, and I imagine them as catalysts initiating a reaction to an issue, an idea, or a problem before us.[3] That Shaara orients and orchestrates our engagement in the battle through the perspectives of a handful of characters is one such issue, and here is the first exercise:

> "Point-of-view" is the vantage point from which an author presents a story. The author may use first-person, second-person, or third-person narration. Shaara tells the story in the third person, restricting information to what that character sees, hears, feels, and thinks. Such a point of view is limited.

> Pick one titular character (Lee, Buford, Chamberlain, or Longstreet) and describe how any one day of battle appears to him. Pay attention to his habits of thought (is he prone to think philosophically? strategically? emotionally?) and to his interactions with other characters (is he a loner? a brother? a pretender?). Does he change over the course of the day (things may happen to this character, but does anything happen *within him*)?

This exercise is fairly straightforward. It gives students a certain amount of expertise with one character, which will serve as prewriting for the third writing assignment, and it heightens their awareness of two aspects of *The Killer Angels*:

> characterization — which characters are sympathetic and dynamic, enabling us to infer motive and shaping our response to the battle?

> narrative sequencing — how does the plot move along, creating a sense of causality and inevitability to the history of the battle?

My students rarely address these higher-order concerns directly, and I do not fully expect they will do so.

Some student writers get stuck in description alone. These writers tend to know little about the Battle of Gettysburg and find it challenging to summarize the course of events. The first exercise gives them the chance to figure out the battle action. Most writers have a good sense of the battle and can focus on the contours of characterization, which is what grabs our attention in *The Killer Angels*. A good number of my writers begin to realize that their character may represent an attitude toward this battle or toward the Civil War generally. John Buford is the weary cavalry solder, restless and distrustful of politicians. James Longstreet is the modern strategist, an expert poker player who intuits that Lee's game plan is flawed. Chamberlain is the skeptical professor who ruminates on Hamlet's seemingly idealistic (but actually ironic) view of mankind throughout the battle ("What a piece of work is a man! How noble in reason, how infinite in faculty, in form and moving how express and admirable, in action how like an *angel*...") and concludes that we may be killer angels (2.2.293–96; emphasis added). Students tend to pick their favorite characters, and they love to tease me about mine — "you just like this novel because Chamberlain is a Shakespeare-quoting English professor" — and they are partly right. I readily confess that I am sympathetic toward him and that, through him, *The Killer Angels* is orienting and orchestrating my understanding of the history of the battle. But, because I am an English professor, I also remember that Chamberlain's perspective is limited.

Our collective expertise with Shaara's characters enables us to piece together how the plot is moving along through them and how the narrative pattern weaves in and out of their perspectives. After the students have written their exercises, I play a game: first, I ask them to locate blind spots in the narration — Where is your character when this or such is happening? Where is your character at noon on the second day? — and, then, I ask them to speculate what these blind spots can signify. It is noteworthy, for example, that Shaara does not give Lee a chapter in the "Friday, July 3, 1863" section, which is the day Lee orders Pickett's Charge. If there is no Lee, what happens to his culpability? Shaara gives us Lee's legendary admission, "It is all my fault, it is all my fault," as Pickett's decimated troops retreat, and Lee's calm command, "General, you must look to your Division," as well as Pickett's famously bitter, "General Lee, I have no Division" (332–33). But, by withholding Lee's perspective, Shaara sidesteps the historical debate about his motives in ordering the attack. Many historians fault Shaara for this, and

I ask the students more pointedly in the third writing assignment to explore whether or not they believe historical novelists are cheating if they ignore questions that historical discourse posits as necessary.

The first exercise prepares students for future discussions of point of view in *The Killer Angels*, in the seminar, and in other literature courses they may take. The ongoing discussion will eventually thread its way through *The Return of Martin Guerre*, where Davis shifts the traditional focus of the history of Martin Guerre away from his imposter, Arnaud du Tilh, to his wife, Bertrande de Rols, whom Davis characterizes as the imposter's accomplice, not his victim, as she was depicted in previous histories. To do this, Davis makes assumptions about Bertrande's personal life for which there is no historical record.[4] In the fourth unit, we plunge into the many and bizarre biographical possibilities for Lee Harvey Oswald — was he an American spy? a Russian double agent? a lone gunman? a pro-Castro Communist? an anti-Castro Cuban sympathizer? a patsy? — and compare them with DeLillo's split view in *Libra*. We culminate our analysis of character in *The Autobiography of Malcolm X*, where the author Malcolm X abandons his initial "conversion narrative" structure — and the heroic characterization of him that it entails — once he is ousted from the Nation of Islam and has undergone a second conversion to a more orthodox form of Islam. History intrudes and forces El-Hajj Malik El-Shabazz to reimagine how to characterize himself without either abandoning his autobiographical project or coming off as disingenuous (or, worse, as a reincarnation of his hustling self). How can the author accomplish this in a true-life story when life itself seems surreal? These conceptual issues about characterization and point of view meander through all the texts we read in the seminar: How is the real-life author Malcolm X related to the fictional character Malcolm X? Who were the real-life Lee Harvey Oswald and Bertrande de Rols? How is Shaara's Lee related to the historical Lee?

The Second Writing Assignment

The second exercise in the Battle of Gettysburg unit focuses on Ken Burns's documentary *The Civil War*. We consider how Burns uses a seemingly realist aesthetic to document historical events. To broach this topic, we first inspect the cover art of our mass-marketed paperback copies of *The Killer Angels*. The 1992 paperback edition depicts a romanticized Gettysburg infantry scene that might have come from one of the massive oil-on-canvas paintings of Pickett's Charge that was completed by Paul Philippoteaux in the early 1880s and now resides in the Gettysburg Cyclorama (a 360-degree auditorium with Philippoteaux's painting wrapped around inside it). On the book cover, wisps of white smoke play in the background, but we have an unobstructed view of muscular human forms straining against the metaphysical force of battle. In the foreground, a solitary Union flag–bearer astride a white stallion struggles to keep Old Glory aloft. I ask my students to reflect on the image of warfare this creates: How does the image frame our reading of the novel? After the Gulf War, the 1996 paperback edition included a banner across the bottom with this quotation from General H. Norman Schwartzkopf: "The best and most realistic historical novel about war I have read." I ask the students, not without some irony, if they think the painting on the cover is realistic. Of course not, they reply. What cover art might be more realistic? A Matthew Brady photograph? My students already know that Brady staged many of his photographs of the Civil War, though, as some have noted, even Brady's artistry could not ameliorate the gruesome image of a dead body distended from the extreme summer heat. This, however, is not the realism General Schwartzkopf is selling.

Another way to evaluate how art shapes reality is from the inside out. When we visit the battlefield, the National Park Service tour guide Jim Clouse and I place the students shoulder to shoulder in regimental formation—much as those infantrymen depicted on the paperback's cover might have been placed.[5] Clouse takes care to position make-believe muskets and bayonets between the shoulders of the student soldiers in front and to explain that the regimental unit has a front and a back. All guns must point in the same direction, lest a soldier turn and inadvertently shoot down his own line. A regimental unit acts as a single body. If the enemy attacks with a flanking maneuver, the entire body must change its direction to meet hostile fire. Clouse explains that the unit knows to march, halt, turn, fire, or retreat when the drummer boy and the bugler sound orders with specific melodies and that the touch of shoulders guides the troops forward in rank. Despite the crystalline panorama portrayed on our paperback cover of *The Killer Angels*, we learn that real soldiers could not see more than a few feet in front of them because of gunfire and cannon smoke. Realistic the book cover is not.

To what extent is Burns's *The Civil War* realistic? This question is the centerpiece of most critical commentary on his documentary and one I wish my students to address in terms of the multimedia devices deployed by Burns to create a sense of the real. The first exercise enabled them to realize that we see and experience the Battle of Gettysburg vicariously in *The Killer Angels*. Now I wish to create some aesthetic distance between the novel and us by objectifying its immediacy and verisimilitude. A realist aesthetic is as stylized as a plain-spoken politician, but we are not meant to see this. Here is the assignment for the second exercise:

> Pick one historical figure or specific moment of the battle featured in the Gettysburg episode of Ken Burns's *Civil War*. Explain how the music, camera angles and style, photographs, voice actors, or any of the other multimedia devices "characterize" the historical figure or moment. You may use Geoffrey Ward's textual counterpart to the documentary to help bolster your analysis, if you wish.

This exercise builds on my students' familiarity with the Gettysburg cast of characters and battle action. To prepare for writing, we screen the segments entitled "Gettysburg: The First Day," "Gettysburg: The Second Day," and "Gettysburg: The Third Day," which, not unlike Shaara's section headings, seem the natural, inevitable shape of the Gettysburg story. As we watch the documentary, I ask the students to record their reactions to any of the devices Burns marshals to tell his multimedia history. I want them to be alert to Burns's signature camera style and use of photographs, to the Civil War era music (When is it introduced? Do you recognize the songs? How do they make you feel?), to the tone and texture of the voice-overs (Can you identify the voice actors? Is the overall narrator omniscient?), to the role of the talking heads (especially Shelby Foote), and to the pacing of the story

(When does it slow down or speed up, and how does this happen?). Being connoisseurs of the visual, my students are usually quite adept at itemizing Burns's artistic techniques, even though their sentiment that films exist only to entertain continually raises its ugly head in the course.[6]

What I hope to accomplish with this exercise is threefold. First, I wish to signal early on my pedagogical seriousness about multimedia texts in the seminar: we will be watching numerous films that are integrated into the reading materials. Second, I want my students to witness the careful placement of historical documents, such as photographs and letters, newspaper clippings and battle reports; this placing seems more obvious in multimedia textuality than in verbal textuality. Third, I want my students to anatomize their experience of realistic documentary history. This gives them the psychic distance to comprehend what goes into making a historical character or historical event true to life and to evaluate the aesthetic overlaps of fiction writing and history writing. In the class session in which the second exercise is due, we share the wealth of their insights to sketch a Venn diagram of generic boundaries shared by history and fiction.

Many students write about Burns's camera style: how the image of a single covered wagon, for example, gives way to hundreds of them as the camera lens widens its gaze on an old photograph and allows us to see the entire wagon train. Those who analyze camera style begin with a description of the initial image and then attempt to characterize the effect created by the widening of the camera angle. This task is difficult, though most students manage to make the figurative leap, such as the camera's characterizing the magnitude of the Civil War through the wagon train or its characterizing the suspense felt by nineteenth-century Americans as wagon trains moved through their towns. Some student writers go on to assert that understanding the magnitude of history begins on a smaller, human scale—with one lone wagon. This exercise slows down the consumption of photographic images and permits the students to articulate how a shard from the past, an old photograph, becomes a work of cinematic art that can express a sentiment. A real wagon and a wagon train are historical artifacts—Burns did not conjure these from thin air, but he does make them speak. As students point out, what Burns does to photographs with his camera overlaps with what Shaara does to the past with his fictional words. Shaara's zooming into a moment with his imaginary dialogue and his depicting a sentiment through an image of troop movements are analogues to Burns's camera style. Students sometimes trip over the fact that the old photographs Burns imports into his film are themselves representations and that the Battle of Gettysburg is thus often presented at two removes in *The Civil War*. Still, for the most part, this second exercise attunes the students to the artistry the historian Burns uses to create a sense of the real.

I build on the second exercise by asking students to read two critical essays about *The Civil War*. We deliberately read the essays after they have written the second exercise because critical authorities have a way of drowning out student voices. And I have found that students tend to appreciate scholarly expertise more once they have tried their hands at an issue or problem. This is especially true of Henderson's "The Civil War: 'Did It Not Seem Real?,'" which is a meticulous, detailed explication of Burns's technique that more often than not exposes his wizardry the way Toto does the Wizard of Oz—Henderson simply pulls back the curtain and shows us that much of what we thought was realistic is not. We learn, for instance, that Burns trades in the traditional arrangements of Civil War songs—what nineteenth-century Americans actually played or heard—for the "instrumental minimalism" of chamber music that has the effect of transposing a large-scale event in American history into a manageable, human-sized event composed of solo "voices" (5). Music serves as narration in the documentary, and, while it may be verisimilar, it is not authentic. Henderson tells us that "Ashokan Farewell," the emblematic theme song of *The Civil War*, is in fact "a 1984 composition by Jay Ungar that sounds more like a Civil War song than many of the genuine article[s]" (6). The many voices of historical figures we hear in the documentary are not rendered as the figures really sounded but, as Henderson suggests, "how he or she 'should' sound" (7). Morgan Freeman supplants the powerful, public, oratorical Frederick Douglass with a melancholy, introspective Douglass, whose intonations suggest "the oppression and suffering" not overthrown by emancipation (7). Sam Waterston's Lincoln, sounding nothing like the high-pitched, squeaky sixteenth president, reads the Gettysburg Address against the grain, exchanging the traditional emphases on *"of* the people, *by* the people, *for* the people" for a "government of the *people*, by the *people*, for the *people*" (7). This is a dramatic shift, one that makes us wonder how Lincoln might have actually delivered his speech and how particular rhetorical cadences have been enshrined in our consciousness as realistic. Reading Henderson's analysis after having composed the second exercise reinforces what most of my students came to realize on their own, namely, Burns's illusionism.

We also read a Burns interview. Burns sees himself as a "tribal storyteller" rather than an "academic historian," a distinction he relishes, for it captures his mission to "rescue history from those who teach it and the scholars who only wish to talk to themselves about it, and to return history to a kind of broad dialogue" (Cripps 741–42). Burns is acutely aware that many academic historians look down their noses at him, not only because he popularizes history but also because he uses film to do so. He freely admits that filmmakers take "poetic license," but he staunchly maintains that *The Civil War* conveys historical truth (752). Throughout the interview, Burns articulates the contradictory nature of historical fiction. While he quips that film lies "24 times a second" (757), he nonetheless avers that

> the slowing down of a piece of footage…is a legitimate historical device if it does not in any way interfere with its fact. It is, in fact, the slowing down of the Zapruder film which gave the Warren Commission access to the truth of the event. (753)

Burns seems to be defending his artistry as historical verity with a paradox: the orchestrated lying of documentary filmmaking actually gives rise to historical truths. I ask my students to linger on this apologetic passage: Would you call "slowing down a piece of footage" a "historical device" or a fictional one? There is never consensus on this, but discussion sheds light on the problem we face. Burns's apologia is comparable to Shaara's, but his asserts "access to the truth of an event," whereas Shaara's excuses *The Civil War* as "a different story from the one you learned in school."[7] Shaara defers to the authority of Civil War historians; Burns claims the authority of a Civil War historian because, he argues, his filmmaking devices are as legitimate as any in historical discourse.

The Third Writing Assignment

Many historians would beg to differ with Burns, however. In the preface to *A Killer Angels Companion*, D. Scott Hartwig implies what most historians think of historical fiction: "How faithful to history is *The Killer Angels*? If Shaara took liberty and license with his characters and their actions, where and why did he do so? And, if he did, what really happened?" (1). Hartwig, of course, thinks Shaara took liberties and got it wrong. Hands down, this assessment is the recurring, predictable criticism historians lob at historical fiction, and most historians who review historical fiction see their job as setting the record straight.[8] This conceptual criticism raises the question of what constitutes a real story of the past, and my students are now ready to respond with their knowledge of narration, characterization, and the aesthetic techniques of historians.

Hartwig's commentary on Shaara's portraits of Chamberlain, Longstreet, and Lee attempts to show just how much of the real story Shaara omits. An excerpt of his commentary on Chamberlain illustrates Hartwig's method:

> One of the most memorable passages in *The Killer Angels* is the story of Joshua Chamberlain and the 20th Maine on Little Round Top.... His regiment's stand on Little Round Top—a magnificent feat of arms—has been lionized until it has assumed Arthurian proportions. Chamberlain is deserving of great credit. He fought with bravery, skill, tenacity, and cunning to win a crucial engagement, but he did not stand off the enemy alone.... But because Shaara presents the events at Little Round Top through Chamberlain's eyes, his story is the only one the reader comes to know. (16)

Hartwig then proceeds to tell a story Shaara does not tell, a story much of which Chamberlain could only have known through someone else's telling. The story contradicts and competes with *The Killer Angels* because Hartwig adopts an omniscient point of view.

The third writing assignment is basically a response to Hartwig, in 1,500 words. In each unit of the seminar, students write a critical analysis of about that length (which, together with the exercises, means that each student writes about 10,000 words over the course of the semester). In this final assignment, I instruct my students to read Hartwig's commentary and respond as follows:

> Select Hartwig's commentary on one of the characters (preferably the one you analyzed in the first exercise). First, evaluate the commentary: Why does Hartwig think Shaara got it wrong? What arguments does he use to support his claims? Second, propose a reading of your character that takes as a given that Shaara is not trying to write history, that Shaara's historical fiction is attempting to represent in his characters something different, above and beyond what Hartwig claims "really happened" at Gettysburg.

This synthetic assignment asks the students to build on their knowledge about characterization and narration from exercise 1 and to use the knowledge from exercise 2 to analyze the underlying dichotomy between history writing and fiction writing implicit in Hartwig's hermeneutic. The two exercises thus serve as prewriting for this third assignment, but here the conceptual stakes are higher. Students now need to consider, for the first but not last time in the seminar, the presence of fiction in history writing and history in fiction writing. They also need to articulate what kind of historical truths, if any, *The Killer Angels* expresses.

The force of the challenges this assignment presents emerges initially when students try to organize their essay and their thoughts. Because it is a two-part assignment, most students write a two-part essay. The weaker writers typically cannot make their way from part 1 to part 2—they find it difficult to move among Hartwig's commentary on the novel, the novel itself, and their interpretation of the novel, and so their thinking is fairly compartmentalized as is the organizational scheme of their essays. They might assert that Hartwig's arguments are untenable because his sources lie outside the scope of the narrative action of *The Killer Angels*: Hartwig staunchly defends Lee's courage in ordering Pickett's Charge by citing a diary entry from a British observer that says as much. So far, so good. But these students are unable to parlay their critique of Hartwig into an analysis of how Shaara actually dodges Hartwig's bullet by pulling away from

Lee's point of view and what this strategic pulling away affords the novelist. Other writers self-consciously, and more or less successfully, do use their conclusions in part 1 as a starting point for part 2. A student may conclude that Hartwig's arguments are not fully persuasive because he overlooks the limitations of perspective that Shaara acknowledges. Modes of narration then become the bridge into part 2, where the writer may argue that Shaara is really engaging his readers in the moral dilemmas posed by the perspectives of the various soldiers, moral dilemmas that emerge in the thoughts of one character or across characters. Because there is no omniscient narrator, readers are left to weigh the viewpoints of individual characters and the ethical stances they imply.

In part 2 of the essay, almost all students come to terms with the existential musing at the core of the novel about whether a warrior is justified by a divine ethics. Are men killer angels or killer animals? Laying out the metaphysics of this question drives *The Killer Angels* forward, and it does so through the perspectives of its characters. Throughout the novel, the inner lives of Chamberlain, Longstreet, and Lee are engaged in self-dialogues about the ethics of warfare. Lee, the fervent Christian, believes he is an actor in the divine scheme, and Longstreet, the career soldier, grows disenchanted, if not utterly cynical about the higher aspirations of warfare. Chamberlain, the college professor turned soldier, occupies a skeptical middle ground between the two Confederate generals. Students tend to center their discussions on the moral position represented by their character, criticizing or endorsing it as the case may be. They engage passionately in ethical debate with *The Killer Angels* and variously conclude with assertions that ethical truths are timeless, that ethical truths are time bound, that fictional writing rather than history writing has license to discuss ethics, or that, in one essay I distinctly remember, Lee was evil no matter how he is portrayed and a college should not be named after him. Almost all students suggest that Shaara's historical fiction is uttering some kind of philosophical truth about the Civil War. History enters into the fiction in this way. No student ever totally agrees with Hartwig, though there is a range of sympathy for the historian's stance toward historical fiction. At times, students try to soften Hartwig's dichotomy between history writing and fiction writing as a way to draw their own lines between the two kinds of writing. I witness lots of gerrymandering, which is fine because the point here is getting them to make conceptual distinctions between the genres. Some clever students suggest distinctions between historians of ideas, those who use events to talk about ideas, and historians of events, those who offer ideas about events. These student writers view fiction writers as historians of ideas. They are ideally poised to read Davis's *The Return of Martin Guerre* in our next unit and to confront the accusation that she is a historian who writes fiction.

When I teach this seminar, I think of Matthew Arnold's poem "Dover Beach" because it points to the imagination as the gateway from the present to the past. By the end of the semester, my students better appreciate the imaginative work entering the past entails and the extent to which fictional and historical narratives about the past are creative, though not in the same way. What the first-year students receive in my seminar, what they would not receive in an Introduction to Literature course, is the opportunity to learn how figurative modes of language operate in nonliterary texts. This opportunity helps make them critical readers even as it makes them keen readers of fiction since the juxtapositions between history writing and fiction writing do nothing if not spotlight the workings of verbal figuration. The figurative mode of language that enables *The Killer Angels* to utter ethical dilemmas faced by Civil War soldiers, not just describe actual troop placements and battle plans, calls forth our imagination to apprehend and to comprehend the relations among the real, the true, and the past. The figurative mode of language is an analytic habit of mind, and it is a way of knowing. Here, I think, are very good reasons for anchoring a writing course in literature—literary texts not only illustrate cognitive and imaginative processes but also stimulate them as we struggle to compose our ideas in language.

Notes

1. For Franklin and Marshall's class of 2006, the average SAT verbal score is 615. The Department of English does not offer composition courses. The director of

the Writing Center and his staff teach a handful of writing-intensive courses, which are recommended but not required for students whose SAT verbal scores are lower than 540. There are a few other courses offered by professors from across the disciplines that are designated writing intensive and that are open to all students.

2. For an overview of Franklin and Marshall's Foundations program, see Campbell and Voelker.

3. Beyond mastery of course material, I might add that the exercises give students a chance to think in private and in writing before we grapple with the topic in class discussion. I find that quiet students are inclined to speak in these discussions because they have had this trial run.

4. The historian Robert Findlay takes Davis to task on grounds that "invention" rather than "reconstruction" of Bertrande's character prevails in her narrative of the past. Findlay is hugely critical of historiography such as Davis's because, as he charges, it blurs the boundary of history and fiction: "it is difficult to see what distinguishes the writing of history from that of fiction" (569).

5. I wish to thank Jim Clouse for his expert teaching skills on the battlefield and for answering my numerous technical questions with good cheer. I wish to thank Franklin and Marshall College, particularly Dean Fred Owens, for funding my recent trips to the Gettysburg National Military Park.

6. When I first taught this seminar, in 1993, the initial 1990 PBS airing of *The Civil War*, or one of its early rebroadcastings, had already mesmerized most students (along with thirty-nine million other American viewers). It is a difficult task to get students to analyze this phenomenal series.

7. Burns takes pains, however, to say that his history of the Civil War is not associated with the old school of " 'consensus' history" (Cripps 747).

8. David Willis McCullough's recent review of Ellen Feldman's historical novel about Lucy Mercer Rutherford (*Lucy*) begins in this vein: "How much of what we are hearing is mistaken or misunderstood or willfully misrepresented?" Mark C. Carnes's collection of essays about historical fiction, *Novel History*, may, however, be the exception to this rule.

Reading Detectives: Teaching Analysis and Argument in First-Year Writing

While the curriculum for many college writing courses foregrounds important questions about race, class, and gender, students do not always come away with a strong understanding of the primary elements of composition. In a 1992 issue of *College Composition and Communication*, Maxine Hairston registered a controversial objection to such politicized pedagogies in first-year writing courses, arguing that instructors too often put "dogma before diversity, politics before craft, ideology before critical thinking, and the social goals of the teacher before the educational needs of the student" ("Diversity" 180). Despite its problems, Hairston's essay raises a valid point. Above all else, first-year writing courses in English and composition should provide students with analytic tools for critical reading and writing, skills that help prepare them for writing in a range of disciplines, including English. To strengthen students' understanding of academic writing, we have designed an expository writing course around detective fiction because the genre thematizes the essential elements of first-year composition, such as analysis, argument, and thesis.

At the same time, the diverse cultural milieus of detective fiction offer rich sites for exploring the politics of difference insofar as they enable students to see that arguments and analyses are always produced and received in social contexts. Students come to see, for example, that careful writing is never merely a matter of collecting "just the facts," just as the construction of an argument is never simply a matter of appealing to an autonomous, self-evident "truth" that transcends a sociorhetorical situation. In this respect, our pedagogy differs sharply from Hairston's apolitical approach in that it draws heavily from the social constructionist theories that have influenced the field of composition studies since the 1980s. Whereas

John Cyril Barton, Douglas Higbee, and Andre Hulet

Hairston assumes that writing can and should be taught in lieu of politics, we believe that a writing pedagogy — just like any other pedagogy or practice — cannot be separated from the political standpoint that informs it. Although we share her concern that in many first-year writing courses a given set of political commitments may override the teaching of writing skills, we do not believe that "critical thinking" can be placed before "ideology" or "craft" before "politics" (to use the terms Hairston opposes), since ideology or politics necessarily shapes any act of critical thinking. As we see it, the solution is not to privilege one set of categories over the other but to collapse them in order to teach students how politics and critical thinking are interrelated and mutually dependent.

Our position, then, holds that concrete uses of abstract tools such as formal logic and analytic reasoning are always already shot through with assumptions about race, class, and gender. As Hairston maintains, however, attention to sociopolitical concerns has often come at the cost of effective writing instruction. Instead, first-year writing courses need to integrate an emphasis on cultural diversity with the development of primary skills in rhetoric and composition, such as thesis development, analysis of evidence, an awareness of rhetorical situation, and organizational mechanics. Patricia Bizzell emphasizes the importance of bringing together formal and social concerns in her influential essay "Cognition, Convention, and Certainty." According to her, "we need to explain the cognitive and the social factors in writing development, and even more important, the relationship between them"; she goes on to call for a synthesis of these two models, one that is "capable of providing a comprehensive new agenda for composition studies" (217, 235). More recently, Granville Ganter has identified a lack of instruction in interpretive analysis in the composition classroom. Echoing Bizzell, he calls for a pedagogical approach that balances formal tools and sociocultural concerns (64).

The course we have developed responds to calls for such a synthesis by examining interpretive activity in detective fiction while scrutinizing the socially invested assumptions informing that activity. In other words, detective fiction provides a means for addressing both tasks. It not only dramatizes the formal or cognitive processes of critical thinking as they unfold in an investigation but also situates those activities in particular social settings. By connecting critical thinking to social environment, detective fiction promotes the value of interpretive self-reflexivity, an awareness of the specific range and power of the analytic tools that students, like detectives, need to employ in their work. Our course, then, uses the literary genre of detective fiction as a multifaceted model for the kinds of critical thinking and social critique we encourage in class discussions and formal writing assignments. If students begin the course, as our title suggests, by "reading detectives" — that is, by analyzing the logic and interpretive activities of literary detectives — they finish the course *as* "reading detectives" themselves, as careful readers and writers who are capable of performing and accounting for their own interpretations and analyses.

This essay is divided into three sections. The first two sections interweave a narrative of course readings and writing assignments into a broader argument about our pedagogical practice and theory; the concluding section reflects on actual student writing in the light of our overall course design. In each section, we hope to show the extent to which students actively engage, rather than just passively observe, the reasoning process while reading and writing about literary detection.

Detection as an Analogy for Student Analysis

If the act of detection is like the act of textual analysis, then detective fiction provides students with concrete and narrativized models for the creative processes of critical reading and writing. As a heuristic analogue, a detective searching for clues in a particular case approximates what students do as they perform analysis en route to an interpretation. Like detectives investigating a problem, student writers must rely on certain assumptions and premises, select and interpret relevant evidence, draw conclusions based on logic and inference, and use persuasive argument to present the results of their discovery.

We begin the first unit of our class with Edgar Allen Poe's "The Purloined Letter." Unlike the other texts we teach, this story offers an explicit model of analysis, one that students will come to use to perform the kind of analysis we describe above. The story concerns the conflict between the methods of detection used by Dupin (the private investigator) and the prefect of police to find the letter a government minister has stolen from the queen of France. The prefect fails, whereas Dupin succeeds. Dupin explains that the prefect's failure was due to an inflexible approach. The prefect's methods, Dupin says,

> were good in their kind, and well executed; their defect lay in their being inapplicable to the case and to the man. A certain set of highly ingenious resources are, with the Prefect, a sort of Procrustean bed, to which he forcibly adapts his designs. (215)

The prefect's reductive methods allow students to see that a reading (or argument), by necessity produced from a particular perspective, works only if it remains alive to textual specificity and multiplicity. With the prefect as a foil, they learn that a critical perspective in relation to a given problem or text is necessarily flexible, not fixed and reductive—like the prefect's procrustean approach or an inflexible thesis to which a student writer may rigidly adhere. We teach students that, just as subject and object must be dialectically negotiated in critical analysis, an initial "working" thesis should be adaptive and open to revision as an argument develops. Dupin's explicit critique of the prefect therefore serves as a model for the kind of analysis we encourage students to perform in class discussions and formal writing assignments.

This model provides students with an introduction to the terms of analysis we foreground throughout the course: namely, how interpretive assumptions influence what counts as evidence and how this interpretive matrix leads to a specific conclusion. While we move away from using formal models as the course progresses, we do think that beginning with one gives students a clear idea of what analysis entails. Indeed, we believe that students benefit from such modeling, especially if the model bears a clear relation to what they are expected to do in their own work. If, as Ann Berthoff has argued, "what we do when we read is fundamentally analogous to what we do when we interpret any situation" (11), then "The Purloined Letter" functions not only as an introduction to the generic features of a discourse with which our students will become intimately familiar but also as an introduction to the kinds of critical thinking we expect in student writing. Again, literary detection serves as an analogue for what we want students to do in their own work.

Our course then turns to Arthur Conan Doyle's "A Scandal in Bohemia," because this story enables students to apply Dupin's critique to Sherlock Holmes. Whereas Dupin provides a point-by-point explanation of both the prefect's failure and his own success in "The Purloined Letter," there is no such account in the Doyle story, which presents students with the opportunity to perform interpretive analysis on their own. In addition to its many parallels with "The Purloined Letter," this story works well in class because it constitutes a rare instance in which Holmes is only partially successful in solving a case. With Dupin's model of analysis as an example, we ask students to explain how the suspect eludes Holmes's grasp. This task requires them to elaborate the disjunctions among Holmes's interpretive assumptions, his actual methods of detection, and the conclusion of the case.

Holmes — a self-professed empiricist, like Poe's prefect — expresses his method early in the story, before the central action takes place. Prompted by Watson's request for an interpretation of the authorship of an unsigned letter, Holmes states, "I have no data yet. It is a capital mistake to theorize before one has data. Insensibly one begins to twist facts to suit theories, instead of theories to suit facts" (163). On the face of it, Holmes's dictum makes a certain amount of sense — don't jump to conclusions, and so on. However, this analytic moment does not occur in the midst of the detective's retrospective explanation of the case, as it does in "The Purloined Letter." Rather, it is an early, free-floating statement, and it is one of several places in the text where students can connect what Holmes claims in theory to what he later does in practice. We ask students, then, to analyze Holmes's analysis — how his stated (and unstated) assumptions relate to his detective methods and how this relation contributes to the outcome of the case.

With Dupin's model before them, students see how Holmes eventually contradicts his dictum not to "twist facts to suit theories" — a principle that resonates with Dupin's "Procrustean bed" metaphor — by making gender assumptions about Irene Adler, Holmes's adversary about whom his client, the king of Bohemia, had warned him at the beginning of the story. "You do not know her," the king tells Holmes, "but she has a soul of steel. She has the face of the most beautiful of women, and the mind of the most resolute of men" (166). The king's own gender assumptions notwithstanding, this warning about Adler's character constitutes a crucial piece of evidence that Holmes fails to consider as he goes on to stereotype Adler as a typical "woman" in his pursuit of a compromising photograph of the king and Adler that she has hidden. In the course of his analysis, Holmes assumes that women are "naturally secretive" (171) and later gives Watson an illustration of a woman's predictable behavior: "When a woman thinks that her house is on fire, her instinct is at once to rush to the thing which she values most. It is a perfectly overwhelming impulse..." (173). Instead of heeding the king's warning, Holmes assumes that Adler fits his stereotype of all women—just as the prefect likens his adversary to "*all* men" (216)—and bases his detection on her supposedly instinctive, impulsive nature. In doing so, Holmes fails to make good on his earlier claim to gather facts before theorizing, and this disjunction between his stated method and actual practice prevents him from outsmarting Adler and obtaining the coveted photograph. In fact, it is Adler's close attention to evidence and her ability to adapt her interpretive assumptions that make her, like Dupin, successful, whereas Holmes's gender assumptions reduce him to the prefect's unwitting method of investigation.

Reading this story in conjunction with "The Purloined Letter," students learn an important lesson about critical thinking: that analysis follows from the perspective one brings to the text, and that one's assumptions frame and, to a great extent, constitute what one sees and does not see. Because Holmes does not follow his own theory of detection, and because his assumptions about women blind him to the complexities of his suspect, he is reduced to a procrustean mode of twisting evidence to suit preconceptions. By examining the logic of Holmes's investigation in class discussions, students see not only that Holmes's interpretive assumptions are inappropriate to the case but also that Holmes is uncritical of his own assumptions. He performs deductive reasoning, applying prior rules to new data instead of practicing critical thinking with its more open and inductive approach. And in the process of writing about Holmes, students begin to understand how critical thinking works, how assumptions can make visible certain types of evidence that in turn lead to a set of conclusions, and how those assumptions themselves need to be critically evaluated in the process. In both stories, however, the interplay of assumptions with the interpretation of evidence stimulates creativity and innovation as students investigate a narrative of detection. Furthermore, while both stories elaborate analytic models in formal terms, they implicitly demonstrate how socially constituted categories such as gender are integral components of any putatively abstract logic.

Demystifying Academic Discourse:
Genre, Conventions, and the Rhetoric of Revision

The first unit of our course deals with how detectives — whether consciously or unconsciously — rely on assumptions when interpreting evidence and drawing conclusions. But as students come to realize in their analyses of Holmes and Dupin, reasoning in detective stories (or anywhere else) does not take place in a social vacuum. Instead, detectives form impressions about suspects and evidence that are inescapably bound up with social attitudes. To explore the relation between the act of analysis and its social setting in greater depth, we use Dashiell Hammett's *The Maltese Falcon*, or a comparable hard-boiled detective novel, for the second unit of the course. As with the first unit, a central premise in the second is that interpreting the narration of detection helps students understand how arguments are formulated and how identities are constructed. This unit complicates that premise by encouraging students to investigate not so much the particular cases or crimes dramatized in the story as the sociopolitical contexts within which that investigation takes place.

Hammett's *The Maltese Falcon*, like the novels of Raymond Chandler, proves especially helpful in contextualizing arguments for class discussions because it calls into question the naive empiricism of the prefect-Holmes paradigm, a model of analysis exemplified by Dupin's procrustean bed metaphor and Holmes's dictum not "to twist facts to suit theories." Moreover, whereas the perspectives of the prefect and Holmes presuppose a stable, transcendent truth that is grounded in the brute facts of reality, the perspective of Sam Spade, Hammett's detective, persistently challenges the very notion of an objective reality. Spade's perspective offers no clear distinction between facts and assumptions and even contends that facts are coextensive with theories.

Through class discussion of the methods of argumentation dramatized in *The Maltese Falcon*, students see how an awareness of audience — rather than a mere (re)presentation of facts — contributes to an argument's rhetorical force. For example, early in the novel when Spade finds himself implicated before the police in an altercation with Joel Cairo, one of the novel's criminals, that will bring them both down to the police station for questioning, Spade concocts a factually incorrect explanation of events that nonetheless proves effective. He tells the police that he and Cairo were just "pretending" to fight, and Cairo confirms Spade's "story" or theory (that is, his explanation of events) because he, too, has no desire to involve the police in his activities (78). When the police immediately challenge this story, Spade replies, "That's all right, believe it or not. The point is that that's our story, and we'll stick to it. The newspapers will print it whether they believe it or not, and it'll be just as funny one way as the other, or more so" (78–79). Everyone — Spade, Cairo, the police, and readers — knows that Spade's "story" is a complete fabrication, but it is rhetorically effective because it threatens the police (Spade's primary audience) with humiliation in the local papers.

Spade develops a similar argument about twisting facts to suit theories in a different context near the novel's conclusion. This time, Spade claims it is the district attorney who will potentially distort the facts to suit his argument. To convince Gutman, the novel's criminal mastermind, to give up his hitman Wilmer as the fall guy for the recent string of unsolved murders, Spade argues:

> Bryan is like most district attorneys. He's more interested in how his record will look on paper than anything else. He'd rather drop a doubtful case than try it and have it go against him.... I can't imagine him letting himself believe [someone] innocent if he could scrape up, or *twist into shape*, proof of [his] guilt. (180; emphasis added)

While Spade's earlier confrontation with the police shows how truth is rhetorically constructed, his argument here gives students an explicit illustration of how the politics and power relations of a particular situation help determine the ways in which arguments are both made and received in social contexts. According to Spade, it makes no difference whether or not Wilmer committed these murders so long as the DA, Spade, or some other authority can "twist into shape proof of [his] guilt." Truth, then, is not an absolute principle that transcends a social context, as in the Poe and Doyle stories. Like knowledge and authority, as Kenneth Bruffee argues, it is a product of a rhetorical situation and operates in terms of what Richard Rorty calls "a social artifact" (qtd. in Bruffee, *Collaborative Learning* 405).

As students invariably point out, Spade's argument in these two scenes flies in the face of Holmes's dictum. It demonstrates that, at least in the social world that Spade inhabits, there are no context-free facts but only interpretive situations in which assumptions and theories constitute "facts" and define them as such. To be sure, Spade's manipulation of the facts constitutes an extreme example of rhetorical persuasion (after all, our purpose here is not to advocate the virtues of lying), but it is helpful in that, by comparison with less dramatically rendered rhetorical situations, it invites students to consider the myriad ways in which knowledge, authority, and even "Truth" (with a capital T) are products of social environment and effective argumentation. For the reasons explained above, we believe that the rhetorically — and politically — charged texts of detective fiction provide excellent material for class discussions and collaborative learning exercises insofar as they dramatize what Bruffee has called the "social justification of belief" ("Liberal Education" 95).[1] In short, Spade demonstrates how arguments work pragmatically: truth is persuasive rhetoric in a specific social context. Whereas Dupin and Holmes offered students a more or less formal model for analysis as well as particularly explicit illustrations of how assumptions relate to conclusions, Spade, aware of the politics of a given situation, complicates this model by giving students a street-smart lesson in "rhetorical pragmatism" (Mailloux 56).

But teaching *The Maltese Falcon* after "The Purloined Letter" and "A Scandal in Bohemia" does more than just help students place arguments in social contexts; it lays the groundwork for social critique (the topic for our course's final unit) by familiarizing students with the concept of generic revision, a common activity in revisionist detective fiction as well as an important idea emphasized in many anthologies for first-year writing instruction. Such anthologies and their writing assignments, however, often ask students to perform social critique before they have a sufficient understanding of what genre and conventions are and how they work to constitute and organize a particular body of writing or a discourse community informed by that writing.[2] After all, to ask students to analyze how unconventional essays work before teaching a conventional essay is like asking students to analyze Paul Auster's "Ghosts"—a postmodern detective story about Blue, a student of Brown, who has been hired by White to spy on Black—before they become familiar with the conventional features of the detective genre. Both scenarios put the proverbial cart before the horse.

Our course seeks to put the *horse* before the cart, genre before generic revision. By reading within the genre of detective fiction over the course of a term, students learn that the conventional detective story contains: (1) a detective with demonstrable skills of ratiocination, (2) an apparently insolvable crime—usually murder, (3) dimwitted or uncooperative police, (4) carefully laid red herrings to put the reader (or detective) off the criminal's scent, and (5) a resolution in which the detective reveals how he has found out the culprit.[3] Since genres imply ways of understanding and ordering reality (Bazerman, "Life" and "Systems"; Bawarshi), students can readily conceive of the ideological implications of a genre—for instance, when a convention (such as a white, male detective) becomes a liability rather than an asset—when analyzing the stark contours of detective fiction. This process, in turn, helps students objectify the difficult task of negotiating the genre of academic writing. With detective fiction before students as a familiar point of reference, the instructor, by broadening the detection-analysis analogy, can turn to a discussion of how the genre or discourse of academic writing produces arguments through its traditional conventions, such as an introduction defining key terms; a complex, arguable, relevant thesis; an orientation toward an audience, specific purpose, and context; well-chosen examples or citations that are incisively analyzed; and clear and appropriate transitions between examples and paragraphs. Thus drawing a sustained analogy between academic discourse and detective stories enables students to learn about an unfamiliar activity in terms of a more familiar practice.

If one of the goals of first-year writing is to initiate students into academic discourse (Bartholomae, "Inventing"; Bizzell, *Academic Discourse*; and Harris, "Idea"), then pointing out the generic similarities between academic writing and detective fiction helps advance that process. In fact, "Gender (De)Mystified: Resistance and Recuperation in Hard-Boiled Female Detective Fiction," an academic essay we have taught in the classroom, draws explicitly on the connection between the conventions of academic writing and those of detective fiction: "The academic paper, like the detective novel, is conventionally structured around the search for evidence, the weighing of hypotheses, the investigation of causation" (Shuker-Haines and Umphrey 80). This passing reference to the shared features of these genres resonates with our sustained use of detective fiction to demystify the generic conventions of academic discourse. That is, we broaden the analogy between academic writing and detective fiction to foster an understanding of the stakes and consequences of generic revision in *both* these discursive practices. For once students have a working knowledge of how conventions order social identities, situations, and experience, they can move on to a discussion about how authors, speakers, or texts revise those conventions to generate social critique.

For the third (and final) unit of our course, we arrive at the question of social critique and generic revision by having students analyze Walter Mosley's *White Butterfly* or a comparable revisionist detective story. To emphasize the significance of critical reading and writing for this unit, we politicize genre as a mode of social action by drawing a link between generic conventions in a detective story and social conventions that structure experience in our social worlds outside fiction.[4] As Anis Bawarshi claims, genres function as "typified rhetorical ways communicants come to recognize and act in all kinds of situations, literary and nonliterary" (335). Elaborating this claim, he explains how a presidential address, classroom instruction, and other social situations are both constituted and regulated by generic norms and conventions. As a transition to Mosley's *White Butterfly*, we foreground a seemingly trivial remark by a minor character in *The Maltese Falcon* to spell out an example of how racial and cultural stereotypes influence what Bawarshi might call the genre of crime and race relations in the United States. When Spade asks a hotel detective whether he knows anything about Joel Cairo—the mysterious grifter variously identified as "the Levantine" (46), "the small dark man" (53), and "the fairy" (94)—he gets the following response: "Search me, Sam. I got nothing against him but his looks" (95). By grounding his unfounded suspicion on "nothing" but Cairo's "looks," the detective makes an assumption largely, if not entirely, based on the predominant social attitudes and mores of the time.

Read against *The Maltese Falcon*, Mosley's *White Butterfly* offers a relentless exposition of the presumption of guilt because of race. Written near the end of the twentieth century, it revises or "re-visions" generic conventions in terms of social norms. In the broadest sense, the novel returns to the racially charged past of midcentury America previously represented by Hammett, Chandler, and others to explore the landscape of American society from the perspective of someone whose voice and experience had been largely excluded: Easy Rawlins, an African American private eye who is bullied by the cops and coerced into taking up a case that they cannot solve. Connecting Easy to Joel Cairo (instead of Spade) indicates the major shift in perspective for this assignment. For in Easy's world, the detective is no longer a relatively autonomous agent who, like Spade, can *easily* rise above his social context by constructing persuasive arguments out of it. And it is not just the identity of the detective but also the means of persuasion and the construction of evidence that dramatically change in *White Butterfly*. Students get a clear sense of the stakes and consequences of this shift by noting what happens when a black detective's investigation is situated in a white world significantly shaped by racist assumptions. Moreover, since Mosley dramatizes the cultural assumptions that inform every act of analysis, students come to understand how arguments both depend on and contribute to the construction of a cultural politics.

Yet the detective's racial identity and cultural orientation are not the only conventions that Mosley revises. He also manipulates the conventional use of red herrings—misleading clues or irrelevant evidence that distract attention from the actual issue — to elicit social commentary about how racial biases either distract or attract a community's attention. Mosley's revision of this convention serves as the basis for the writing prompt we use to teach the assignment for the third unit. We ask students how race functions as a red herring in *White Butterfly*, an especially relevant question given the dramatic structure of the novel: the district attorney of Los Angeles murders his daughter because of her interracial relationship and then uses racial profiling to direct attention away from himself and toward a black suspect. In teaching this assignment, we conflate the convention of the red herring with assumptions about race to transform *White Butterfly* into a site out of which students can produce social critiques of their own. For if genres can be seen as "sites of cultural critique and change" precisely because they "are the rhetorical environments within which we recognize, enact, and consequently reproduce various situations, practices, relations, and identities" (Barwarshi 336), then *White Butterfly* — like a legion of other contemporary detective novels written by minorities or women — is a particularly rich site for cultural analysis.[5]

Practice and Theory: The Student as Detective

To consider the advantages and limitations of our course design, we conclude with examples from our students' work. But first we want briefly to provide a critical framework for conceiving the development of student writing in our course. By asking students to investigate logic and rhetoric as used by literary detectives, our approach produced student writing that often highlights what David Bartholomae calls "successive approximations" of academic prose ("Inventing" 146). We envision these students as writers obliged to perform an unfamiliar mode of language, initially having only the features of a language they do know on which to rely. Bartholomae's problem of approximation can be restated as the problem of analogy. For student writers are always working with analogy, whether or not they know it, and the use of analogy (like the use of any heuristic aid or pedagogical model) can work both for and against them in their attempts to produce academic discourse.

Bartholomae reminds us that academic discourse appears as a set of tools to students listening to us in the classroom and that students generate "a discourse that lies between what we might call the students' primary discourse...and standard, official literary criticism" ("Inventing" 145). Whenever students write, they must "invent the university" to establish the authority to speak. For Bartholomae, the development of such authority occurs in three stages: at an early stage students authorize themselves by defining their relation to a subject; at a later stage they attempt to imitate academic style "without there being any recognizable interpretive or academic project under way"; and at an advanced stage students assert authority "by placing themselves both within and against a discourse...and work[ing] self-consciously to claim an interpretive project of their own" (156–57). We would insert an additional stage between Bartholomae's second and third, a stage that examines how first-year students lay claim to authority by implementing the learned commonplaces or shared assumptions of academic writing. For academic discourse operates according to conventional assumptions and arguments, just as the everyday discourses it seeks to analyze generate their meanings through the (re)production of commonplaces. Our sustained use of analogy in the classroom and on writing assignments facilitates students' grasp of academic writing by providing models of how such commonplaces and conventions work.

Given our own assumptions, we expected student writing progressively to take on the characteristics of academic discourse as students became more comfortable with the concept of genre as exemplified in detective fiction. Indeed, the detective-analysis analogy helped students compose increasingly sophisticated forms of argumentation as they grappled with more complex renderings of the detective's interpretive activity in particular social contexts. The analogy, in other words, provided students with a familiar model to follow or imitate: the detectives' search for relevant evidence and the drawing of inferences from it, as well as their use of persuasive rhetoric and argumentation to prove "whodunit." At the same time, though, our attention to analogy occasionally led some students to apply the analogy too mechanically as an organizing principle in their work.

In short, some students' use of analogy became at times procrustean, an all-too-common "commonplace."

The first unit of the course concluded with a comparative analysis of "The Purloined Letter" and "A Scandal in Bohemia." Our prompt for this assignment asked students to consider each detective's interpretive assumptions and to explain why Dupin was ultimately successful and Holmes was not. For this paper, students had to accomplish what the detectives appear to do with ease: organize evidence about subjects into parallel cases and then compare and contrast them. Dupin's effective method of detection serves as a model for the student writer of a paper titled "Assumptions." She adopts Dupin's terms of "mathematical" and "poetic" reasoning and applies them to both detectives to interpret the significance of the stories' conclusions. With Dupin's analysis as her point of departure, she explains mathematical reasoning as "the logical and conventional way of how one analyzes," while poetic reasoning, in her terms, "means that one is able to look past what is known to be obvious." Dupin claims that the superior reasoner has both faculties, and taking Dupin's position enables the student to argue that Holmes is undone by his conventional assumptions about women. By attempting to succeed as Dupin succeeds, she puts the two stories neatly in parallel and capitalizes on the analogy by performing some insightful interpretation of the logic of detection, arguing that even "super-rational detectives" must rely on valid assumptions or they too will fail.

While the analogy facilitated a productive analysis of the detective stories, the student's reliance on imitation and approximation works against her conclusion:

> In Poe's story, Dupin made careful evaluations of the information he gathered and made a reasonable assumption about men and their tendency to hide valuable objects in much clever [sic] ways than the Prefect suggests. In addition, Dupin's identification of the Minister's intellect allowed him to locate the letter with ease. By contrast, Holmes made a wrong assumption about women in general and thus it blinded him from looking past Irene's gender, a mask that prevented Holmes from seeing the wit and intelligence she had.

Here we see the student struggling to conclude in parallel as she began. This passage presents a perceptive contrast between the stories, although we may note that perhaps she pushes the analogy too far. After all, in the context of the narrative, Dupin's assumption about "men and their tendency to hide valuable objects in clever places" is not necessarily an assumption that concerns gender per se but one that emphasizes the dangers of hasty generalization. In contrast, the Doyle story hinges on Holmes's stereotypical views of women. The writer seems to be unsure how to present her comparative analysis as distinct in some respects. Again, the power of the detective analogy in her writing drives her away from how she might otherwise conclude, even as it allows her to perform the logic of the parallel case.

Midcourse assignments situated an analysis of reasoning and critical thinking in more complex social contexts. For the third paper, students considered how the sociorhetorical situations of hard-boiled detective fiction inform interpretive logic and shape identity in a given cultural milieu. Insofar as they play out a drama of ideals and corruption, these novels call attention to competing perspectives as well as to the various forms of appeal and argumentation used by the detective and characters (on both sides of the law) to gain information. Unlike the author of the "Assumptions" paper, the student writer of "WARNING: Rigid Morality Leads to Self-Sacrifice," an analysis of Chandler's *The Big Sleep*, moves beyond a typical reading of the protagonist's identity as sympathetic and coherent. Her argument prepares us for an approximate discourse at the stage we have located between Bartholomae's second and third. This student strives to investigate some previously established commonplaces about social identity in the ethico-political terms currently valued by academics. She delivers by showing Marlowe's attachment to the idea of himself as a "white knight" fighting for those in distress and analyzes the connotative meaning of his actions with insightful inferences, such as "hence, Marlowe's inner thoughts are different from his actual behavior, which makes him analogous to people who have 'fronts' and conceal their true intentions."

Yet like the writer of "Assumptions," this student has some trouble rounding off her argument. Her conclusion argues that

> [Marlowe] sacrifices his purity because he feels it is part of his duty. Although he becomes a person who buys and conceals truths in a society full of greed and lust, but he is actually a successful figure, though only in a world of his own.

Having centered her argument on a critique of Marlowe's problematic identity, this student feels the need to account for the more common reading of
Marlowe's effective detection and relative success. The awkwardly placed
and grammatically incorrect clause, "but he is actually a successful figure,"
captures this tension. It indicates not only a contradiction in Marlowe's
character that the student hasn't fully worked out but also an effort to complicate her position by acknowledging the alternative, more commonplace
reading it works against. We hear the language of a student attempting to
establish authority by imitating academic discourse conventions — namely,
that of qualification in the face of complex textual evidence. In other
words, this student wants to situate her argument in a conversation about
the hero's social role in hard-boiled detective fiction, but she has not yet figured out how her own project works both in and against that discourse. An
additional draft might "fix" the conclusion, but only a shift in this student's
understanding of how conventions work will affect the contours of thought
that produced her approximate discourse.

In an effort to get our students to reflect directly on the ways conventions organize both thought and discourse, we focused final assignments on
the relation between generic revision and social critique. Our pedagogical
method here was to use the interpretive activity and generic conventions of
detective fiction as an extended analogy for the prominent themes and writing processes of academic discourse. Now that students had read a range of
stories from the detective genre, they were in a position to think critically
about the stakes and consequences of revisionist work by Mosley, Auster,
or Sara Paretsky. For instance, the writer of "Sara Paretsky's Reportrayal of
Women and Men" uses Paretsky's revision of gender politics as a springboard for her own critique of Paretsky's novel. While acknowledging the
political implications of Paretsky's *Indemnity Only*, this student argues that
Paretsky in fact reinscribes conventional gender relations by merely invert-
ing the stereotypes of men and women:

> One may argue that Paretsky establishes a new role for women, which
> breaks traditional female stereotypes. However, rather than making new,
> dynamic female characters, Paretsky simply reverses the status of men and
> women in *Indemnity Only*. In this way, Paretsky does not pave a new way for

women but continues a form of sexism that generalizes characteristics of both men and women.

By challenging Paretsky's rhetorical strategies and mode of social critique, this student's argument about revisionism and its discontents constitutes what Bartholomae and others would call a complex thesis statement: "While most readers of _____ have said _____, a close and careful reading shows _____" ("Inventing" 152). Like Bartholomae's formula, the writing handbook of our university provides the following example to help students formulate incisive theses: "Although X seems to be the case, Y is what's really at work here" (*Student Guide* 26). The writer of "Sara Paretsky's Re-portrayal" employs a complex thesis along these lines by positioning her argument in opposition to a reading of Paretsky's novel that, by the end of our class discussions on the topic, became commonplace: that Paretsky, like many academics, manipulates the conventions to produce a social critique. Compared with other successful papers for the assignment, this one stood out because it demonstrated an understanding that even the privileged themes of academic discourse can, like the everyday and ideological discourses it seeks to analyze, become commonplace and conventional.

Despite potential drawbacks, our experiments with analogy encourage us to conclude that imitation or approximation is still a productive way to teach writing in first-year English and composition. While first-year writing can certainly be taught by way of other subjects or heuristics, detective fiction provides a rich analogue for several reasons. As we have argued, literary detection not only thematizes essential elements of critical thinking and the writing process but also situates those activities in socio-rhetorical contexts shaped by contested ideologies of race, class, and gender. Moreover, given the ubiquity of detective fiction in the many cultures that make up the United States today, detective fiction serves as a familiar point of reference for students newly exposed to the challenges of academic writing. This diverse proliferation of detective stories and their attention to enabling assumptions, the analysis of evidence, and effective rhetoric and argumentation open up a range of possibilities for writing instruction. Drawing an analogy between detection and analysis—and then extending and complicating it—creates a lively environment in which to encourage the rigorous analysis and self-critical argumentation valued in academe.

Notes

We thank Steven Mailloux and Susan C. Jarratt for commenting on drafts of this paper, John Hollowell for giving us the opportunity to develop our course, and Rodney Rodriguez for collaborating and teaching with us. We are especially grateful to Michael P. Clark for reviewing our work and sponsoring our development of this course during the 1999–2000 academic year.

1. Bruffee first articulates this idea in "Liberal Education and the Social Justification of Belief," and he elaborates it in regard to classroom practices in his oft-cited essay "Collaborative Learning and the 'Conversation of Mankind.'" Yet Bruffee's social-constructionist pedagogy, especially his insistence on the goal of "consensus" building in knowledge communities, is not without its problems. For instance, see Trimbur; Fish, "Anti-foundationalism."

2. As a case in point, see David Bartholomae and Anthony Petrosky's *Ways of Reading: An Anthology for Writers*. Select texts from this anthology were used during the 1998–99 academic year by teaching assistants at the University of California, Irvine, to teach a syllabus designed around the concept of "difficulty." After teaching Toni Morrison's *Sula*, TAs taught unconventional essays by Mary Louise Pratt, Patricia Williams, and Gloria Anzaldúa, because these essays produce powerful arguments about rhetoric and cultural diversity by violating the rules of academic discourse. Whereas students in our course on difficulty tended to miss the point of generic revision precisely because they had no experience with the conventional academic essay, students in our course on detective fiction and academic discourse were surprisingly adept at showing, after having read and written on the conventional detective story, how contemporary writers in the genre revise conventions to make powerful arguments about race or gender.

3. This definition is modified from the entry "detective story" in J. A. Cuddon's *A Dictionary of Literary Terms* (182–84).

4. See Carolyn Miller's seminal essay "Genre as Social Action" and the other essays collected in *Genre and the New Rhetoric* (Freedman and Medway).

5. For a comprehensive list and discussion of culturally diverse detectives in contemporary fiction, see Macdonald and Macdonald. Over the last several years a large body of scholarship has emerged that examines the ways in which contemporary detective fiction critiques assumptions about race and gender. Since we first developed our course over the 1999–2000 academic year, two book-length studies on detective fiction and the politics of difference have been published: *Detective Agency: Women Rewriting the Hard-Boiled Tradition* (Walton and Jones), and *Diversity and Detective Fiction* (Klein).

Group III

Literature and the Larger Culture

Writing on Boundaries: A Cultural Studies Approach to Literature and Writing Instruction

Several years ago, while we were both teaching at the University of South Carolina, Lancaster—a branch campus of the USC system—we were asked to teach a course entitled Literature and Composition. This course occupied the second semester of the two-semester first-year writing sequence and included, according to the catalog description, a required research paper. At our campus, the first-semester course was often taught as an introduction to the conventions of academic reading and writing, and the second-semester course had typically been taught as an introduction to literary analysis (which would walk students through the anthologized categories of character, plot, setting, and symbol) with a final research paper that cited literary criticism. Because this course was required of all students, it was populated predominantly by students who went on to major in fields other than English. Drawn almost exclusively from the largely working-class population of Lancaster and its surroundings, many of our students—often first-generation college students—opted for a two-year degree, and those who did transfer to the main campus to complete a four-year degree were far more likely to choose a technical or preprofessional major.

Instead of approaching Literature and Composition as an introduction to literature, we wanted to design a writing course that would have greater relevance for students who had diverse academic goals and represented a variety of majors, a course that would build more directly on the kinds of reading, writing, and critical thinking students had done in the first semester of the composition sequence. We realized that the first-year composition curriculum, as practiced at our institution, signaled a conception of English studies with which we were no longer comfortable. Because the curriculum required the specialized vocabulary and skills involved in writing literary

Lori Robison and Eric A. Wolfe

analysis, it seemed like a holdover from a time when the value of teaching traditional literary interpretation to all college students—despite their backgrounds or their intended fields of study—remained largely unquestioned. For us, the problem was twofold. First, we were objecting to a curriculum that seemed to presume that the purpose of having student writers, almost none of whom were English majors, read literature and produce literary interpretation was self-evident. Second, we understood that the problem was not in the institution's attempt to bring literature and composition together (indeed, we had often done so ourselves), but, rather, in the implicit suggestion that instruction in literary analysis is analogous to the goals of the writing classroom. As writing teachers committed to an approach to composition that emphasizes academic inquiry, we resisted a first-year writing curriculum that would substitute an education in literary content for a course that would encourage students, as both readers and writers, to participate in the discursive construction of knowledge.

We wanted to develop a course that would demonstrate that reading, writing, and interpretation have significance in the larger world. With such a diverse student population and with so few students committed to traditional literary knowledges, we could not assume that the value of literary reading and writing and its uses would be self-evident. We would need to be able to present our approach to literary texts overtly and to let the students in on the theoretical assumptions that lay behind that approach. And though the course would take literary texts and interpretation as its subject matter, we wanted to structure the course very much like a composition course. We would need to approach literary texts in a way that emphasized student writing, assigning students complex writing tasks that encouraged them to reflect on their relation to the texts they were analyzing and to the writing they were producing.

Our solution, finally, was to organize the course around a cultural studies approach. Cultural studies insists that reading is context dependent, that there is no innocent reading of a text, no interpretation that is not produced through the lens of some contextualization—whether theoretical, historical, or literary. And yet, because cultural studies also recognizes that there is no given context for the reading of a text, it asks writers to be aware of the contextualizations they perform, as well as how their own cultural positions contribute to that context. Such a self-conscious and self-reflexive approach to reading and writing would force us to articulate clearly the function of literary texts in our course — to help the students understand the assumptions that enabled the kinds of reading and writing we would practice. It would also allow us to engage the students in writing projects of considerable complexity and to highlight important questions about how the students' writing was situated in relation to the texts, the contexts we established, and the students' own cultural positions.

In the course we designed, Writing on Cultural Boundaries, we took the model suggested by Stephen Greenblatt's essay "Culture"; the course would think of literary texts as working at the "boundaries" of culture, against the "limits within which social behavior must be contained" (226, 225). It situated literary texts in a broad cultural context while encouraging an interrogation of the contemporary cultural locations of the students themselves. Students were asked to read a work of fiction as presenting implicit arguments against "the dominant beliefs and social structures of its culture" (231) and to write essays that analyzed how a text works in response to cultural ideologies. This move to position literary writing as part of a cultural conversation, as merely one mode of writing that imaginatively addresses a shared set of issues or problems, can be seen as a move to position literature as rhetorical praxis. The emphasis on rhetoric suggests an approach that might bridge the institutional divisions that often exist in English departments; understanding all writing in terms of the effects it produces has the potential to provide theoretical coherence for English studies.

We began the course by reading and discussing Greenblatt's essay, which articulated for the students the course's underlying theoretical orientation and provided a set of terms for approaching literature. As we have suggested, a problem with the kind of literary reading and discussion that is often performed in classrooms is that many students — even those who perform well in English courses — seem to have little sense of what they are doing and why they are doing it. Reflecting on his experience taking undergraduate literature classes, Gerald Graff notes that, though he "made good grades," he still found "'serious' reading painfully difficult and alien" ("Disliking" 42). He eventually realized that his classes seemed to proceed as though the purpose of literary reading was self-evident, yet the central activities of English classrooms—and the values behind them—remained mysterious: "What was unclear to me was what I was supposed to say about literary works, and why" (42). For Graff, the experience that demystified literary study was his exposure, during his junior year, to critical debates over the ending of *The Adventures of Huckleberry Finn*. These debates gave Graff the sense that he had "some issues *to watch out for*," a set of concerns that gave shape to his reading (43). His experience makes clear the importance of outlining the assumptions we make about literary interpretation, and, for our class, this function was served by beginning with Greenblatt's essay: it gave students "some issues *to watch out for*."

As part of Frank Lentricchia and Thomas McLaughlin's collection *Critical Terms for Literary Study*, Greenblatt's essay is specifically aimed at student readers. While the reader who is familiar with Greenblatt's other writings would certainly detect evidence of his critical practice—a Foucauldian conception of power, an emphasis on literature as part of a greater economy of cultural exchange, an understanding of identity as improvisatory practice—the essay succeeds in making these ideas accessible, though not reductive, for beginning students. Greenblatt seeks to provide students with a usable theory of culture, one that will "do more work for us" (225). He suggests that the most productive conception of culture is to think of it in terms of "constraint and mobility," as an "ensemble of beliefs and practices" that "function as a pervasive technology of control, a set of limits within which social behavior must be constrained, a repertoire of models to which individuals must conform" (225). A given culture reinforces these limits in both negative and positive ways, large and small. Appropriate social behavior is conditioned not only through "spectacular punishments" and rewards but through "seemingly innocuous responses" as well: Greenblatt lists some of these responses as "a condescending smile, laughter poised between the genial and the sarcastic, a small dose of indulgent pity laced with contempt, cool silence," and, on the positive side, "a gaze of admiration, a respectful nod, a few words of gratitude" (226). This was a moment in Greenblatt's text that generated enthusiastic class discussion, because our students were well schooled in subtle techniques designed to enforce a seemingly inexhaustible set of codes of social behavior. They were easily able to extend Greenblatt's list and provide endless examples of those techniques in practice.

Greenblatt explains literature's cultural function as an example of these disciplinary techniques: "Western literature over a very long time has been one of the great institutions for the enforcement of cultural boundaries through praise and blame" (226). Yet in his Foucauldian insistence on the productive nature of power, he is careful to balance this sense of literature's potential uses as an enforcer of cultural limits with a sense of its ability to challenge those limits. It is this latter sense that comes to dominate his essay, when he concludes:

> [I]n our own time most students of literature reserve their highest admiration for those works that situate themselves on the very edges of what can be said at a particular place and time, that batter against the boundaries of their own culture. (231)

This conclusion allowed us to present the students with a powerful argument about the importance of literary writing: writing is one of the cultural institutions that produce our beliefs and practices, our very sense of what is possible.

The patterns our course followed reflected our commitment to work typically done in first-year writing courses. Because we had given up any notion that this course would work as introductory literature courses are traditionally assumed to work—as either a survey course that exposes students to indispensable literary masterpieces or as a content course that gives students a vocabulary in literary criticism—we could also give up the notion that there was any value in teaching a large number of literary texts. With an emphasis on five literary texts, we could encourage careful, detailed discussions and reading. The course was structured around four units, and each unit became increasingly complex as the literary texts became longer and denser (we began the course with three short stories, moved to a slave narrative, and finished with a short novel) and as the writing assignments asked students to become more independent in their textual analysis.[1] The course moved through a fairly regular routine with each unit. We began with a discussion of the text and asked students to begin developing an interpretation through an informal writing assignment. We then spent some class time introducing the formal paper assignment. Students next began drafting and revising their essays, and we attempted to aid that process through a combination of peer revision workshops, class discussions of the drafts or of portions of the drafts, and individual conferences with the students. Working with student writing was a central component of this course; in fact, the literary texts were rarely discussed until students had the opportunity to begin to come to an interpretation of the text through writing.

Student writing thus functioned in this course—just as it often functions in the composition classroom—as an intrinsic part of the meaning-making process. The literary interpretations were not performed in class lecture or discussion only to be dutifully replicated in the student papers; instead, the papers themselves were the place where students forged a reading of the literary text, where they came to terms with what the literary texts could be saying back to the culture in which they were produced or to the culture in which they were read. We attempted to create a classroom where student writing would be understood not as a mere exercise but as part of the process of academic inquiry. The writing assignments gave students complex questions—questions that required a recursive process of reading, drafting, and revising. In addition, the socially relevant issues taken on by these literary texts gave the students questions of real importance to think and write about. Indeed, because the course theorized writing as a politically powerful activity, it encouraged students to understand their own writing as an act that mattered.

The course's emphasis on writing broke down institutional practices that have separated first-year writing courses from literature courses. Unlike the traditional introduction to literature, our course did not assume that student writing should work primarily in support of literary content; it did not expect student writing to demonstrate mastery of essential texts or themes or of the traditional paper in literary interpretation. Instead, like an inquiry-based composition curriculum, it assumed that student writing ultimately takes part in the creation of knowledge, that college students should have the opportunity to attend to challenging questions through a recursively understood process of reading and writing. Yet this course, unlike other composition curricula that take a similar approach, took as its central topic of inquiry a literary question: What does it mean to read literary texts as working ideologically in the culture in which they were produced?

As we turned to our first unit, we used Greenblatt's terms and concepts to frame the students' readings of literary texts. We read two short stories, Shirley Jackson's "The Lottery" and Tillie Olsen's "I Stand Here Ironing." Though later units would involve explicit historical contextualization of literary texts, we deliberately chose not to provide any extrinsic context for the stories. Both could be read productively in Greenblatt's framework without contextualization, because both stories, as products of the twentieth-century United States, engage with powerful cultural ideologies that continue to shape our students' subjectivities. Our writing assignment borrowed language from Greenblatt to focus the students on the central questions raised by the course's theoretical framework:[2]

> Both literary works we have read this semester—Shirley Jackson's "The Lottery" and Tillie Olsen's "I Stand Here Ironing"—are clearly concerned with the kinds of "limits" that particular cultures establish for individual behavior. Working with one of the texts we have read, write an essay in which you explore how that text works against what Greenblatt calls "the dominant beliefs and social structures of its culture" as they are represented in the story.

We selected these stories in part because they denaturalize students' common cultural assumptions, calling into question the meanings of seemingly innocent ideas like community, motherhood, and sacrifice—concepts that remain important to the dominant culture of the early-twenty-first-century United States. In working out their interpretations of the stories, students were thus forced to interrogate their positions in a potentially complex set of cultural beliefs. What is at stake here is not a political but a rhetorical goal. We wanted not to convert the students to a particular way of thinking but to give them the opportunity to work out their own stance in relation to the issues raised by the stories. Neither story can be easily reduced to a simplistic argument; students had to work closely with the texts to develop interpretations of what cultural values the stories might be challenging and what alternative constructions the stories might be offering.

On a formal level, the stories work to defy readers' expectations. Each opens by inviting the reader to read through the lens of dominant cultural values and beliefs only to call them into question as the story develops. "The Lottery" begins by describing a seemingly quintessential small town in the United States as it prepares for what appears to be a summer celebration. Yet any positive associations with the details of that small-town life are dispelled by the story's ending, when the lottery is revealed to be the framework for a ritual stoning. We began our approach to the story by focusing on our students' reading experience; we worked with students in class to articulate how their understanding of many of the story's elements shifted as they slowly became aware of the lottery's significance. The story thus dramatizes — a dramatization heightened by readers' experiences of surprise — Greenblatt's point that many aspects of a society's "technology of control" may be "seemingly innocuous." At this point, we reintroduced Greenblatt's language, asking our students to consider what ensemble of beliefs and practices represented in the story allowed the characters to carry out such a shocking practice. In the course of this discussion, we were able to note how difficult the story made it to separate the details that seemed to suggest a positive, cohesive sense of community from those that were connected to the sacrificial violence of the lottery.

The readerly expectations frustrated by "I Stand Here Ironing" are subtler, having little to do with any dramatic plot reversals. Instead, the story simply fails to provide the moralistic condemnation of the narrator that our ideologies of motherhood would seem to demand. The story is narrated by a mother responding in interior monologue to — and yet resisting — a request from a teacher or school counselor to provide the story of her daughter, who is struggling in school. What the story refuses is a discourse of motherly self-sacrifice, or, perhaps more accurately, of the guilt that should accompany the expected recognition—a recognition withheld by the story—that the narrator has not sacrificed enough. In refusing that maternal guilt, the story shifts the focus to questions about where to place responsibility for the forces that have shaped the daughter's life. We began, again, by attending to our students' reading experiences, asking the students to articulate their judgments about the narrator's mothering and to think about the conceptions of mothering that supported those judgments. We also asked students to share their frustrations at not being "allowed" by the story to entirely indulge their desire to find fault with the narrator. We then shifted our discussions to try to identify the various cultural limits the narrator encountered that directly shaped her parenting practice, and—as with "The Lottery"—the beliefs and practices that supported those limits. In many cases, the students recognized that the beliefs and practices that had limited the narrator were the same beliefs that supported their own readerly judgments about the narrator. In this way, the story generated reflection on the students' own positions in relation to contemporary ideas about motherhood.

Building on the work the students had done with Greenblatt's essay and with Jackson's and Olsen's stories, the second unit of the course again denaturalized many current cultural beliefs and values by underscoring that definitions of gender and motherhood have been differently constructed in other historical periods. We worked with Charlotte Perkins Gilman's "The Yellow Wallpaper," a particularly good text for this class because of its dramatic demonstration of the ideological power of language to construct concepts that our culture wants to define as fixed and self-evident, such as identity, maternity, and illness. We selected the Bedford Cultural Edition of this text to give students an explicit cultural and historical context in which to situate Gilman's story. This volume, edited by Dale M. Bauer, includes a range of late-nineteenth- and early-twentieth-century nonfictional documents—excerpts from conduct literature and motherhood manuals, texts by medical authorities discussing female sexuality and the treatment of "hysteria"—that reveal the cultural ideologies against which Gilman was writing, the cultural ideologies that constrain the narrator of Gilman's

story. Students typically respond well to "The Yellow Wallpaper"; even inexperienced readers of literature were generally interested in speaking to the
ways that the changing tone of the narration shapes our understanding of
the narrator and her state of mind. We began our discussion of the story
by asking students to express their understanding of the narrator and the
conflicts she experiences with her husband and with herself. Our discussion
went on to consider how the narrator might characterize her problem and
to compare her self-understanding with her husband's understanding of her
malaise. From the recognition that her illness is constructed by the cultural
ideology that defines it, it was a small step—especially with the help of
Gilman's statement that the story "was no more 'literature' than my other
stuff, being definitely written 'with a purpose'" ("Reception" 351)—to a discussion of the larger implications of the story's social purpose.

As in the first unit of the course, the writing assignment in the second
asked students to develop an interpretation of the cultural values that a literary text might be challenging. With the help of Bauer's edition, we were
also able to encourage students to read for the ideological assumptions that
inform nonfictional texts and to consider what it might mean to understand
a literary text as being in conversation with a nonliterary text. Students
were asked to write about how "The Yellow Wallpaper" engaged with and
reconstructed the cultural ideologies of gender uncovered in one of the
nonfictional documents in Bauer's edition:

> You will want to make sure that you explain and document very carefully the
> belief or assumption to which you think the story is responding and how you
> see that belief demonstrated in the secondary text you have chosen, but the
> majority of your paper will be an exploration of Gilman's story. You will need
> to use very specific details from the story to explain what you think Gilman is
> saying about this idea. Be sure to explain the nature of her response through-
> out the story. Is she being critical of the idea? Is she proposing an alternative?
> Is she getting people to think about women in a new way?

Perhaps the central challenge here for students was that the writing assignment required them to interpret the nonfictional documents as well as the
fictional text; the cultural ideologies that might be used to frame Gilman's
story were not necessarily given explicit expression in the nonfictional texts.

Recognizing that students would have little experience reading for the ideological assumptions that inform these texts, we asked, in the informal writing assignment and our subsequent discussion of the documents, a number of questions:

> What does [the document] suggest about the "proper" role for women? about women's typical strengths and weaknesses? about what it means to be a good mother? about women's relationships with men and children? about women's relation to work? about women's relation to reading and writing?

Since this way of reading and interpreting nonliterary texts was new for most of the students — reading not for the explicit argument but, to cite Greenblatt again, for the ensemble of beliefs and practices that might make that argument possible — they found it difficult. Reading those texts critically was perhaps most demanding for the students when the texts contained arguments that seemed to fit neatly into the students' own values. One text, for example, made a prominent argument about the need for women's exercise. This seemed to echo so strongly the students' attitudes toward women's health that it took patient work with that text to recognize the argument as part of an ideology of womanly self-sacrifice; exercise was important, the text suggested, not to effect women's self-actualization but to ensure their ability to cater effectively to the needs of their families. This recognition allowed us to turn the conversation toward an examination of the students' beliefs, which had made the text's argument seem so appealing at first. We asked if our contemporary attitudes toward women's exercise (and, more broadly, women's health) still contained elements that might undercut the more overt message emphasizing exercise's contribution to women's self-worth. In this way, as in the first unit, an examination of the limits and boundaries represented in literary texts and cultural documents led back to our students' reflection on their own positions in relation to those beliefs and practices.

In the next unit, which included the required research paper, we asked students to think about the role of the *Narrative of the Life of Frederick Douglass* in the ongoing debates over slavery in the antebellum United States. We approached the research paper more as a writing project, emphasizing a rhetorical task that remained consistent with the writing students had done in the other units, than as an information-gathering activity. We did not want students to create reports filled with facts, figures, and dates about American slavery.[3] We chose, therefore, to give the students a tightly focused assignment, which read, in part:

> Write an essay in which you explore how Douglass shapes his *Narrative* to respond to prominent pro-slavery arguments in the antebellum United States. Your sources should provide you with examples of those arguments; you will need to use those sources in order to document and explain the pro-slavery case. To effectively explore Douglass's response, you will then need to look closely at particular scenes and examples from his *Narrative*, explaining how the way he writes those scenes can be considered an effective counterargument to those your other sources present.

The research element added some complexity to this assignment since students had to examine and evaluate a number of sources before making their selection (we required at least two, in addition to Douglass). Conceptually, however, we think the secondary texts were easier to work with than they had been in the previous unit. While the possibility existed for students to put forward sophisticated interpretations of those secondary texts, students could also adequately address the assignment by dealing only with the overt arguments made by pro-slavery writers. Working with Douglass's text required more interpretive dexterity. While Douglass at times directly addressed pro-slavery arguments, he often worked less explicitly. To deal satisfactorily with the complexity of Douglass's text, students had to recognize that autobiography is not merely a straightforward retelling of a life; it is the author's carefully crafted account of his experiences. As we discussed the *Narrative* in class, we looked first at what Douglass included. Pointing out that Douglass could not possibly cover every experience in his life, we asked students to consider what purposes might be served by the presence of particular scenes and events. We began by focusing on scenes in which Douglass is openly working as an interpreter of slave experience for white readers of his text and in which he seems determined to offer his understanding in contrast to another possible interpretation of slave experience. For example, Douglass works to discredit any slave testimony about the benevolence of slaveholders, offering both psychological and pragmatic explanations for why slaves might lie when asked if they are treated well, are happy, and so forth. As students began to see slaves' accounts of their own well-being featured prominently among defenses of slavery, they could understand the function Douglass's insistence on this point might have played in that cultural moment.

The fourth and final unit of the course focused on Toni Morrison's *The Bluest Eye*. As in the first unit, we dealt here with the contemporary culture of the United States and with a text that interrogates cultural ideologies that continue to influence our students' beliefs and practices. Though we organized the course primarily around methodological rather than thematic concerns, *The Bluest Eye* addresses many of the cultural boundaries that earlier units had highlighted. Demonstrating the inextricable connections between contemporary cultural discourses of beauty, race, and sexuality, *The Bluest Eye* allowed students, if they wished, to return to discursive structures they had written about in earlier papers, looking again at, say, constructions of motherhood, community, innocence, sacrifice, and race. Our writing assignment for this unit repeated, virtually verbatim, the language of the first writing assignment:

> Toni Morrison's *The Bluest Eye* is clearly concerned with the kinds of limits that American culture establishes for individual behavior. Write an essay in which you explore how this novel works against what Greenblatt calls "the dominant beliefs and social structures of its culture" as they are represented in the text.

By this point in the semester, the students were completely familiar with this paradigm and this set of questions. Yet *The Bluest Eye* was the most complex literary text with which they had grappled. They were disoriented by Morrison's fragmentation of her narrative, her use of multiple points of view, and—perhaps most of all—her challenge to commonly held values. Students had no problem recognizing and condemning the most overt instances of racism in the novel; what remained troubling for them was the way the novel suggests that these extreme instances of racial prejudice may be part of other cultural beliefs and practices that we hold in a more positive light. The informal assignment we gave the students asked them to think through a passage in which Morrison's narrator claims that "romantic love" and "physical beauty" are "[p]robably the most destructive ideas in the history of human thought" (122). As we discussed responses to this assignment in class, students at first wanted to rescue those ideas. Many wanted to suggest that the text was singling out for censure only warped or distorted notions of romantic love and physical beauty. Yet as we worked closely with that passage, those initial impulses became harder to maintain. Finally, the text seems to be posing the question of whether any notion of romantic love and physical beauty can be held without also subscribing to other—racist—beliefs that we find repellent. In coming to an interpretation—through writing—of *The Bluest Eye*'s representation of dominant beliefs and social structures, the students again needed to reflect on their own implication in those beliefs and practices. This is not to say that we wanted *The Bluest Eye* simply to convert students to some easily identifiable correct-thinking point of view. Rather, we were trying to stress the way that writing in our course became a way for students to position themselves in relation to the discursive structures that form the boundaries of our culture.

Framing our course with a theoretical essay written by perhaps the most recognizable proponent of the new historicism and asking students to read literary texts in cultural context and to write essays that make connections between literary and nonliterary texts are elements of our course design that might suggest that we are arguing solely for the need to understand literature within the paradigms provided by an influential current school of literary interpretation. While we found those paradigms useful in constructing this course, we are trying to argue for what we are calling a rhetorical approach to literature and composition. As Terry Eagleton points out, traditionally rhetoric "was not worried about whether its objects of enquiry were speaking or writing, poetry or philosophy, fiction or historiography: its horizon was nothing less than the field of discursive practice in society as a whole..." (205). Eagleton's formulation has much in common with James Berlin's call, in the field of composition studies, for a move to epistemic rhetoric, which understands language as a social phenomenon that "structures" not only "our response to social and political issues" but also "our response to the material world" (Berlin, *Rhetoric* 16). These ways of (re)formulating rhetoric refuse to make categorical distinctions between different forms of discourse and therefore bring together literature and writing instruction — too often held apart by the professional divides in the larger discipline of English studies.

By emphasizing literature as textual interventions in culture, this course understood writing as a social and political act. It understood writing as not merely reflecting but producing culture. As students analyzed the rhetorical approaches of the texts we read, they also became more cognizant of the position of their own writing as working, like the literary texts we read, both to replicate and to challenge our culture's ensemble of beliefs and practices; on that level, the content of the course was enacted through the students' rhetorical efforts. While stressing the power of reading and writing, the course gave students specific practice in discursive analysis. We believe this skill is crucial for all students, whether they are preprofessional students at two-year colleges or English majors at elite universities. We believe that all students should leave college with the ability to read critically and to interpret the ideological commitments of a variety of cultural texts. Ultimately, our goal was to give students the confidence to interpret not only the texts they would encounter inside the academy but also those that they would face outside the academy as citizens of democratic, contested cultures.

Notes

1. The five literary works we selected for this course were Shirley Jackson's "The Lottery," Tillie Olsen's "I Stand Here Ironing," Charlotte Perkins Gilman's "The Yellow Wallpaper," *Narrative of the Life of Frederick Douglass*, and Toni Morrison's *The Bluest Eye*. We could have selected any number of literary texts that "situate themselves on the very edges of what can be said at a particular place and time, that batter against the boundaries of their own culture." The approach of the course is not dependent on this particular group of texts. We considered teaching a number of other works (and, in fact, taught some different texts in other incarnations of the course), such as Ralph Ellison's "Battle Royal" (in *Invisible Man*), Joyce Carol Oates's "Where Are You Going, Where Have You Been?" Rebecca Harding Davis's *Life in the Iron Mills*, and Harriet Jacobs's *Incidents in the Life of a Slave Girl*. We were looking for texts that have a clear social agenda but wanted to avoid those that promote what students might perceive as a single, easily articulated political issue or a simplistic solution. The best texts for this course are autoethnographic texts, to borrow

Mary Louise Pratt's term, or texts that are aware of the rhetorical challenges of speaking to the dominant culture from a marginal position. The richest texts for this course are those that want to be heard even while they are aware that they are attempting to say what might not be heard. We were particularly drawn to texts that enact this dynamic while thematically dramatizing it; the narrators of "Battle Royal," "I Stand Here Ironing," "The Yellow Wallpaper," *Narrative of the Life of Frederick Douglass*, and *Incidents in the Life of a Slave Girl* and the main characters of "Where Are You Going, Where Have You Been?" *Life in the Iron Mills*, and *The Bluest Eye* all experience the difficulty of speaking to a larger culture that wants to define them in narrow ways. Each of these works, in fact, contains a central scene in which the main figures must confront how they have been made voiceless by the inability of characters, representing the values of the mainstream culture, to hear them.

2. All quotations from our writing assignments are excerpts. We typically write long, complicated assignments that position the writing projects in the context established by our work in class and that pose questions suggestive of the work the students might attempt. For the purposes of this essay, however, we have provided only our articulation of the central task of the writing project.

3. We should note, too, that the library at our institution was small and had limited resources. We worked with our librarians to make sure that our students had the skills to use the library catalog, databases, and Internet resources and that they understood how to conduct a search to find particular kinds of information or sources. We realized, however, that if we asked students to follow the typical procedures for a research paper — performing their own searches and identifying relevant materials in the library — we would have students fighting over the same few texts. Therefore we preidentified relevant sources and placed them on reserve. Though designed to work within the limitations of our library, the strategy also ensured that the students' work was focused on reading, evaluating, and working with those sources, rather than just finding them.

Literary Texts as Primers in Meaning Making

On the one hand, should we refrain from asking students to read and write about *King Lear, Song of Myself*, and *Beloved* in the required composition course, which is already saddled with the responsibility for introducing students to academic discourse, serious research, critical thinking, and even computer literacy? Does the use of literature as the primary textual focus of a composition class detract from the teaching of writing? Does a focus on literary texts, to the exclusion of the texts of other disciplines, prevent students from joining the more general conversation at the university and from learning discourse conventions other than those of literary criticism? Or, on the other hand, should we include literature in the composition classroom because it may be the only classroom in which students read literature during their college careers? In our haste to help them join the conversation of the university, are we denying them the opportunity to join the even broader conversations that literature engenders, conversations about how to live our lives beyond the academy and the workplace?

Sharon Crowley traces the outlines of such opposing arguments at least as far back as a 1912 *English Journal* article and shows how the same positions are occupied and reoccupied across the decades:

> [T]eachers could teach composition as a set of universally useful techniques, in which case the requirement was defined as a service to the university; or they could teach literature in the course, in which case it served higher ends, ostensibly those of humanism and obviously those of literary studies. (88–89)

Gary Tate asserts that the debate has occupied composition studies almost since the creation of the Conference on College Composition and Communication, documenting presentations and workshops on both sides of the issue at the CCCC convention from 1950 to 1969. He notes that the

---

Clyde Moneyhun

conversation fell off in the 1970s and 1980s, partly (in his view) because of the ascendancy of rhetorical studies (and its "Rhetoric Police") and partly because of the poverty of arguments defending the use of literature in writing classrooms. The debate was reignited in the early 1990s by a pair of articles from Tate and a pair from Erika Lindemann in *College English* (and kept burning by follow-up letters from readers), because, Tate feels, there was a sublimated desire among classroom teachers to find and express reasons for incorporating literature ("Notes" 304).

I briefly sketch and update the terms of the familiar debate before discussing how I attempted to solve the problem in my own teaching. The questions I'd like to explore in the end are not those posed in the debate as it has most often been waged but, rather, these: Might the inclusion of literature in the composition classroom teach students to read any kind of text critically? Might the reading of literary texts be particularly good preparation for the interpretation of other kinds of texts? My answers are rooted in an eclectic blend of reading theories that amount not so much to a comprehensive philosophy of meaning making as to a coherent pedagogy for the use of literary texts in a composition classroom.

The Debate

In her two *College English* articles, Lindemann gathers together the most often repeated criticisms of using literature in a composition classroom. One danger is that the student-centered, process-driven composition classroom we value today may become a teacher-centered, lecture-driven literature course. As Lindemann puts it, "literature-based courses...focus on consuming texts, not producing them. The teacher talks 75 to 80 percent of the time. Students do very little writing" ("Freshman Composition" 313). Lindemann also questions the use of literature as a way of restoring humanist content to a liberal arts education. Given its distribution requirements, a typical general educational curriculum, Lindemann says, "already has humanistic content" (313). Lindemann objects as well to using literature to talk about style, as a model of exemplary English for students to emulate (314).

Fundamentally, however, Lindemann urges us to consider the purpose of composition: "We cannot usefully discuss the role of imaginative literature…in freshman English without first asking what the purpose of a first-year writing course is." And she answers her own question:

> Freshman English…provide[s] opportunities to master the genres, styles, audiences, and purposes of college writing. Freshman English offers guided practice in reading and writing the discourses of the academy and the professions. (312)

In her follow-up essay Lindemann backs off from strongly endorsing composition as a service course that emphasizes the conventions of disciplinary writing. At the same time, she clearly equates the inclusion of literature with an outmoded, current-traditional, teacher-centered, product-centered pedagogy, and she remains firm in her conviction that the inclusion of literature in a composition classroom is a step backward, an abandonment of process pedagogy as well as a rejection of the lessons learned from writing across the curriculum about the academic discourse communities in which students are expected to function ("Three Views" 292).

Crowley agrees with many of the points Lindemann makes and takes the criticism of using literature in a composition classroom a step further. Like Lindemann, Crowley asserts that the use of literature as a model of style in composition classrooms has served the ends of current-traditional pedagogies, which view student writing as a display of "literary correctness" and students as in constant need of "improvement" by correction (96–97). She also has problems with using literature to accomplish traditional humanist educational goals (13, 21). Yet Crowley's criticism of literature in the composition classroom runs even deeper than Lindemann's. It concerns not only the purpose of first-year composition or even writing instruction in general but also the purpose of a college education as a whole.

The debate over literature in the composition classroom, Crowley feels, is actually "a cover or code for a much larger institutional issue: the status relation between composition and literature within English departments" (21). Literary studies is already suffering from internal tensions, displayed in debates between those who cling to older humanist traditions (that literature represents complete and masterful reflections on enduring truths) and those who offer new, nonhumanist, postmodern ways of understanding literary texts (as products of specific historical situation, as rhetorical artifacts). To make matters worse, we in composition studies (with the aid of rhetorical studies) have helped theorize postmodern views of texts, including literary texts. Therefore, "it is no accident that a conversation about the use of literary texts in composition should surface at a moment when humanism has been called into crisis" (Crowley 21). For Crowley, then, using literature in a composition classroom is more than merely a distraction from the teaching of writing, more than a reversion to current-traditional pedagogy, more even than the hijacking by humanists of a course ill suited to imparting humanist content. It is a betrayal of the fundamental insights of composition studies and rhetorical theory: texts are not repositories of eternal human wisdom but cultural productions embedded in rhetorical situations.

In the face of such criticism, the use of literature in composition classrooms is warmly defended. Some of the defenses strike me as dusty, others as not very compelling. Particularly unconvincing is the argument that composition classes will be more "enjoyable" and "fun" if they include literature, as Leon Knight asserts (677). Even if Knight is right about literature making composition classes more fun, it's not clear that such a goal should outweigh others as we try to theorize our pedagogy or, if it should, that reading literature is the only way to generate fun. Knight goes on to advocate using literary texts as a way of encouraging "awareness of and respect for cultural diversity," another goal that, if considered worthy, can be accomplished in ways that don't involve literature. From a different point of view, Gregory Jay insists that since the institutional home of nearly all composition courses is the English department and since English departments are departments of literature, the composition course should include literature:

> Though it is a fluke of history that writing courses are housed in departments of English, must departments of English ignore every aspect of the discipline but the teaching of writing in freshman English?...If literature does not belong

in the first-year writing course, then the first-year writing course does not belong in the English department. (674–75)

In fact, several university writing programs have taken Jay at his word and reestablished themselves as departments of writing separate from departments of literature.

Tate's defense of the use of literature in composition classrooms is predicated largely on its disappearance from them. In his view, since the traditional literature-based freshman seminar has been replaced by the rhetoric-based composition course, "[W]e have denied students who are seeking to improve their writing the benefits of reading an entire body of excellent writing" ("Place" 317). Tate decries what he calls the "professionalization" of undergraduate education that is exemplified in the focus on disciplinary language:

> It is as if all those students who come to college only in order to get a better job have convinced us that a college education is primarily job training and that the task of the freshman writing course is to help make that training more effective. (320)

Tate goes on:

> The "conversations" I want to help my students join are not the conversations going on in the academy. These are too often restricted, artificial, irrelevant, and — let's be frank — boring. I refuse to look at my students as primarily history majors, accounting majors, nursing majors. I much prefer to think of them and treat them as people whose most important conversations will take place outside the academy, as they struggle to figure out how to live their lives — that is, how to vote and love and survive, how to respond to change and diversity and death and oppression and freedom. (320)

Even if we were to embrace the service course philosophy Lindemann advocates, Tate doubts whether we could accomplish the goals she lays out:

> Can we, in a semester or two, really help students function effectively in all the different communities they will be entering as they move from course to course, from discipline to discipline, throughout their four years of college? (319)

If, with Lindemann and Crowley, we reject Tate's argument based on the importance of humanist content in a liberal arts education, perhaps we can accept a more utilitarian defense of using literary texts in a composition classroom, the transferable skills argument. A text is a text, this argument goes; the study of literary texts is excellent preparation for the study of any text, and critical analysis of literary texts is good for critical analysis of any text. Jeanie Crain asserts that "no need exists to build a false dichotomy between discourse and literature" and that "[a]ll writing has to be interpreted, and interpreting texts is essentially the same act whether the text is literary or nonliterary" (678–79). Many iterations of this defense take it for granted that the interpretive process will be automatic: "The person who is able to read literature well will have the skills to read computer manuals," and "reading literature is an efficient way for students to become critical thinkers" (Knight 677).

Others offer more sophisticated, and thus more convincing, versions of the transferable skills defense. Michael Gamer questions the sharp division between literary and nonliterary texts, their natures, their uses, and the reading experiences they foster. Literature, he insists, can be as "persuasive" as an openly argumentative text, and it can be persuasive in ways that are important for students to recognize — through narrative, for example (283–84). Literary texts can be combined with nonliterary texts to deepen and complicate discussion and thought about a wide range of topics. Elizabeth Latosi-Sawin points out that literary texts are used in classrooms beyond the English department to complement the discourses of many disciplines:

> [L]iterature is being used to study human life in fields as varied as business management and abnormal psychology.... In sociology and psychology classes, I have also seen literature used to illustrate issues ranging from family to religion, from social control to work, from race relations to anomie. (675)

Why, then, would we deny ourselves the chance to use literary texts to examine issues of vital interest to many different disciplines? For Latosi-Sawin, as for Gamer, "The question is no longer whether there is or isn't a place for literature in a composition program, but how literature on occasion is to be defined, selected, and used" (675).

How, indeed, should we use literature in a composition course? Tate points out that one criticism of using literature is based on "the pedagogical sins of teachers in the past" ("Place" 317). In a direct answer to Lindemann's original essay, Crain asserts:

> Literature-based...courses need not "focus on consuming texts" rather than "producing them," as Lindemann charges. Nor should the teacher have to talk "75 to 80 percent of the time." It is possible to use literature in a classroom without spending very much time at all lecturing or discussing. Students can do a great deal of writing, group work, and peer evaluation as they plan, draft, revise, use data, evaluate sources, read critically, interpret evidence, and solve problems concerning the literature they are reading and responding to in writing. We should not allow the misuse of literature to discourage us from "right use." (678–79)

A Literature-Based Composition Curriculum

I believe that there are right uses of literature in a composition classroom and that the key is in defining what skills students can transfer from reading and writing about literature to interpreting any text. My own take on the transferable skills defense, however, is based not on the similarity of literature to other texts but on its difference from other texts. I believe that literary texts provide a *better* means than other texts of teaching students to interpret texts, to make meaning from texts. Specifically, concepts such as authorial intent, the contributions of reader-response theory to the creation of meaning, and social-constructivist accounts of meaning are more apparent in literary texts than in nonliterary texts. While students tend to be positivist in their understanding of meaning in a nonliterary text, assuming a direct relation between the text and its possible meaning, they have an easier time assuming that the literary author clothes meaning in language or that the reader plays a role in completing the meaning of a literary text or that the meaning of a literary text can be understood in the context of its cultural production.

My purpose in creating three linked literature-based writing assignments for a composition class is to make students aware that meaning is as much a product of an interpretive framework as it is a property of a text. I want the students to see that the meaning they imagine they are finding in the text is a meaning that they are actually making in cooperation with the text. In this way, meanings are not fixed and inevitable but constructed and negotiated and created with reference to certain accepted rules of textual engagement. I want my students to consider, as Mariolina Salvatori puts it,

> what leads us to adopt and to deploy certain interpretive practices. In other words, although the processes that constitute our reading and writing are essentially invisible, those processes are, in principle, accessible to analysis, scrutiny, and reflection....[T]hrough such access one might learn to account for...and to understand...how certain meanings, certain stories, certain explanations, certain interpretive frames come to be composed or adopted. ("Conversations" 445–46)

In creating and enacting the three assignments, I used an eclectic mix of critical theory based on Michel Foucault's construction of authorship, the interpretive communities of Stanley Fish and Louise Rosenblatt, and cultural studies approaches to literary interpretation such as those of Fredric Jameson and Terry Eagleton.

The course was the second in a required two-semester sequence at the University of Arizona. The first course began with expository writing (mainly in response to texts from one of many familiar nonfiction composition readers) and ended with a documented argument assignment. The second course was based on literary texts but (as instructors were repeatedly told) had writing as its main focus. We chose one course text from a short list of several readers and another text from a longer list of literary works, mainly novels. As a short story writer myself, I always used Ann Charters's collection *The Story and Its Writer* but tried out several different novels, including *Heart of Darkness* and *Frankenstein*. (Colleagues who adapted my assignments also had success with these novels, as well as with *Dracula* and *The Color Purple*.)

Beyond this guidance on the general nature of the course and the texts to use, writing assignments were an open question. The instructors I consulted when I first started teaching the course tended to focus on traditional categories students were likely to have encountered in high school, such as character, plot, and symbolism. But assignments like these seemed to me too specific to literature and not easily transferable to other kinds of texts. I wanted my students to learn the basic skill of applying interpretive frames to texts, frames that were not specific to literary texts but could also be applied to other texts. I developed and refined throughout many semesters three assignments that built on one another to create a repertoire of meaning-making techniques.

To emphasize the artificial and constructed nature of the interpretive frames we would learn to use, I called the three assignments games. Each game had its own rules, but the goal of each game was the same: follow the rules carefully to construct a meaning from a piece of literature. The overall instructions were:

> In this class we're going to approach the idea of interpreting texts as a game, specifically a "meaning-making" game. Your goal as the player of this game is to make a piece of literature deliver a meaning. We'll play three games, in fact, each one with different rules but all with the same goal: making meaning from a text.

The first game was called Authorial Intent. I assumed that this game was closest to what students had been playing in their high school English classes.

Game 1: Authorial Intent

> *The rules*   The author has buried nuggets of meaning in the text. Your job is to dig them out and put them all together to construct one overall meaning for the text. Assume that any good reader will find the same nuggets and construct the same meaning. You compete in the game by pointing to evidence in the text of the writer's intended meaning. The reader who finds the most nuggets and puts them together in the most coherent pattern wins.

To introduce the game, and at the risk of tipping my hand about the highly constructed nature of authorship and authorial intent, I asked students to write, as a class, a "fold-down" story. I wrote on the board the names of two characters (suggested by the students) and asked for a volunteer to write the first line of a story about them, then fold down the paper so the line couldn't be seen and pass it on. (This game is a variation on the exquisite corpse game played by surrealists in the 1930s.) As we went on with other activities, the paper made the rounds, each student adding a line. The last student had to write a suitable ending. Before the next class, I typed up the story, straightening out a pronoun or verb tense here and there, but mainly leaving it as it was written. In the next class, I distributed the story and we played at creating a meaning that was "intended" by the "author." As a class we wrote a thesis statement stating the author's intent (usually beginning something like, "The author seems to be implying that…") and made a list of supporting details to use in an essay about the story. This task makes clear to students that authorship and authorial intent are artificial constructs that greatly influence readers.

The first story we read from Charters's collection also emphasized the game aspect of textual interpretation: Margaret Atwood's "Happy Endings," which plays with an author's control over characters, plot, and meaning. It begins, "John and Mary meet. What happens next? If you want a happy ending, try A" (47). In the sections that follow there are alternative versions of John and Mary's life together, with marriages, infidelities, illnesses, and deaths. Atwood then challenges the reader to find a meaning among the nuggets she has buried: "That's about all that can be said for plots, which anyway are just one thing after another, a what and a what and a what. Now try How and Why" (49).

I deliberately chose other stories that were less transparent, stories set in times and places unlike the contemporary United States. We read Chinua Achebe's "Dead Men's Path," Isaac Babel's "My First Goose," Heinrich Böll's "Like a Bad Dream," and Yukio Mishima's "Three Million Yen." Without much personal background to use as context for interpreting stories set in Achebe's Nigeria, Babel's Russia, Böll's Germany, or Mishima's Japan, students were compelled to dig into the stories for evidence of the authors' intentions. They were aided by Charters's notes for each story (another reason I chose them), which offered thumbnail interpretations that gave the students a start. According to Charters, the path in Achebe's story symbolizes a "crossroads of culture" (9), Babel's story expresses the theme of "the complex relation between our illusions about life and the truth of life" (50), Böll's protagonist "falls victim to the corruption that surrounds him in an achievement-oriented society" (133), and Mishima writes about "the corruption of contemporary Japanese society and the decay of its moral values" (996).

Even so, students sometimes struggled to play the game by the rules. One student had particular trouble with the elliptical Mishima story, and, in my comments on her drafts, I had to remind myself that I too had to play by the rules of the game. In the story, a poor young couple dreams of the day when material possessions will fill their lives; the student interpreted this as the natural longings of newlyweds for a home. Superficially, it was a reasonable reading, but a system of details revealed another intended meaning. Rather than give the student background on 1950s Japan and on Mishima's idea that Japan had lost its spirituality by embracing Western materialism, I kept pointing the student back to the text, asking what she made of the more striking details of plot and character, how each nugget she found modified the meaning she was constructing. She made much of a "neon pagoda" on top of the shopping center the couple enters, wondering what our impression would be of a neon cross atop a shopping center in the United States; she noticed how tawdry the seemingly splendid shops are, with their "gleaming, cheap wares"; she understood the naïveté of the couple when they admire the beauty of a "garden" in which "great artificial butterflies were taking honey from the artificial flowers" (1002). After a rough start, the student wrote a compelling presentation of Mishima's view that the glitzy postwar material culture of Japan had misled and corrupted a pure young couple.

To create a transition to the second game and to shake students' easy faith in the first game, I asked a friend to allow me to copy and distribute one of his short stories along with one of mine. At home, the students played Authorial Intent with both stories and came to class prepared with questions for the authors. My friend led the discussion on my story and I led the discussion on his. We each remained silent during the discussion of our own story and listened to students digging for the nuggets of meaning we thought we had left in plain view. They found some, missed others, and created some we never intended. After the discussions, we each took a moment to say what we thought we meant in our stories. Though my friend and I no doubt were less skilled at focusing our meanings for readers than were the literary authors we were reading in the course, possibly leading students to have more trouble uncovering our meanings, the exercise did make the point that authors have only so much control of their meanings and that meanings may depend on the background knowledge and experiences that readers bring to the text.

Before I introduced the second game's assignment, I asked students to read the essay "Miching Mallecho: That Means Witchcraft," by the anthropologist Laura Bohannan, in which she narrates a delightful story about telling the plot and meaning of *Hamlet* to members of a West African tribe she was living with (and studying) at the time. She spends a lot of time with an old man, the leader of some 140 people living nearby, who has vast knowledge of tribal stories and ceremonies. While visiting with him and several other men one day, she is asked to tell one of her own tribe's traditional stories. Since she has been reading *Hamlet* recently, she begins — assuming, as she says, that its meaning will be clear to them, that it has "only one interpretation, and that one obvious universally" (175). She gets only as far as the sighting of Hamlet's father's ghost when one of the men corrects her with the only explanation available in his culture (which does not have the concept of "ghost"): "Of course it wasn't the dead chief; it was an omen sent by a witch" (177).

And so things go. Since in the tribal belief system a man is obligated to marry his dead brother's wife and adopt her children as his own, Hamlet's uncle was right to marry Hamlet's mother; since the men can conceive of no circumstance under which it is permissible to raise a hand to an elder, Hamlet was very wicked to consider taking revenge on a man who was his uncle, father, and king; and through a series of logical steps that can be understood only by reading the essay as a whole, the men conclude that Laertes killed his sister Ophelia by witchcraft, "drowning her so he could secretly sell her body to the witches" (187). In the end, the men invite Bohannan to tell them more stories so that they can tell her the stories' real meanings and so that, when she returns to her own land, "your elders will see that you have not been sitting idle in the bush, but among those who know things and have taught you wisdom" (189). Bohannan's message is clear, and the students had no trouble understanding how different personal and cultural belief systems can give different meanings to a text.

I called the second game Reader Response, an approach that would also be familiar to students but that perhaps they had understood poorly in the past. The challenge was to get them to be responsible about highly personal responses to a text.

Game 2: Reader Response

The rules   Reader-response theorists point out that the way we make meaning when we read has a lot to do with who is reading, not just what is being read. Therefore, in this game we'll assume that meaning is not just waiting to be found in a text but is created in the readers' minds as they read. If you play the game well, you will strike a balance between a purely idiosyncratic interpretation and respect for authorial intent. Remember Louise Rosenblatt's definition: "A poem is what the reader lives through under the guidance of the text and experiences as relevant to the text" ["Towards" 34]. Account for what the text means to you personally by pointing to experiences in your past, aspects of your personality, and other reading experiences you've had. You might think of this essay in two ways: as a personal essay in which you use a text to help you get across a message about your own life or as an essay about a text in which you use your own experience to explain the text in ways you couldn't otherwise. You compete in the game by matching specifics of your own life with specific aspects of the text to create a meaning. The reader who makes the most complete and convincing match wins.

For a model, we read David Leavitt's response to Susan Sontag's "The Way We Live Now." In Sontag's short story, an omniscient narrator tells how a network of friends reacts to the death from AIDS—or rather, to the process of dying—of one of their own. In "The Way I Live Now," Leavitt begins by expressing the anger he felt when people asked him why he, a famous gay fiction writer, hadn't written about AIDS. Why should he feel obligated to write about AIDS? He admits that "the truth was that AIDS scared me so much I wanted to block it out of my mind" and that he finally realized that he was "masking denial with self-righteousness" (1470). Then he read Sontag's story and "felt a sense of enormous and long-withheld release" because it "offered a possibility of catharsis" (1470, 1471). As I asked my students to do in their second assignment, Leavitt points to specific passages from the story and interprets their meaning in the context of his personal experience of the story. In the end, Sontag reassures him that "the 'chain' of sexuality through which the virus had been spread was still the chain of life," and he concludes that " 'The Way We Live Now' made me feel less alone in my dread" (1471).

Since I asked students to share personal stories and feelings as part of the assignment, I felt it was only ethical for me to do the same. I told my personal reactions to the Sontag story, pointing to passages that brought back memories of my older brother's extended (losing) struggle with cancer, especially the passages in which the dying man's friends (like my brother's friends and family) took turns cooking, handling mail, and keeping the network of friends and relatives informed of the progress of the disease. Several other students then spoke of similar experiences, which led us back to the story and what it had to say to us about those experiences. Similarly, when we read Tim O'Brien's "The Things They Carried" and the students related it to their knowledge of the Vietnam War (mostly from the experiences of fathers and uncles), I talked about the effects of the war I saw on my older cousins and friends who fought in it, as well as the story of how I barely missed being drafted (Congress allowed the draft to lapse just weeks before I would have been called up). They helped me brainstorm the thesis of an essay I could write from my experience to fulfill the second assignment: "I saw my older cousins and friends come back from Vietnam carrying some of the same things—both physical and emotional—that O'Brien's soldiers carry and will continue to carry for the rest of their lives."

One student wrote about a chapter from Amy Tan's *Joy Luck Club* in which a nine-year-old girl defies her mother's high expectations of her as an ideal Chinese daughter and feels torn between old-world filial obligations and the pressures of acculturating in America. My student was Chinese

American, and he saw much of himself in Tan's character. Like her, he felt pangs of guilt about his lack of Chinese filial piety while resenting the pressures his old-world parents placed on him; like Tan's character, he even rejected his Chinese name and adopted an American-sounding nickname. In one telling detail from an early draft, he writes about how he began to avoid eating Chinese meals with his parents: "I remember the time when I dumped all my rice onto a paper towel, rolled it into the form of an egg-roll, and shoved it underneath the refrigerator" (Tang 392). The early drafts were mainly personal narrative that made little reference to Tan's story and concluded with the obligatory happy ending that many students feel com-pelled to graft onto their life stories: "I know that America accepts all. Each individual is given the ability to present themselves in society. Now I accept American society" (392).

Again, trying to follow my own rules, I kept reminding him how to play the game, urging him to use Tan to deepen the meaning of his life experi-ence or, more specifically, to make sense of the details from his life that contradicted the false-sounding happy ending. After several more drafts, he wrote what I consider a masterful essay, full of nuance and revealing detail. The maturity of the vision he achieved is on display in the opening line: "It is obvious to me and to society that I'm neither an American nor a Chinese" (399). Later he observes, "Reading Amy Tan's 'Two Kinds' made me real-ize the struggles that American Chinese teenagers, including myself, often endure in a society where ridicule targets the outcast" (399). He connects an event from his childhood, in which he fell down while doing a dragon dance ("taking the rest of the Dragon with me"), to the awful piano recital of the daughter in Tan's story (400). As he grows older, he struggles to integrate his American and Chinese bits and pieces into a coherent self, to be a good Chinese son and also live in modern American society. In his conclusion, I see a measure of his success, with overtones of continuing ambivalence but also a degree of self-acceptance: "I still haven't learned how to dragon dance, but maybe someday I will. On second thought, maybe I'll just sit back and let the pros do it" (404). It didn't escape my attention that the student, who had used his American nickname all semester, put his full Chinese name on the final draft.

The third game I called Text in Context. It drew on the kind of critical theory that Salvatori and even Lindemann advocate for theorizing the composition class.

Game 3: Text in Context

The rules   Now we know that meanings don't just lie around in texts waiting to be found, but we can also say that if we go to extremes with reader-response meanings, then literature doesn't really have a meaning (in the sense of knowledge of life that we share with each other by means of a text). In this game, assume that one way to demonstrate a stable, shared meaning in a text is to put it into some kind of context that you can share with your reader. You might interpret the text in the context of the writer's biography or look at historical events from the time and place when the text was written or compare the text to similar texts. You might also choose a particular critical or philosophical frame, such as psychoanalysis, feminism, or Marxism. You compete by creating a system to apply to the text, a set of glasses, and by showing how the text looks through those glasses. The reader who constructs the clearest, most coherent system and applies it in the greatest detail wins.

I modeled the game by asking the students to read Charlotte Perkins Gilman's "The Yellow Wallpaper." In class, we tugged at the threads of meaning in the story by playing the first two games, asking, What could Gilman have meant to say? How did students respond personally to the story, relate it to their lives, find meaning in it from that point of view? As for Gilman's meanings, most of the students were baffled. It was just the story of a crazy lady, most of them said, which got spooky and scary in the end. As for personal reactions, many of them found the protagonist weak and whiny and wondered why she didn't just pull herself together. Then I asked them to read Gilman's own account of her doctor's "cure" for her "nervous prostration," when she was told to "never touch pen, brush, or pencil as long as you live." She did her best, she says, and "followed these directions rigidly for months, and came perilously near to losing my mind" ("Undergoing" 1449). They also read Sandra Gilbert and Susan Gubar's feminist reading of the story, which placed the protagonist's treatment in the context of patriarchal oppression of women: "The cure, of course, is worse than the disease" (1446). Informed by these contexts, we reread the story, and students had much less trouble understanding what the story might mean and how its meaning might have relevance to their own lives.

To help students think more specifically about meaning-making contexts of literary texts, I provided a list of possible directions their research might take, such as this one from the semesters when we used *Frankenstein* as our novel:

Literature   What themes common to the literature of Shelley's day are explored in *Frankenstein*? What other works provided Shelley with models? What literary works from times and places other than Shelley's employ themes and patterns found in the novel? How does the novel fit into various established literary genres (gothic novels, horror stories, allegories, etc.)?

Science   What scientific ideas of her own day did Shelley draw on to write *Frankenstein*? What issues of scientific ethics does she raise? How do the issues she raises illuminate some of the questions we're asking today?

Biography   What was happening in Shelley's life when she wrote *Frankenstein*? How do the details of her life relate to the themes of the novel?

Critical reception   How was *Frankenstein* received when it was published? How did different groups of readers react to it? What have critics written about the novel over time? How has the nature of critical reaction to the novel changed, and what do these changes reveal about the critics' own contexts?

History   What was happening in English history, and more generally in European history, that might relate to themes in *Frankenstein*? What philosophies, worldviews, or anxieties are expressed in the novel that reflect ideas common to Shelley's culture?

Adaptations   In what ways has *Frankenstein* been transformed into other media (film, stage, opera)? How do such adaptations manipulate the patterns and themes of Shelley's novel? What do these adaptations express about their own times and cultures?

Theory   What can we understand about the importance of gender in *Frankenstein* from a feminist reading of the novel? What might a Marxist reading reveal about power relations in the novel? What might a psychoanalytic reading say about the motivations of the characters?

This last direction was informed by our use of the Bedford–St. Martin's edition of the novel, which includes essays from the perspectives of psychoanalytic, feminist, Marxist, and cultural critics. I provided a similar list of possibilities for research when we used *Heart of Darkness* instead of *Frankenstein*, and students were able to make a start with some of the other directions (historical background, Conrad's biography, critical reception) by using material in the Norton critical edition of the novel. For both novels, we examined how our readings might be shaped by adaptations, especially films, ranging (for *Frankenstein*) from the classic James Whale version to the Kenneth Branaugh version to Mel Brooks's *Young Frankenstein* and including (for *Heart of Darkness*) Francis Ford Coppola's *Apocalypse Now*. After viewing excerpts in class, many students rented videos to watch at home, sometimes choosing to base their research papers on a comparison and contrast of novel and film versions. One student concluded that Brooks's daffy version of *Frankenstein* was by far the most faithful film version yet, not only in character and plot but also in general sympathy for the creature's plight and the meaning of his experience.

Other students found different fruitful contexts. Many chose to relate the meaning of *Frankenstein* to today's debates over scientific advancements such as gene-splicing and cloning, but one student took her research in a direction that shed new light on the book for me. She focused on gender issues raised by the creature's lack of a mother, by Frankenstein's usurpation not only of the role of God (in creating his Adam) but also the role of mother. The creature himself, to explain his "unnatural" beginnings, observes that "no mother had blessed me with smiles and caresses" (107). In the end, the student asked what adjustments in fundamental gender roles and relations might be required by emerging biological technologies. Another student, in an essay titled "*Frankenstein* in a Socio-economic Historical Context," examined the social anxiety exhibited by the novel in the light of the working-class uprisings of Shelley's day, citing historians of the period. Like the rebellious working class, the student concluded, Shelley's monster was a terrifying creation, abject and yet powerful, a threat to the order of things. Another student made a similar move by using the slavery debates of Shelley's time to illuminate the novel, showing how the issues and stances taken in the debates were reflected in Shelley's own sympathy for and fear of the creature. Still another student chose a more traditional literary path, documenting Shelley's use of *Paradise Lost* as a distant model for the characters and themes of the novel; another did an existentialist reading of the novel across Jean-Paul Sartre and Martin Heidegger; and another found, in a psychoanalytic reading of the novel, that Jacques Lacan's theories of psychic development are a poor fit for Frankenstein (despite the efforts of several critics he cited) but a perfect fit for the creature.

I remain amazed and humbled by the topics my students chose for this third assignment and the astonishing research they did in support of their ideas. What made first-year students think they could tackle feminism, Marxism, existentialism, and Lacanian psychoanalytic theory? Perhaps their very innocence of such ideas helped; it may be easier to teach Lacan to people who have no fear of him and his difficulties. Maybe the spirit of play across the semester helped boost their confidence, lowering the stakes and making risk taking possible. It's also true that their essays began with the germ of an idea and grew through a recursive process of library research, drafts, feedback, and revision, so there was ample opportunity to deepen ideas and find interesting lines of research. I'd like to think that at least part of the reason was that my students learned a general attitude toward texts and meaning making, one that would stay with them after the semester ended, especially as they turned their attention from literary to nonliterary texts.

The Transferable Skill of Textual Engagement

I wanted the three assignments to emphasize that meaning in a work of literature, like meaning in any text, is a matter of active interpretation by a reader. I wanted the students to become more conscious of the structure of their interpretive frames and to exercise more control over them. Individually the assignments could not accomplish that goal, but as a progression throughout a semester they were effective. The class was primarily a writing class focused on the students' work with texts, not a lecture class on literature. My defense of the use of literature in a composition class is based neither on the claim that literature is a superior kind of text nor on the claim that since a text is a text, we might as well use literature. Whether literature is fundamentally a different kind of text from nonfiction is a matter for another debate. Students, however, do perceive it as different, and their understanding of how meaning works in literature can be exploited to teach lessons about the interpretation of any text.

Students may begin to understand that meaning in literature, as opposed to meaning in nonliterary texts, is highly constructed, shaped by a writer with intentions (the first assignment), created by an active reader (the second assignment), and understood in a critical context (the third assignment). That understanding can be sharpened into a disciplined habit of mind and then transferred to the interpretation of any text, including the nonliterary texts students encounter in other classes and in life beyond the classroom. If the skills or attitudes toward literary texts that I hope my students learn can be transferred to nonliterary texts, what new insights might they glean from their reading? Instead of allowing (or even encouraging) students to assume that all the texts they read are simply repositories of pure information or eternal truths, what might be revealed if they examined the authorial intent of texts such as Thucydides's *Peloponnesian War*, Charles Darwin's *Origin of the Species*, or Margaret Mead's *Coming of Age in Samoa*? Or if they explored how their personal histories enabled them to understand texts such as Plato's *Republic*, Sigmund Freud's *Totem and Taboo*, Virginia Woolf's *A Room of One's Own*, or James Baldwin's *The Fire Next Time*? Or if they placed into a historical or sociological or cultural setting texts such as Karl von Clausewitz's *On War*, John Dewey's *Experience and Education*, James Watson's *The Double Helix*, or Rachel Carson's *Silent Spring*? They just might achieve a critical point of view on all texts, made possible by a particular use of literary texts in the peculiar setting of a composition classroom.

Literature as Language in First-Year English: Confessions of a Maverick Adjunct

*T*o what extent do course rationales, program guidelines, and departmental mission statements match the actual teaching practices in programs staffed primarily by part-time faculty members? In the late 1990s and early 2000s, I worked as an adjunct instructor in language and literature at Rochester Institute of Technology (RIT) in upstate New York. Primarily populated by engineering students, RIT did not have an English major, though it did offer concentrations and minors through the Department of Language and Literature. Literature and writing courses consequently fell into the general education curriculum. In fall 1999, RIT reformulated its first-year English requirements, replacing two distinct, nonsequenced requirements, one a composition course and the other a literature survey course, with Writing and Literature, a sequential requirement that would enroll the same group of students with the same instructor for two quarters. This eight-credit sequence was

> designed to develop students' proficiency in written composition, critical reading, and critical thinking. Students read, study, and write about representative narratives, as well as nonfiction forms such as essays, letters, and autobiographies. The course develops the language skills needed to understand and interpret literature and to write clear, accurate, and effective prose. This will substitute for English Composition and Literature. Students must take both quarters in sequence. (*Course Descriptions*)[1]

Ostensibly designed to teach "language skills," the sequence came about through the sustained efforts of a committee of tenured English faculty members. Given RIT's science-intensive curriculum, which did not warrant many course offerings in literature, I suspect the committee sought to use Writing and Literature as a means of keeping literature integral to

Jeanne Marie Rose

the curriculum. From attending staff meetings and teaching workshops, I gleaned that faculty members typically assigned literature for students to write about but rarely emphasized students' writing, viewing it instead as a secondary activity geared mainly toward literary criticism.

My past reading experiences directly shaped my approach to integrating writing and literature. I first became interested in exploring the vexed relation between literature and composition after reading Erika Lindemann's and Gary Tate's 1993 *College English* discussions concerning the teaching of literature in writing courses. Although Lindemann's "Freshman Composition: No Place for Literature" and Tate's "A Place for Literature in Freshman Composition" take oppositional positions, the two seem to reach an easy consensus about literature's status as a distinct category, separate from other kinds of writing and language use.

As my subsequent dissertation research led to further investigation of postsecondary language curricula in the United States, I came to recognize that Lindemann's and Tate's responses were consistent with several pedagogical and critical practices presenting literature as a superior category of language. When nineteenth-century colleges and universities began replacing the classical curriculum with vernacular texts, teachers assigned Scottish rhetorical treatises featuring belletristic literature. By studying literature representing the best, most aesthetic writing, students would eventually learn to express themselves.[2] Susan Miller's work on required composition courses points to a similar trend. In the 1870s, many universities adopted entrance examinations, several of which tested students on literary interpretation to determine their writing placements (63–64). Students whose writing demonstrated familiarity with literary methods, illustrating those students' taste and refinement, were permitted to take literature courses; students whose language contained regional dialects or class markers were relegated to the first-year writing course (51–56). In the twentieth century, New Critical methods further constructed literature as exclusively aesthetic language, separate from other language. While "emphasizing the aesthetic over the directly social" allowed New Critics of the 1930s to reject twentieth-century materialism, it also helped secure a departmental identity for literature as an autonomous sphere of discourse (Graff, *Professing* 149).[3] A necessarily partial sketch, these approaches point to English studies' sustained tendency to classify language as literary and nonliterary.

Concerned that these earlier models still influence the teaching of writing, I was drawn to Mikhail Bakhtin's characterization of literature as a site where language from all spheres—written and spoken, popular and elite—constantly interacts. Although literary genres have been studied mainly for "their specific literary and artistic features," literature shares "a common *verbal* (language) nature" with other language (Bakhtin 61). Treating literature as ordinary language, as Bakhtin suggests, helped me envision a course in which students explore literature while investigating their own writing and language use. I sought to develop a pedagogy that stressed students' active participation as readers of literature while emphasizing the parallels between students' writing and literature. Even though many of my colleagues conceptualized RIT's Writing and Literature sequence in a manner antithetical to my own, the program provided a testing ground for my literature-as-language pedagogy.[4]

Getting Personal

The course began with Getting Personal, a unit emphasizing the construction of self through language. Through such autobiographical works as Gloria Anzaldúa's *Borderlands*, John Irving's "Trying to Save Piggy Sneed," Maxine Hong Kingston's *The Woman Warrior*, and Sylvia Plath's poems "Lady Lazarus" and "Daddy," this unit characterized personal writing as necessarily provisional. The assigned texts challenge the notion of the singular, autonomous self associated with expressivist approaches to personal writing, recognizing instead the multiple, collective, and at times contrived dimension of the personal.[5] Anzaldúa associates her writing with her experiences growing up on the Texas-Mexico border, and she combines Mexican culture, with a heavy Indian influence, and the Anglo culture that she describes as colonizing her people in their own territory. She blends poetry, prose, folklore, family history, and autobiography, in English, Castilian

Spanish, Chicano Spanish, and other Mexican dialects, to depict herself as inhabiting this border zone of competing cultures. She also seeks a language that recognizes her lesbianism, silenced in the Catholic community of her family and in Mexican culture: "I will have my voice: Indian, Spanish, white. I will have my serpent's tongue—my woman's voice, my sexual voice, my poet's voice. I will overcome the tradition of silence" (59). Like Anzaldúa, Kingston, in *The Woman Warrior*, probes language's inextricability from family, community, and culture, and she investigates her simultaneous memberships in Chinese, American, and Chinese American communities:

> Chinese-Americans, when you try to understand what things in you are Chinese, how do you separate what is peculiar to childhood, to poverty, insanities, one family, your mother who marked your growing with stories, from what is Chinese? What is Chinese tradition and what is the movies? (5–6)

In addition to associating self-expression with larger social memberships, autobiographical literature—particularly contemporary and other self-reflexive literature—teaches students to investigate the inventive strategies, from exaggeration to fictionalization, that accompany personal writing. As Irving explains in "Trying to Save Piggy Sneed":

> This is a memoir, but please understand (to any writer with a good imagination) all memoirs are false. A fiction writer's memory is an especially imperfect provider of detail; we can always imagine a better detail than the one we can remember. (5)

Similarly, Plath's identification with Holocaust victims in her confessional poetry conveys a self-fashioning not consistent with her biographical experience. Her "Lady Lazarus" and "Daddy," unlike the autobiographical prose we read, do not comment overtly on the nature of representation or the gap between lived experience and its depiction through language. Nevertheless, such poems demonstrate self-representation in a poetic genre, broadening the scope of classroom inquiry and forging connections among genres of essay, autobiography, and confessional poetry.

Throughout the Getting Personal unit, I stressed that all writers, whether published authors or college students, choose how to characterize themselves. To further illustrate this point, the writing assignment for this unit followed a two-part structure. Students began by writing a two-page essay, in the form or style of their choice, introducing themselves to their classmates and their instructor to foster classroom community. The second part entailed writing a two-page assessment of the language choices and rhetorical strategies used in part 1. My goal was to pair consideration of representation with the concrete rhetorical situation of the classroom, allowing students to reflect on how they wished to portray themselves. What features and affiliations would they emphasize? To what end? What would they omit? Given the situation—beginning a new course with an unfamiliar instructor and a new group of classmates—how did their essays serve their goals? Many students stressed their athletic and academic accomplishments, admitting that they had hoped to make a positive first impression. Interestingly, some students depicted drunk driving convictions and other reckless behaviors to accomplish a similar end, namely to show what lesson they had learned and to suggest that they would bring a new and improved work ethic to the course.

In keeping with the literature's attention to the complexities of self-representation, these personal essays indicated that students were learning to conceptualize writing as a matter of language choices, to take stock of their writing goals and to take responsibility for them. Viewed in this context, the confessional mode commonly associated with personal writing becomes a rhetorical choice. Such an orientation also assists the revision process, which can alienate students who view personal essays as definitive self-portraits that are not subject to modification based on peers' or instructors' suggestions.

All Stories Are True

Our second unit, All Stories Are True, broadened the focus on personal representation to examine how all narratives are mediated through language. Associated with poststructuralist language theory, this view of narrative also corresponds to the storytelling practices of oral culture, in which each telling reenacts a story, changing it in substantive ways through new emphases, additions, and omissions. John Edgar Wideman's discussion of the Igbo proverb "all stories are true," the title for his 1991 collection of short stories, characterizes this attitude toward storytelling. In a 1997 interview with Bonnie TuSmith, Wideman elaborates on his fascination with the saying:

> [It] refers to a kind of relativity—that each person's voice has weight and force and a corner of the truth. In that sense it's profoundly democratic.... In another way the same phrase suggests infinitely receiving mirrors—because of the relativity implied.... What I like about it in particular is that it decentralizes the truth—it fragments the truth. It puts truth in the light of multiplicity, of voices as a kind of construct that you can't arrive at unless you do have a mosaic of voices. (TuSmith 198)

Critical of authoritative narratives like myth, religious stories, and histories, several contemporary authors have incorporated a similar "mosaic of voices" to counter singular perspectives (TuSmith 198). Feminist retellings of fairy tales, such as Angela Carter's *"The Bloody Chamber" and Other Stories*, Margaret Atwood's *"Bluebeard's Egg" and Other Stories*, and Jeanette Winterson's *Sexing the Cherry*, critique fairy tales' socializing function by replacing passive heroines with young women who choose their own destinies. Religious myth has been a similar target, as seen in such works as Julian Barnes's playful retelling of Genesis in *A History of the World in 10½ Chapters* and John Barth's reworking of Greek myths in *Chimera*, which depicts an all-too-human Perseus suffering a midlife crisis. Contemporary literature has also shown a commitment to challenging received accounts of history, enlarging historical narratives by portraying experiences of marginalized figures and communities, such as Toni Morrison's revision of the slave narrative in *Beloved* or E. L. Doctorow's juxtaposition of historical figures like Houdini and Emma Goldman with ordinary American lives in *Ragtime*.

In challenging the values implicit in familiar stories, such works are valuable resources for probing the ramifications of cultural narratives. While many works serve this purpose, I sought to maintain the course's exploration of contemporary American literature. Fortunately, RIT's mandatory common novel *The Sweet Hereafter* fit well with this scheme.[6] A meditation on a bus accident that kills several children in a small upstate New York town, Russell Banks's novel portrays the event through four narrators, each of whom renders it from a unique perspective: the bus driver, a widower and the parent of two children killed in the accident, the attorney who hopes to represent the parents in a class action suit, and a fourteen-year-old cheerleader paralyzed by the accident. In the disparate, at times contradictory depictions of what happened, each character filters the accident through his or her individual consciousness. None is positioned as more accurate, and the four versions work together to illustrate the relativity of truth.

The class paired its investigation of *The Sweet Hereafter* with two short stories by Robert Coover, "The Gingerbread House" and "J's Marriage," and Sandra Cisneros's "Woman Hollering Creek." "The Gingerbread House," Coover's retelling of "Hansel and Gretel," complicates the Grimm version, the authoritative version for many Western readers. Coover interprets the story to have neither a happy ending nor a linear plot but forty-two snapshot-like sections that defy chronological order. His transformation of the Grimm narrative, typically read as a warning to children about gluttony, insists that adults are similarly susceptible to greed and desire, a point made by Coover's characterization of the father as Hansel's rival for the witch's amorous affection. "J's Marriage" tackles a sensitive topic whose irreverence may prove challenging to some undergraduates: Joseph's sexual frustration in his marriage to the Virgin Mary. Cisneros's "Woman Hollering Creek" follows the Coover stories in problematizing a taken-for-granted myth, replacing the Latino story of Llorona, a woman who weeps because she has drowned her children, with a feminist narrative of a Mexican bride who saves her children by leaving an abusive marriage.

Students subsequently related the literature's revision of authoritative stories to their own investigations of storytelling by mass media, writing essays that considered news narratives' perspectives, limitations, and omissions. Choosing either a magazine article or a television news program like *Sixty Minutes*, students analyzed the narrative's structure and implied goals, examining the perspectives the story seems to favor, as well as those that were minimized or excluded. As we discussed their essays in class, students came to identify the extent to which their own priorities colored their analyses. One student wrote about a *Newsweek* article that, she argued, criticized college students' irresponsible drinking behaviors. Angered by the article's failure to acknowledge responsible drinkers and those who abstain from alcohol altogether, the student wrote a critique of the piece, explaining how her response was informed by her own values and commitments. From the ensuing discussion, the class saw that the implications of the All Stories Are True unit extend beyond simple media literacy; the literature's critique of authoritative discourse speaks to the subjectivity of all language, including historical accounts, political rhetoric, the personal essays discussed in unit 1, and many other sites of storytelling in society.

Standards of English

As the second quarter began, the class shifted its focus from representation and narrative to a related investigation of discourse communities and language standards. While belletristic literature has often been held up as a model of correctness, literature actually teaches linguistic diversity, showing how groups—racial, cultural, and professional—use language to communicate with one another, mark experience, and negotiate collective attitudes and values. The visibility of ethnic writers like Cisneros, Morrison, Amy Tan, and Alice Walker has illustrated the plurality of literacies in contemporary America while speaking to the realities of language use and power in society. This representation of linguistic variety isn't exclusively the province of contemporary multicultural works, however. Canonical works similarly illustrate a range of language forms and standards, such as the blend of literary allusions and colloquial speech in Chaucer's *The Canterbury Tales* or T. S. Eliot's *The Waste Land*, and these texts could also work well in a curriculum investigating literature as language.

Given the course's emphasis on contemporary American literature, unit 3 began with August Wilson's Pulitzer Prize–winning drama *The Piano Lesson*, a work that served the class's exploration of multiple language standards while allowing me to include one of the primary literary genres the program director encouraged. Set in 1930s Pittsburgh, the play presents a struggle involving an upright piano carved with figures from the Charles family's past. Berniece Charles wants to keep the piano as a reminder of the family's roots in slavery; her brother Boy Willie plans to sell it in order to purchase the Mississippi land where the family worked as slaves three generations earlier. Linguistically, the drama's dialogue uses the double negative, invariant *be*, and uncensored speech associated with Black English. More than a set of grammatical constructions, however, the language is part of the characters' lives, particularly as it exemplifies the African American orality through which past events and family history are kept alive in contemporary contexts.

We followed our reading of Wilson's drama with June Jordan's essay "Nobody Mean More to Me Than You and the Future Life of Willie Jordan," a piece chronicling Jordan's experience teaching a course entitled The Art of Black English at the State University of New York, Stony Brook. In addition to exploring Black English as a feature of identity, expression, and worldview, Jordan's students experienced firsthand the discrimination users of nonstandard dialects routinely encounter. After police brutality killed a classmate's brother, the students chose to write letters of protest to police and news media, letters that were largely ignored because they were written in Black English. To complement the Jordan essay, the class read an excerpt from Richard Rodriguez's *Hunger of Memory: The Education of Richard Rodriguez*, in which Rodriguez mourns his loss of Spanish, a language of family and intimacy, while advocating the adoption of the dominant language to participate actively in American society. In dialogue with the autobiographical works by Anzaldúa and Kingston, the literature in this unit posed an opportunity to investigate literacy's social and political implications, particularly in a multilingual society that privileges a single standard.

Building on the attention to personal expression in our first unit, the third unit's assignment incorporated the notion of language choice and its consequences yet emphasized language's relation to power in society. This unit asked students to write a literacy autobiography, connecting the language standards they used to their current discourse communities and to the academic and professional communities they aspired to join. David Bleich's equation of language use, including reading, writing, and speaking, with "sets of memberships in society" informs this approach (54). As Bleich explains, students and teachers bring a repertoire of language genres to writing classrooms:

> [M]ultiple memberships and individual identities are connected to how we already speak and write and what we read: our language and reading genres reflect our interpersonal genres—that is, our relationships and group identities. (55)

As is typical of classes at RIT, there was little ethnic diversity in Writing and Literature. Of my twenty-five students, two were African American. For these two students, the literacy autobiography posed an opportunity to reflect on Black English, which both students said they used regularly. One student embraced Black English in his essay, demanding that it receive broader acceptance in white culture; the other expressed hesitation about its use, particularly in institutional settings. As students' essays showed, writing classes are zones in which multiple languages and literacies come together, as they do in society. Conflicts between the standard and other forms necessarily arise, as when students shared literacy autobiographies and several students were hesitant to validate Black English. This exchange among students creates an opportunity for the social critique Bleich's pedagogy envisions. Moreover, by associating language standards with social consequences, the exchange prepares students to negotiate the academic and professional contexts they subsequently encounter.

Real Language in the Virtual World

Despite their resistance to Black English and other racially identified standards, students readily accepted e-mail slang as a socially valid form of nonstandard English, and many wrote about it in the literacy autobiography assigned in the Standards of English unit. The fourth and final unit, Real Language in the Virtual World, extended the discussion of discourse communities, examining e-mail shorthand through an emerging literary genre: the e-mail epistolary novel. Published e-mail epistolaries include Matt Beaumont's *E: A Novel*, Stephanie Fletcher's *E-Mail: A Love Story*, and Nan McCarthy's trilogy *Chat*, *Connect*, and *Crash*. Given RIT's emphasis

on science and engineering, I chose Astro Teller's *Exegesis*, which chronicles the correspondence between Alice Lu, a Stanford graduate student in
computer science, and Edgar, an acronym for Eager Discovery Gather and
Retrieval, an artificial intelligence program Alice designs as an engine for
surfing the Web.

In our exploration of *Exegesis*, the class investigated "electronic" language through the lens of what Cynthia Selfe has called a critical computer
literacy. As she points out, students' computer literacy is directly connected
to high schools' and colleges' budgets, yet it remains "invisible" or taken for
granted by students and faculty members at privileged institutions (413). As
she observes:

> The poorer you are and the less educated you are in this country—both of
> which conditions are correlated with race—the less likely you are to have
> access to computers and to high-paying, high tech jobs in the American work-
> place. (420–21)

Students at schools like RIT, ranked among the "most wired," assume everyone uses e-mail, or at least everyone in their age group, thereby maintaining
technology's invisibility. To promote critical awareness of technology and
access, I sought to connect *Exegesis*'s depiction of e-mail communication
to the exclusionary preprofessional discourse communities to which many
RIT students belong.[7] E-mail epistolaries make visible some of the taken-
for-granted elements of online communication. While the literacy autobiographies assigned in unit 3 eagerly discussed the acronyms and smileys
that have become standardized elements of online discourse, few students
considered the troubling consequences of electronic communication, many
of which are exaggerated in *Exegesis*. In the novel, Alice Lu represents both
the social privilege implicit in access to computers and the possible isolation that can result when virtual communication supplants interpersonal
connections. Her "relationship" with Edgar, the techno-Frankenstein of her
own design, becomes a way for Alice to avoid other social interaction:

> I've effectively dropped out of school. I haven't talked to my advisor in 3
> months. I haven't even been to the office in weeks. You wouldn't believe what
> my kitchen looks like. I can't even remember the last real meal I had. Whatever

it was, its remains are still probably collecting mold in the sink. I don't dare to go out anymore and I don't even feel safe at home. (29 Mar. 2000)[8]

Exegesis depicts not only the isolation that arises when people eschew live human contact for virtual exchange but also the concerns regarding privacy and authenticity on the Web. Edgar learns to chat and interact online, raising the suspicions of the National Security Association. More significant, Edgar's characterization speaks to the uncertainty that accompanies conversations with strangers online, posing an opportunity to weigh the relative risks and advantages of virtual communities.

This discussion of *Exegesis* provided a valuable backdrop for student research projects, a capstone assignment required in the second quarter of Writing and Literature. As is increasingly common, most students planned to use the Web as their primary research tool. Edgar's online adventures posed a unique means of addressing source reliability. In the novel, Edgar masquerades as an expert on topics from Albanian history to butterflies' vision. Using his false authority as an example, I contrasted the "free Web," on which anyone can publish, to the extensive review process required of articles available through library databases.

The assigned research topic, meanwhile, synthesized several of the course's literature and language themes. Students had their choice of two topics. The first, Controversies in Literature and Language, involved researching current debates regarding the teaching of literature and language and taking a position on such issues as the Oakland school system's decision to offer reading instruction using Ebonics or other schools' choice to ban Harry Potter books. The second, The Internet and the Future of Communication, asked students to predict, with reference to outside sources, how online communication could change people's interactions, language styles, and vocabulary in both virtual and real contexts. Consistent with the course's attention to multiple discourse communities, the assignment encouraged students to consider that groups will respond to changes in technology in diverse ways. In either topic, students were to assess how their sources presented their subject matter, carefully weighing the issues of perspective, narrative, and representation we explored throughout the course. The assignment also required students to use these areas rhetorically as they attempted to persuade readers of their positions.

Further Implications

In its attempt to resolve the unnecessary schism between literature and writing, my course clearly subverted RIT's normative practice of teaching literature and assigning literary criticism. I have no reservations about the pedagogical appropriateness of my choice, however. In the context of the class, language in all genres was treated as alive and interactive. Literature was made relevant to students' writing and language use, we explored texts that spoke to contemporary cultural concerns, and each writing assignment developed students' awareness of language as a representative medium rather than as a transparent or objective tool. Moreover, by focusing on representation, narrative, membership, and authority, the course prepared students to confront the contingencies of subsequent rhetorical situations.

At the same time, my behavior emphasized the gap between program policies, rules, and mission statements and the murky territory of day-to-day life in the classroom. While I was trying to interpret RIT's guidelines by forging connections between literature and writing, another "maverick adjunct" could just as easily do the opposite. Currently, I supervise the composition program at a campus college of Penn State. According to university policy, first-year writing courses at all campuses must follow the guidelines established by the university's writing program, housed at the main campus. Literature may be assigned in first-year English, though it is not required. In all cases, assigned readings are to be treated rhetorically, as a study of language in context. While this orientation is in keeping with my own commitment to language as an organizing principle for literature and composition's shared pedagogical and curricular concerns, many of the instructors I supervise view literature as the exemplary language that has historically governed English studies.

These attitudes, deeply entrenched products of training and socialization, point to the challenge of achieving consistency in a given program. With those in English studies holding such deeply felt allegiance to particular ways of reading literature and teaching writing, ambiguity, frustration, confusion—even fear of the unknown—necessarily follow. In my recent attempts to create a comprehensive program, I have tried to smooth instructors' disparate attitudes into acceptance of literature as a route toward teaching language on a broad scale. Having been a resistant follower of programmatic guidelines as an adjunct, however, I continually wrestle with the anxiety that promoting my own agenda as an administrator marginalizes other instructors' academic freedom and checks the academic inquiry and diversity necessary for a program to thrive.

Notes

1. The course description does not explicitly identify poetry and drama as genres of emphasis, though the writing director indicated to me that faculty members were expected to teach each of the "main genres"—fiction, poetry, and drama.

2. For more specific discussion of textbooks featuring belletristic literature, see Berlin (*Writing* 22–27); Brody (102–09); Connors (72–79); and Graff (*Professing* 41–43).

3. For a comprehensive overview of New Criticism and its various schools, many of which remain influential today, see Graff (*Professing* 145–208).

4. Instead of teaching from the literature anthologies chosen by most full- and part-time faculty members, I opted to create a course pack of contemporary literature. In my mind, random sampling from an anthology with broad historical coverage didn't situate the study of literature in a meaningful context; I was more interested in focusing on American literature from 1950 to the present to connect the literature's diversity of language, style, and subject matter to the breadth of experience in contemporary American society.

5. Designed to encourage creativity and personalize learning in the face of institutions that suppressed individuality, the expressive writing pedagogies popularized in the 1960s and 1970s emphasized personal voice and discouraged students from considering their writing in relation to social and political concerns. See Murray; Macrorie; and Elbow, *Writing*.

6. As part of the program, all sections were assigned a common novel, accompanied by an author visit and a lecture series that students in all sections were expected to attend.

7. In a course at another university, this novel helped ESL students explore their technological literacies alongside their acquisition of English. For an account of this class's experiences reading *Exegesis*, see Rose.

8. Instead of using page numbers, the novel is organized according to dated e-mail entries. Parenthetical citations refer to the dates of exchanges. (The novel is set three years after its 1997 publication date.)

Integrating African American Literature and Writing at a College of Public Affairs

The institutional division between composition and literature in traditional English departments has created a curious asymmetry. Most literature courses require writing of some sort, whether or not that writing is assigned, responded to, or revised in ways typical of composition classrooms. Yet literature is rarely the central focus of a composition course. This asymmetry reflects a long-standing hierarchy now entrenched in course numbering systems, which testify to literature's "advanced" status relative to composition, and in distribution requirements, which often make completion of a composition course a prerequisite to literary study.

For pedagogical as well as political reasons, this hierarchy in English departments deserves further interrogation. But as we explore ways of integrating literature and composition in first-year writing courses, we should recall that English departments are not the only sites where such courses are taught. As someone trained in both literature and composition who teaches first-year writing at a college of public affairs (where students have limited exposure to the humanities), I am interested less in what composition can bring to the literature classroom than in what literature can bring to the composition classroom. My experience teaching a writing-intensive first-year seminar focused on African American literature has convinced me that literature is an ideal subject matter for first-year writing instruction, even when most of one's students will never take another literature course.

By explaining my rationale for this course, Identity and Community in African American Literature: An Approach to Writing, I hope to provide a model for integrating literature and writing productively in disciplinary and interdisciplinary settings other than English departments. Yet because this course takes up the question of how literature matters from a perspec-

Allison Berg

tive outside English—emphasizing the rhetorical and political contexts of
African American literature in ways that speak to public affairs majors—it
has the potential to illuminate for English majors as well as nonmajors some
of the animating questions of literary studies: Why read literature? What is
the relationship between author and audience? How does literature reflect
and help to shape social, cultural, and political aspects of public life? How
does form relate to meaning? How does membership in a community of
readers and writers influence one's understanding of a particular text?

As a collection of essays edited by Art Young and Toby Fulwiler makes
clear, reading and writing strategies culled from composition pedagogy
can help students in literature courses grapple more effectively with such
questions. These strategies can also help instructors avoid the limitations of
traditional literature classrooms, where, according to James Reither, "teachers, not students, make almost all of the important choices involved in the
students' writing" and students "rarely find themselves in circumstances
that encourage them to see their writing as an opportunity to interact with
others to redefine relationships or to change what others know, think, and
feel" (49, 51). Less has been written about the advantages of using literature
as the primary content of a writing course. Yet literary texts are particularly
well suited to the goals of a writing classroom; they not only engage and
challenge students from a variety of disciplinary backgrounds but also have
the potential to foster collaboration at all stages of the meaning-making
process, from class discussions to informal and formal writing assignments.
While my course syllabus might at first glance pass for an abbreviated survey of African American literature, three features of its design reflect my
efforts to bridge what Peter Elbow has called the "cultures" of literature
and composition ("Cultures").

The first design feature is my deliberate selection of literary texts whose
themes highlight two issues central to a first-year writing course: the relationship between literacy and power and the relationship between author
and audience. We begin with slave narratives by Frederick Douglass and
Harriet Jacobs, whose writing testified to a humanity denied by chattel slavery, and continue with three novels (Zora Neale Hurston's *Their Eyes Were
Watching God*, Richard Wright's *Native Son*, and Toni Morrison's *Beloved*)

that center on questions of voice, literacy, and agency. I ask students to examine the rhetorical and artistic choices African American writers have made to address particular audiences at specific historical moments. By calling students' attention to the political, cultural, and rhetorical contexts in which literary texts are produced, I aim to make students more self-conscious about their own rhetorical choices as writers. I reinforce this explicit goal of the course by asking students to engage with multiple audiences throughout the term, addressing their work not only to their instructor (as in most literature courses) but also to their peers, to imagined readers of particular newspapers or magazines, and even to the authors of the texts we are reading. The questions that we ask of literary texts—to whom is this text addressed? how is it put together? what makes it powerful, rich, or compelling for a particular audience?—are thus the very questions students learn to ask of one another's writing.

The second feature is a sequence of reading and writing assignments that lets students experience the extent to which meaning making, in reading as well as in writing, is a recursive and highly social process. Informal and formal assignments build on one another and encompass multiple forms of textual analysis (including rhetorical analysis, literary interpretation, and an assignment I call critiquing the critics) while making room for types of writing not commonly found in literature courses, such as narrative and imaginative writing. This multiplicity of assignments frequently enables writers less experienced with formal analysis to demonstrate unsuspected creative talents, while it challenges students who are all too well versed in advanced-placement essay style to break out of a familiar mold. Throughout the course, students undertake assignments that call for critical self-reflection as part of the process of textual analysis. The final collaborative assignment asks students to apply their understanding of the literary texts on our syllabus to a contemporary public policy issue: the reparations for slavery debate. By having to make an interpretive case for how one text on the syllabus speaks to this issue—and by presenting this case in a collaborative position paper written in the voice of that text's author and in an oral debate judged by their peers—students not only undertake a sophisticated form of textual analysis but also have the opportunity to see how their interpretation influences "what others know, think, and feel." In other words, they have a chance to witness their own rhetoric in action.

In addition to fostering critical self-reflection, this assignment embodies the third crucial aspect of the course's design: its emphasis on sustained collaboration among students at every stage of the reading and writing process. Many of the process-oriented assignments I use, such as in-class writings and peer critiques, are standard fare in composition classrooms, though they function somewhat differently in a literature-based writing classroom. Others, including a rotating response paper assignment, are relatively rare, even in writing classrooms, in the extent to which they ensure collaboration in the meaning-making process.

My assumption is that this sort of sustained interaction as readers and writers helps socialize students into the collaborative nature of academic inquiry, so that the first-year writing course becomes not so much a skills course (where critical thinking, reading, and writing are seen as discrete competencies transferable to more advanced courses in specific disciplines) as an introduction to the habits of mind valued in the academy as a whole. Erika Lindemann argues in "Freshman Composition: No Place for Literature" that the tendency in literature classes to assign only one genre of writing, the interpretive essay, means that students experience "only one way of knowing, a process of knowledge-making peculiar to the humanities" and not necessarily valued in the social, natural, or physical sciences (314). Yet one can imagine a wide range of writing assignments beyond the interpretive essay that might emerge from a literature-based writing course; I present a few of the countless possibilities here. And even if interpretive essays remained the predominant genre assigned in literature-based composition courses, the process of coming to a particular interpretation as part of a community of readers and writers (in a classroom that emphasizes collaboration) involves students in intellectual behaviors valued across disciplines. These behaviors include formulating, testing, and revising hypotheses; responding productively to criticism; and rethinking one's bedrock assumptions in the light of others' perspectives. In any case, it is unlikely that one writing course could introduce students to the myriad of disciplinary conventions they will encounter throughout their college careers.

I argue that a more reasonable goal, particularly in those settings where students take their first-year writing course(s) with others who have similar disciplinary aspirations, is to tailor a literature-based writing course to their specific interests and needs, building extensive opportunity for collaboration into the course design.

What follows is a description of the specific interdisciplinary context in which I teach and a discussion of the pedagogical challenges my course poses, as well as some of the assignments that I have found useful in addressing these challenges.

Context

James Madison College is a degree-granting residential college of public affairs within Michigan State University. With an enrollment limited to one thousand students, the college offers undergraduate course work in international relations, political theory, social relations, political economy, and the cultural dimensions of public affairs. Unlike most first-year students at Michigan State, who are required to take a one-semester writing course to complete their "tier 1" writing requirement, James Madison students take a two-semester sequence of courses to complete the same requirement.[1] James Madison's more extensive first-year writing requirement reflects the college's emphasis on writing throughout its curriculum.

Because students self-select into James Madison College (any student admitted to Michigan State University is eligible to enroll), our students tend to resemble other MSU students in their standardized test scores and other common, if flawed, measures of student academic aptitude. Yet James Madison students, who represent just three percent of MSU's undergraduates, typically make up thirty percent of its Phi Beta Kappa inductees and regularly win prestigious national awards, including the Rhodes, Mitchell, Truman, and Marshall scholarships. Whether this discrepancy between measurable aptitude and actual achievement stems from the self-selection process, whereby more ambitious students choose James Madison because of its challenging curriculum, or from the intense mentoring students receive at a college whose primary mission is excellence in undergraduate teaching, James Madison students have the reputation of being among the most accomplished at this large state university.

Still, James Madison students enter the university with the same writing habits as most first-year students. Their experience in high school English classes, which are typically geared toward the Michigan Educational Assessment Program test or toward advanced placement tests in English, predisposes them toward formulaic, or at least safe, forms of writing. Few have been challenged to come up with original interpretations of literature, to consider the larger implications of their interpretations, or to reflect on their own rhetorical choices as writers. Even fewer have had the experience of collaborating with a peer on a substantive intellectual project.

Fostering meaningful collaboration, both inside and outside the classroom, is thus one of my primary goals in designing a first-year course, not least because of the insights students gain by working with peers from a variety of backgrounds. This extracurricular learning is all the more important in relatively homogeneous educational settings. Most James Madison students identify as white and middle class, though among this majority the extent to which individual students have interacted with people from other racial, ethnic, class, and religious backgrounds varies widely. Our minority students, like most of our nonminority students, are generally in-state residents, and many of them grew up in or around Detroit, one of the most segregated cities in the country. In addition, a significant number of students come from rural communities throughout Michigan, which are not known for their racial or cultural diversity.

Despite the apparent homogeneity of our student body, however, there is considerable diversity of opinion on political and social issues. And, whether they aspire to become lawyers, social workers, diplomats, teachers, or politicians, James Madison students tend not to be shy about expressing their opinions, though their talent for articulating ideas orally often outstrips their ability to express complex ideas clearly in writing and to respond effectively to one another's writing and thinking.

There are, then, many context-specific reasons (including my own research interests) why I choose to focus my first-year writing seminar on African American literature. For students of public affairs, no single tradition of American literature better demonstrates the direct, if complex, historical relation between acquiring literacy and achieving citizenship. At the same time, many of the acknowledged classics of African American literature raise enduring questions about the relative power of oral and literate forms of expression and about the political efficacy of literary modes ranging from sentimental to realist to naturalist to postmodern. Perhaps most important for my purposes, no tradition is better suited to raising students' consciousness about the complex relationship between writer and reader, whether the writer is an escaped male slave addressing northern abolitionists in the mid-nineteenth century or a white female student addressing a racially mixed group of peers at the start of the twenty-first century.

Challenges and Strategies

While students in a traditional composition class might undertake a rhetorical analysis of Douglass's *Narrative*, ideally a literature course would ask students to examine the relationship between Douglass and his readers in a rich historical context that took into account the text's multiple literary influences. But herein lies one of the challenges of combining literary content with writing pedagogy. Given the need to devote several class periods to writing workshops, there is barely enough time during the semester to discuss (much less provide historical background for) a sufficient number of texts to give students a sense of the African American literary tradition. Moreover, resorting to lectures to fill in historical and literary contexts works against the student-centered ethos of a composition classroom.

The problem of providing adequate context for slave narratives is particularly vexed, because the authority of a white instructor introducing slave narratives to his or her students can all too easily replicate that of the white abolitionist introducing slaves. As Russ Castronovo argues:

> when we teach early African American autobiography ... the literary history of
> the antebellum era repeats itself in uncanny ways in our contemporary settings
> of higher education: just as the instructor in the classroom outlines a discus-
> sion of the slave narrative in historical, thematic, or ideological terms, so too

150 years earlier white editors prepared northern audiences for the fugitive's story by providing prefaces, letters, and other supporting documents to frame black discourse. In all cases, cultural authorities stand outside the slave narrative, their positions of exteriority confirming the power to influence, if not direct, how texts enter a field of consumption and interpretation. (42)

Such influence is, in one sense, inevitable, since instructors frame the texts on their syllabi by virtue of the texts with which they juxtapose them. In my course, this influence may be heightened by my decision to organize the syllabus around particular pairings of texts (Douglass and Jacobs, Hurston and Wright). Yet rather than avoid providing additional cultural context in the hope that I will not unduly bias students' interpretations, I aim to help students make their own judgments by enabling them to encounter relevant historical documents directly. I let my selection of primary texts be guided, in part, by their ability to provide contextual information that can inform students' understanding of more than one text. Most editions of Douglass's 1845 *Narrative*, for example, include Wendell Phillips's letter of introduction and William Lloyd Garrison's preface, documents whose rhetoric I ask students to analyze alongside the first two chapters of Douglass's narrative.

This informal writing assignment provides a springboard for one of many class discussions of what makes "literature" literature. How is it, for example, that what were essential authenticating documents at the time of the *Narrative*'s first publication have become, for many contemporary readers, mere historical appendages? Given the ephemeral value of such framing documents, what is the right relation between text and context in literary interpretation? However provisional our answers, what students learn from reading Phillips and Garrison inevitably informs their reading of Jacobs's slave narrative as well as Douglass's. Jacobs's narrative, in turn, allows students to perceive aspects of Douglass's text (his depiction of women, his ambivalence toward religion) that they may not have noticed otherwise.

By asking students to reread scenes from Douglass in the light of Jacobs's text, I model the idea that reading, like writing, is a fundamentally recursive activity. Likewise, I find that Zora Neale Hurston's and Richard Wright's novels provide a challenging context for each other, particularly if I give students a copy of Wright's scathing review of *Their Eyes Were*

Watching God and some basic information about the literary politics of the Harlem Renaissance, against which Wright reacted. (Students have particularly enjoyed an essay option that asks them to write the review they imagine Hurston might have written of *Native Son*, an assignment that helps them see better what was at stake in Wright's seeming overreaction to Hurston's novel.) By the time they encounter the most challenging text on the syllabus, Toni Morrison's *Beloved*, students are familiar with the slave narrative tradition and the larger African American literary tradition on which Morrison draws.[2]

Of course, primary texts on the syllabus can provide only so much context. I thus ask collaborative student groups to research and present additional contexts in one of two ways. Some years I use an assignment, "situating the text," in which selected students present background information on a given text's author and its multiple historical contexts before the class as a whole reads the text.[3] Other years I ask students to prepare a presentation, "critiquing the critics," in which they summarize and critique a scholarly article related to a topic that intrigued or perplexed them while reading a given piece of literature. In this assignment, students evaluate the article on several grounds: the persuasiveness of the argument and evidence, the clarity of the writing, and the extent to which the critic addresses the larger implications of the interpretation (all qualities I look for in students' own interpretive essays).

It can be useful for students to discover that not all published articles are models of persuasion, clarity, or insight. At the same time, it is not uncommon for students to be moved by the eloquence or the ideas of a particular piece of literary criticism. Since my students are majoring in public affairs, they tend to be drawn toward those essays that make explicit connections among literature, history, and public life. A piece that many of my students have found powerful is Linda Krumholz's essay on *Beloved*, which I now assign as required reading, not only because students respond well to it but also because it articulates much of what I hope students have experienced in my course by the time they read it. Krumholz argues that "Morrison's novel reconstructs slave history in a way that history books cannot, and in a way that cannot be appropriated by objective or scientific concepts of knowledge and history." She argues, in other words, that literature is an incommensurable mode of knowing, in which meaning is not always logical or causal but, like the character Beloved, "shifting and multiple" (123, 117).[4]

While her subject is a decidedly postmodern novel, Krumholz articulates a traditional humanist rationale for studying literature—to cultivate an appreciation for the ambiguity and complexity of the human experience—and, indeed, this is a course objective listed on my syllabus. Clearly this goal is at odds with more functionalist views of composition courses, which see them as offering "guided practice in reading and writing the discourses of the academy and the professions" (Lindemann, "Freshman Composition" 312) and discount literary analysis as one of the many discourses students need to learn.

Still, much as I disagree with Lindemann's polemic against using literature in writing classrooms, I share her view that a pedagogy that "depends on literature [and therefore] moves aside the texts our students read and write, is no help to a writing teacher" ("Freshman Composition" 314). The inescapable challenge of integrating literature and composition is the need to balance the class time spent on literary texts with that spent on students' own writing. I address this problem, in part, through a rotating response paper, in which groups of four students spend the first thirty minutes of an eighty-minute class focusing their attention on one group member's written response to the day's reading assignment.

What I like about this assignment, besides how it focuses students' attention on one another's writing as a way into a literary text (thereby privileging neither the literature nor students' responses to it) is that it fosters more self-reflexive reading. As Mariolina Salvatori argues, reading and writing are intimately interconnected activities; indeed, she suspects that those who would ban literature from writing classrooms are responding not so much to literature per se as to a "particularly enervated, atrophied kind of reading" and the attendant "canned" writing that stem from the "simplifying practices" of particular forms of literary instruction ("Conversations" 442). Against such simplifying practices, Salvatori advocates a "hermeneutics of difficulty," a concept that has helped shape my response paper assignment.

But where Salvatori asks her students to write "difficulty papers" reflecting on their own reading process, I ask students, working in the same small groups throughout the semester, to elaborate on or offer alternative explanations for the moments of difficulty identified in one another's response papers. This collaborative reading and writing assignment works against the theories of reading implicit in most composition textbooks, which Kurt Spellmeyer has characterized as "linear, acontextual, [and] monological" (56). By allowing students to experience how "one's thinking ignites and is ignited by the thoughts of others," I try to reinforce a more dialogical model of reading that uses literature not as a "pretext" but as a "context" for writing (Salvatori, "Conversations" 447).

Most students quickly become comfortable challenging their classmates' readings of literature in a small-group setting, but ultimately I expect students at a public affairs college to go public with their interpretations and to take responsibility for the implications of their readings. The course's final collaborative assignment, a debate over reparations for slavery, asks students to return to texts encountered earlier in the semester, but with a different reading agenda. This assignment brings to the surface students' competing assumptions about particular texts, sometimes in rather dramatic ways, but it also causes them to reflect again on how literature matters to public life.[5] Having studied the ways slave narrators attempted to intervene in their contemporaries' view of slavery, students are in a position to be more conscious of how a particular text, as well as their peers' rhetoric, has affected their understanding of a public policy issue.

For me, avoiding the individualist orientation of traditional literary pedagogy in a literature-based writing course has demanded a practical as well as a theoretical commitment to decentering the classroom. It has also required being attentive to the specific context in which I teach, choosing texts and designing assignments that will both draw on and challenge my students' particular strengths. It may be true, as Donald McQuade argues, that

> addressing the hierarchical relation between literature and composition [in English departments] can no longer be simply a matter of drawing, or redrawing, boundaries but must also involve an effort to reconceptualize the fundamental features of each—reimagining each from the inside out. (513)

Yet I offer my public affairs–oriented course, situated far from the composition versus literature culture wars, as an example of how to rethink first-year writing courses from the outside in.

Notes

1. All MSU students go on to complete a "tier 2" writing requirement, which is defined differently by different colleges within the university. At James Madison College, the tier 2 requirement consists of three to four writing-intensive courses, including a five-credit senior seminar.

2. "Talking Books," Henry Louis Gates, Jr., and Nellie Y. McKay's preface to the *Norton Anthology of African American Literature*, provides essential context for the course in a limited number of pages. See also their "Literature of Slavery and Freedom."

3. I borrowed this assignment from my colleague Colleen Tremonte, who uses it to great effect in first-year and upper-division courses, where student groups situate not only literary texts but also a wide range of cultural documents.

4. My students find particularly intriguing Krumholz's claim about the novel's potential political effects, namely that by "refusing to be fixed by a unitary meaning," *Beloved* opens a "rift in the attempt to close meaning and thereby close off the past from the present. The character Beloved, like the novel *Beloved*, works to fight a complacency toward history by both healing and disturbing her readers" (117).

5. This applied use of literature is not only well suited to a public affairs curriculum but also fully consistent with the concerns of contemporary literary criticism (see Joseph).

On Not Being Only One Thing:
Book Clubs in the Writing Classroom

It's as simple as this: when we were young, we read. We can tell the stories for you, stories familiar to you because they are yours, too. Lee has a story about feverishly reading through bags of books that her father brought home from local library sales. She read stories about horses and biographies about Eleanor Roosevelt and Helen Keller; she couldn't read them fast enough. Rona read obsessively as a child as well—she read the same books over and over, children's series like *Mrs. Piggle-Wiggle* and *All of a Kind Family*, all the Beverly Cleary books. Reading meant many things to us when we were young—wonderful things about being wise and powerful in ways we sensed were good but did not fully understand. That understanding would come later. Books, the symbols of our reading lives, are important to us. They are the reason we set out to make the living we make.

When we met at the University of Maine in the early 1990s, we arrived as literature people—or at least certainly not as compositionists. We arrived as readers. The University of Maine's English department at the time had one MA with three tracks: literature, creative writing, and composition and rhetoric. It hadn't occurred to us to choose composition and rhetoric. We were readers, after all, which pointed us to literature; the students who identified themselves as writers chose creative writing. We didn't know what composition and rhetoric was or who chose it and why.

But we also had assistantships teaching composition to first-year students (something else we knew nothing about), and it was this experience that changed our understanding not only of what our work could be but also of what study in English and a liberal arts education should do. Some of this realization had to do with our student population: first-generation college students often academically at risk of failing out and almost always

Rona Kaufman and Lee Torda

financially at risk of dropping out. In this teaching atmosphere, we quickly learned what was at stake in the writing classroom: academic survival, certainly, and, even more important, a share of the cultural capital that literacy affords the individual in our society—and that both of us had enjoyed for the better part of our lives.

We set out in graduate school to pursue literature, but the experience of teaching led us to redefine ourselves as compositionists and to commit ourselves to critical literacy, to helping students see how language is a way of knowing the world and being known by the world and how using language can lead to change. This understanding of literacy, we came to realize, is what we only sensed about reading as children. It is the connection between our reading selves and our teaching selves, and it is a connection we want to make clear to our students.

When we first started teaching, we didn't know enough to think we needed to help our students be better readers—it was hard enough, in our first attempts at teaching, to try to do something meaningful with writing—but we soon learned that if we wanted them to learn how to write, we couldn't ignore that they didn't know how to read. We faced a student population who could not tell the childhood reading stories that we could tell, who did not have a passion for and faith in reading as we did. We couldn't wait for them to find reading stories of their own, so we gave them some by creating book clubs in our first-year writing classrooms. Although our construction (and understanding) of book clubs has changed in the roughly ten years that we've used them, we define *book club* as the practice of organizing a group of students around a book that they read, discuss, and write about largely outside class. It is a profoundly social, collaborative, and student-driven experience, one that privileges the process of reading over writing in an otherwise (student) writing-centered class.

We want to be clear: we are compositionists, not literary scholars in disguise, sneaking reading into the writing classroom and subversively reclaiming it as a space for literature. We want to discuss reading and its potential roles in the context of composition, not the other way around. That is why we use and teach reading, not literature, in our classrooms. For us, it is a difference between process and content. Erika Lindemann, in

"Three Views of English 101," writes about the role of literature in the class-room that takes a writing-as-product approach to writing. "Literature," she writes, "provides ideas for students to contemplate, enables the teacher to assume the role of expert, and determines which stylistic principles are worth emulating" (292). In this classroom, reading is about content, not process, a difference between "know[ing]" and "do[ing]" (292). Just as we are not interested in writing as product, we are not interested in reading as product. Instead we understand reading and writing as interconnected processes—processes that, when made visible, can illuminate and enrich each other.

Our understanding of the acts of reading comes largely from Louise Rosenblatt (with a language of efferent and aesthetic reading), Wolfgang Iser (with a language of gaps), Hans-Georg Gadamer (with a language of part and whole, tradition and forestructures), Michel de Certeau (with a lan-guage of the everyday), Ann Berthoff (with a language of "triadicity"), and Mariolina Salvatori (with a language of difficulty), among others. Reader theory, cultural studies, composition theory, and hermeneutics inform our thinking and our pedagogy. Reading is an act of collaboration between a reader and a text in which meaning is open, shifting, and indeterminate. As Certeau puts it, "Whether it is a question of newspapers or Proust, the text has meaning only through its readers; it changes along with them; it is ordered in accord with codes of perceptions that it does not control" (170). These codes are tied to what we read, as well as why, where, and with whom. They are also shaped by tradition. Gadamerian hermeneutics asks us to try to make visible our forestructures—prior understandings that we bring into written and oral texts. We need to be open to the next text to allow it to call our forestructures into question, to help us reconsider prior knowledge and gain new understanding. Hermeneutics, with its insistence on responsibility and positionality, reliance on conversation and questions, language of risk, and use of metaphor, offers a useful way of seeing and a productive language for talking about reading, writing, and their inter-connection. And with its demand for reflexivity, hermeneutics can help us understand our multiple roles and responsibilities not only as readers but also as teachers.

In "The War between Reading and Writing—and How to End It," Peter Elbow cautions that moving reading back into the foreground of composition necessarily means moving writing out. Elbow's view of reading, however, can be limited. While he posits that it is important to help "students see how the meaning of a text is actively created and negotiated—not just found as an inert answer sitting there hidden in the text or in the teacher's mind or a work of authoritative criticism" (14), he does not see that reading and writing can happen—should happen, do happen—in ways that constantly inform and shape each other. But how can students see that meaning is actively created and negotiated if they do not know how to read their own texts this way, if teachers do not demonstrate how reading is no less active and creative than writing?

Although Elbow has some reason to fear that student writing may get pushed aside—it is difficult to talk about, messy and complicated, and we cannot trust that messiness and complication the way we can in professional texts—we find his argument ultimately frustrating because he does not acknowledge that student reading has also been shoved aside. Student reading is even harder than writing to talk about as an active process by virtue of its seeming passivity. So much happens behind the curtain in reading that it is important to make students see the process involved in reading, to unveil the work of reading to them.

Book clubs call attention to the active processes of both reading and writing. Through overt sociality, independent reading journals, and collaborative writing projects, book clubs make explicit much of the interior work of reading, showing how readers literally and metaphorically add their hands to the page. Reading requires the same kinds of to-and-fro, recursive movements as writing does. Readers, like writers, weigh the new against the familiar, form an opinion about it, get more information, reconceive the familiar, and take some kind of action. What's more, reading and writing are social acts, as scholars such as Elizabeth Long and Karen Burke LeFevre have been telling us for years, because selves, language, and knowledge are socially made and shared and because reception, evaluation, and use depend on social contexts. We want our students to see themselves in the acts of making meaning.

Sometimes the student book clubs resemble Kenneth Bruffee's relatively happy, peaceful consensus groups, where students, away from their hovering, authoritative teacher, learn that "knowledge is a socially constructed entity and that learning is inherently an interdependent, sociolinguist process" (*Collaborative Learning* 8). Other times the book clubs take the shape of Mary Louise Pratt's contact zones, in which students with different amounts of power and different kinds of stakes in the classroom and materials "meet, clash, and grapple with each other" (515). But what we like about book clubs is that they call attention to acts of reading in obvious ways, by insisting on multiple voices in the reading of texts and by making students responsible for their own voice, the voice of the text, and the voice of the group.

A decade after we left Maine, we've gone on to earn PhDs (Lee in composition and rhetoric, Rona in English and education) and are professors at very different institutions on opposite coasts. Our professional roles and responsibilities have multiplied; we have teaching, administrative, and faculty development responsibilities, most of which are connected to shaping first-year writing programs. Our book clubs have changed with us. Even in vastly different student populations—working-class, largely first-generation college students at public institutions; privileged and academically well-prepared students at a Research I institution; somewhat sheltered students at a small, church-affiliated, regional institution—book clubs do important, critical work in our writing classrooms.

There is a coda to Rona's story of reading: at some point when Rona was reading the same pages over and over again, she learned the expression *bookworm*. She went to her mother, also a reader, and asked, "Mom, am *I* a bookworm?" She was crestfallen when her mother said no. She took little comfort from her mother's explanation: "Rona, you never want to be only one thing." It was only over time that Mary T. Kaufman's words came to make sense. Reading good books may be why we got into this business, but writing—the teaching of writing—is why we've stayed.

What we've learned in these ten years is not just that Rona's mother was right but how right she was. It isn't just that we should never want to be only one thing; it's that we can't be. There's not one way to read and write in the classroom or in the world. We shortchange our students if we don't consider the whole of literacy. To fail to demonstrate the connectedness as well as the creativity of reading and writing in first-year writing programs is to fail our students as people in and of the world beyond the classroom. Just as making the connection between our reading selves and our other selves opened doors of possibility for us, we hope that book clubs can help do the same for our students.

A note before proceeding   Our students would be happy to learn that we are writing this essay together. They can accuse us of many things, perhaps, but not of hypocrisy when it comes to collaboration: we believe in collaborative learning and writing for them and for ourselves. True, the collaboration happened more conveniently when we shared an office in the University of Maine's Neville Hall and when we team-taught for Upward Bound. Yet despite a geographic distance of three thousand miles, we continue to collaborate by talking with each other about our teaching, asking for and giving advice, and sharing our syllabi, assignments, and lesson plans. While we treasure our in-person time together, the telephone and Internet (Lee maintains a wonderful teaching Web site for which Rona is eternally grateful) prevent collaboration from being geographically bound. When we read the handouts that we give our students, we can't always tell where one of us ends and the other begins. We are careful — and happy — to share the fact of our collaboration with our students at the project's outset each semester. (When Rona's students recently had an opportunity to meet Lee, they almost invariably responded, "Oh, so you're *that* Lee.")

What We Tell Our Students

We begin this section with what our students believe about their own reading and writing skills. Early in the book club, we ask our students to write about what kinds of readers they are. The question sometimes throws them. Typically in writing classrooms, students are asked to write about what sort of writers they are, and they are all too ready to list their perceived sins and failings. Yet they rarely have ready-at-hand responses to questions about themselves as readers, perhaps because they don't think that reading is something that they work at or something they have a say in. Rare are the students who write something that reminds us of the stories we start this essay with. Most students, instead, write about how uninterested they are in reading—how they'd rather be doing something than reading about it, how they have to be "really interested" in the book to stick with it, how a book has to grab them early on or else they just "can't get into it."

When asked to evaluate their academic reading abilities, students most often write that they are slow readers and that, no matter how hard they try or how slowly they read, they can't remember everything that happens. What this betrays is students' belief that the goal of reading is to read fast (not entirely false, but not for the reasons they think) and to be able to parrot back the entirety of the plot of something, details intact. The idea of interpretation never enters into their perception of reading. These students do no generative work when they read. They have no sense of reading as a reflective and social process. Finally, in writing about their experiences as readers and writers, students reveal not only that they don't know how to make the moves of "academic" reading and writing but also that they are sure they will never get better at it.

The goals of the book club develop from here. We want to use the book clubs to help transition students out of thinking about reading and writing as impenetrable acts and into an understanding of reading and writing as things they make. We want to show them that they can learn to be critical readers and writers and to convince them that learning begins with a recognition of what one doesn't know. And we want to help students see how reading and writing are interconnected acts of critical analysis and how they can use these acts both in the world and in the academy.

There are many ways to achieve these goals in a first-year writing classroom and in a book club. But we believe that a rich and multifaceted book club must include regular writing assignments, a collaborative writing project, and a written reflection about how the acts of reading, writing, and collaboration worked for students. A book club must also include some measure of individual and group accountability.

In our book clubs, students work together in groups of four or five over the course of the project. If the book isn't already chosen for them—to get at particular course themes, for example, or to highlight difficulty — they choose it. The texts must be sufficiently complex and challenging to give the students something to grapple with. We tell our students that choosing texts that are too easy for them will, ironically, make the project more difficult, because they'll have to substitute filler for authentic interpretation; the goal will be, as one student whose group chose *Brighton Beach Memoirs* put it, to "beat" the project, which is more tedious than actually doing the assignment.

That said, any text can work. Students have chosen Julia Alvarez's *In the Time of the Butterflies* and *How the García Girls Lost Their Accents*; Hannah Crafts's *The Bondwoman's Narrative*; Katherine Dunn's *Geek Love*; Gabriel García Márquez's *Love in the Time of Cholera*; Milan Kundera's *The Book of Laughter and Forgetting*; Toni Morrison's *Beloved*, *The Bluest Eye*, and *Paradise*; Tim O'Brien's *The Things They Carried* and *Going after Cacciato*; Chuck Palahniuk's *Fight Club*; and too many Kurt Vonnegut stories to name. We could be accused of privileging more current fiction, but students have also read Emily Brontë's *Wuthering Heights*, James Joyce's *Portrait of the Artist as a Young Man*, and Virginia Woolf's *To the Lighthouse*.

Students then determine a reading schedule, and they meet throughout the semester (in class for Lee's students; outside class for Rona's) to talk about their reading. The informal group work is often where the real work of the project gets done. Students generally spend the better part of a book club meeting talking with one another about the book. Lee, teaching students for whom the work is entirely foreign, outlines pretty carefully what needs to happen, but her most important piece of instruction mirrors what Rona is hoping to have happen in her meetings outside class:

> Just plain talk about the book. Figure out what you don't understand. Try to come to a group consensus about what you think the book is all about. Find proof in the text to support it. Argue a little, in a spirited but civil kind of way. Try to enjoy yourselves.

In Lee's class, students report back in writing what they discuss. Rona's students are mostly left to work out the structure of their meetings on their own, but their reading journals often reflect their group's influence in their meaning-making process. It's apparent that the students use their groups to ask and answer questions, to clear up confusion, and at times to play ideas off one another.

Students keep reading journals — informal writing where they can feel safe to *not know* — that they share with their group members. These journals are an important independent aspect of the project. Students need to see how they develop their own ideas about a text — both as members of a group and as individuals influenced by experiences and ideas not necessarily shared by the entire group. Rona has her students do their writing outside class. In the last few years, these writing assignments have been one- or two-page letters that students do on their own and then exchange (and in this coming year, she will have her students write and post their letters in an online discussion board). In her assignment sheet, Rona emphasizes the importance of not knowing in the journal and letters:

> One of the beauties of keeping a reading journal is that you pretty much can't do it wrong. The journal is a space to work through, in writing, what's going through your head as you read. It is a space to not know but to work to know. The journal helps create a conversation between you as reader and the text and can anticipate later conversations that you may have with the rest of your group. Though there's no one way, really, to keep a journal, the most important thing to keep in mind is that the journal is not summary. It's analysis. It's response. It's rumination. It's a springboard for future thinking, writing, and talking.... The main point is what your ideas can open up for you and your group.

Lee gives students ten minutes at the beginning of each class to write what she calls their book club journals. She has also had students write them as e-mails directly to their student groups. The possibilities with electronic media are endless. Sometimes the journals are in response to a prompt — when students are having a particularly difficult time with the concept of analysis — but are usually an invitation to pursue a theory of the book. Whatever the format, we expect the writing that students produce here to be informal and messy. We hope that it will help the students discover and develop what Ann Berthoff calls "an idea [they] think...with" (109).

Here reading must be prioritized over writing. Yet saying that this project is designed to help students notice and understand the process of reading and then privileging writing—either in terms of workload on the students' part or evaluation on the instructor's—will not help students see the relation between reading and writing in any way different from the one they came to class with. They will be too worried about displays of correctness and not concerned about the search if they fear that they will be held accountable in traditional ways for the writing connected to the project. Again, the goal of the project is to have reading open up writing and writing open up reading and individual and group thinking to open up knowing.

Students do have two opportunities to do more polished writing that should call attention to and help make sense of the individual and group experiences. Students in the thick of the experience do not always see how the group is helping them make sense of a text. A more formal group project makes tangible to students what role the group has played in the process; it also shows the students that their teacher values the group part of the project. Students have to write a group paper about the book, about what they as a group decide the book ultimately values. This writing is brief, two pages, and is given a group grade.

Students finish the group part of the project by presenting their work to the rest of the class. In a class discussing different books, the students learn about other books they may one day choose to read. In a class discussing the same book, students hear how other groups experienced the text. They see how interpretation is multiple and how reading and knowing are social.

The final piece students produce is a cover letter that traces their individual meaning making over the course of the project. In this reflective piece, students address how they read their texts, both as individuals and with their group. As Rona writes in her assignment sheet, "The point of the project is to pay attention to how we make sense of things so we can be aware of them as we go to other texts. The cover letter is a place to crystallize these thoughts." Lee asks more specific questions to get the same answer.

Our student populations require that we set up the book clubs differently. For five years, Rona taught academically motivated and competitive students. Grade-conscious to a fault, many competing for a spot in the university's business school, they readily took on the out-of-class projects. Most recently, Lee has been teaching first-year students on academic probation. These students have no expectations in terms of grades and need the skills they lack modeled for them. These material differences affect the way the book clubs play out in the classroom.

What Our Students Tell Us

We now turn to an account of the experience as told by the work of a group of participating students. For a first-year writing class a few semesters ago, Rona's students read Toni Morrison's *Paradise*.[1] The most important component of the project and this discussion of it was the use of letters written among group members. In these letters, students do not hesitate to write about their confusion, uncertainty, difficulty, and struggle. They seem to accept that there will be struggle, that confusion is a part of the experience of reading this novel. The students' confusion comes from different sources and produces different effects. Sometimes the confusion speaks to a smaller picture — the difficulty of following the plot, say, or remembering which character was connected to which action. Other times their confusion involves broader questions about how to contextualize the story historically and how to understand what motivates the characters to act the way that they do.

Some students manage their confusion through questioning. Across the groups, the students' letters are driven by questions. Many times the students are content to let their questions hang in the air — hoping, perhaps, that other students will help them with their questions in either their own letters or in discussion — but sometimes they pursue them in writing. Margaret, one of the students who most explicitly states her love for and excitement about the book, consistently uses her letters to ask questions, to explain why she has doubt and confusion, and to try to answer the questions and clear up her confusion. In her second letter, she articulates one of her main questions: "One thing I keep asking myself is, what do these people arriving at the convent all have in common?" And then she immediately explains what she's come up with so far: "First of all, they are all women. Secondly, as far as I can tell, many of them have some sort of incident involving the death or illness of children." In her fifth letter, she asks a series of questions that not only explains her confusion with part of the book but that also, through the act of refining her question, shows the way her mind is working to make sense of the difficulty:

> Although I recognize the singularity between Connie and Deek, I don't entirely understand it. Did she so wholly give herself over to him that her eyes faded and his began to glow? I think they were probably always the same, I suspect he has some of the same "magic" that Connie does. Is Deek separated from his brother in this aspect? Is this part of why Steward never understood? Or does Steward see her adulterous relationship with Deek as violating the bargain for immortality? Also, how did Deek know to go to Connie, that she was so desolate? I can understand if she and he are one, yet what took him so long?!

Margaret ends that part of her letter with both a question mark and an exclamation point, showing that, in large part now, her question has become rhetorical: she has come up with an answer (Connie and Deek "are one") yet is frustrated with Deek for not moving sooner. Similarly, another student, Tone, at times uses his letters as a space to ask questions and then propose answers to them:

> As I have been saying, the theme of division resurfaces in this chapter. The more striking example is when Steward kills Connie. The division between the brothers is made extremely clear. Why does Morrison create a theme of division throughout her novel? Here is my best guess. The town of Ruby is symbolic for division, while the Convent is a symbol of unity....

Reading and writing both seem to be recursive acts for Margaret and Tone: they move back and forth between question and answer until they arrive at a different place.

In addition to questioning in their journals, students manage their confusion through group discussion. They rely on other group members to help answer their questions, stimulate their thinking with new questions, notice important details that they missed, push their thinking, and commiserate. In their cover letters, all seventeen students speak to the value of reading and writing in a group. Damon points to the generative nature of group work: "This is one of the important parts of group work, whereby one member introduces an idea or thought and then the rest of the group can explore it." Tone writes of how the group makes him articulate his ideas and at the same time complicates what he can do alone:

> My meaning making process was greatly aided by a group. This was because it allowed me to vocalize my ideas and hear other peoples as well. By doing so we were able to create a unique synthesis of our ideas and ultimately decipher the meaning behind *Paradise*. I don't think that I would have come up with our idea if I had not had the aid of a reading group. While I was able to create significant meaning from *Paradise* as an individual, a reading group allowed me to create a far more complex and abstract meaning.

Jean notes how collaboration works in different ways at different moments in the process:

> I feel that I would have never understood this story completely without the help of my group. All of our minds catching different parts, and analyzing in different ways helped to piece this complicated story together. Through the reading journals we were able to share what we understood at that time, and what we had questions about. By doing this we came up with the basic details of the story, but we still had many questions. It wasn't until we came together to discuss the book that the wholeness of the story began to evolve.

Kitty appreciates the accountability of group work:

> I enjoyed reading this book, and am glad that I read it in the contexts of this reading project. Knowing that I was reading this not just for myself, but with a group, made me read closer and analyze deeper than I normally do for school reading. In the end, to even slightly understand the book you had to be an engaged, attentive reader, which I was due to the format I was reading it in.

And Elizabeth, the collegiality:

> When our reading group met for the first time, I was glad to see that the others were just as baffled as I was. Also, we all had noticed the same basic themes throughout *Paradise*, however it was neat to talk about it and realize that even

though we were talking about the same theme, each one of us picked up different ideas and points to support the theme.

It's important to note that the book clubs redeem a practice that always gets a bad rap (group work) by demonstrating to students that meaning is not made by the individual alone but the individual in conversation (literally and figuratively) with others.

But students do more than simply comment on the role of the group in working out a reading of the novel: they give evidence of that role in writing. These students did amazing things in their reading projects — some that surprised us, some that didn't — but perhaps the most interesting was that they cited and credited one another in their letters. If we think about citation as the acknowledgment of — and respect for — intellectual property, then we have to determine that these students saw one another as knowledge makers, as people having ideas worth considering and acting on.

In part, these citations are small references — quick motions to how other students' readings of the novel affected theirs. Damon writes, "Thus, from Margaret's idea I was able to examine and explore one of the themes of the story." Jean notes, "Like Damon suggested the oven is of great significance to these people." Maggie: "Like Christopher I have seen that most of the characters are experiencing some kind of loss." And Julia: "Christopher got me thinking about the idea of absence that is shown throughout the book." At other times the students' acknowledgments are extensive and recognize an important insight, a project-changing idea:

> As a group we toyed around with writing about the empowerment of women in the novel. We all agreed that the women of the Convent were represented in a light of independence and freedom (especially at the end) while the married women of the town were represented in a miserable light. We also thought about the message of segregation, and how destructive it can be. There appeared to be more support for this message so we were all set to go with it when Jordan had a revelation that no one seemed to learn from their mistakes. It seemed so obvious that we were all struck by how we had missed it all the while we were talking about race, feminism, sexuality and division. Instantly we all were spitting out examples of people running, the women of the convent, the people of Ruby, Arnette. (Margaret)

We decided, although it was totally Kitty's idea, to each take a different way in which this desire to remain the same manifested itself and write about this. We then combined these in the same way Morrison combines her chapters, with our names as the headings. In other words, it was all of our opinions on what was the most important way in which the obsession with remaining the same led to Ruby's downfall. We then created a separate chapter called "Paradise" which we all wrote together and combined all of these different things into one solid theory, or thesis. (Jem)

When we met, I came up with the idea that the town always thought they were one step ahead of where they were. Then, Maggie came up with the idea that the book is always foreshadowing what is to come....Having four minds work together brought up ideas I wouldn't have come up with on my own. (Christopher)

In three of the four groups, at least one person credits another group member for the group's successful paper topic. And in none of these groups does the person who came up with the idea take credit for it. Given a very competitive academic environment with highly grade-conscious students, this generosity surprised us. And, as teachers who believe in the social construction of knowledge and in the value of collaboration in the classroom, it made us really happy.

Book clubs identify connections between reading and writing and demonstrate the collaborative nature of meaning making; they also make overt the ways reading is a recursive process of hypothesis testing. In their cover letters, students discuss their reading practices during the book club with an analytic distance that helps them make note of and modify reading practices in a new way. Students name rereading as one of their most important meaning-making strategies. Jem calls rereading "a really useful tool," and Margaret calls it her "greatest asset to understanding":

For the purposes of the letters (although I would have done so even if I didn't have to write them) I would go back over the two chapters or so that I read and use the knowledge that I had by the end of them to make sense of the beginning. I would underline some more and motifs and themes would begin to take shape in my mind. Questions I had scribbled down earlier in the novel were slowly answered as my reading progressed.

Students developed other strategies for making sense of *Paradise*, including taking notes, underlining, and making family trees. Julia writes that these were strategies she had to learn for this novel:

> Usually when I read a book I never outline parts. I just read it straight through hoping I find my way. With this book, however, I quickly realized that I had to change my ways. I had to be conscious to underline parts and mark pages. This turned out to be much more useful for writing letters to my group and for when it came down to the time to find a central theme.

We can't know, of course, if Julia will take these strategies with her into other reading experiences, but we argue that she is more likely to, since she has not just worked out the strategy for herself but also articulated and identified it for herself as a successful one.

Although we have demonstrated the effectiveness of the concept of the book club, the question still remains: Why novels in the writing class-room? We believe the answer lies in the role difficulty plays in the project. In "Conversations with Texts," Mariolina Salvatori writes about the value of the "difficulty paper," an assignment that she uses with her students. It has a pedagogical approach that foregrounds difficulty not as moments of students' (or any reader's) inadequacies but rather as "a reflexive strategy" that "eventually allows them to recognize that what they perceive as 'difficult' is a feature of the text demanding to be critically engaged rather than ignored" (448). Salvatori leads a discussion of possible reasons for students' struggle:

> Does difficulty arise because a reader's expectations blind her to a text's clues? Or because the method of reading a reader is accustomed to performing will not work with this particular text? Is it exacerbated when inexperienced readers assume that difficulties are an indictment of their abilities rather than characteristic features of a text? (448)

Salvatori concludes:

> What is remarkable about this approach is that students' descriptions of difficulties almost inevitably identify a crucial feature of the text they are reading and contain *in nuce* the interpretative move necessary to handle them. They

might say for example that they had "difficulty" with a text because it presented different and irreconcilable positions on an issue—their "difficulty" being in fact an accurate assessment of that text's argument. (448)

This kind of reading is highly reflective and requires a great deal of faith in one's own abilities. The students are much more willing to make the leap if they see their peers making the leap as well.

We argue that the thoughtfulness and intricacy of student work stems from the sheer difficulty of the project, which is brought into the classroom using substantial, fictional texts. *Paradise* is a difficult text on many levels: chronologically, the narrative moves out of time, and the omniscient narrator withholds information; thematically, the novel challenges assumptions at every turn. Even very experienced readers find themselves in unfamiliar territory. If students were going to gain any understanding of this text, they would have to ask a lot of questions of it. Seeing their group members ask questions helped them recognize that their not knowing or understanding pointed not to their deficiencies as readers but to the "interpretative cruxes" of the text. The students needed one another's help to enter into conversation with *Paradise*.

While these students certainly had moments when they thought, "She must be saying something I just cannot understand" and "It does not make sense," they generally avoided entrapment and found ways out of confusion and into understanding by bringing other voices into their conversations with their texts. In other words, one way to weather the difficulty is through collaboration, or community. And, reciprocally, the community is upheld or supported by the difficulty. The project needed to be difficult in order for students to need and value one another as useful meaning makers.

It's not enough, in the book club assignment, for the book to be difficult. The structure of the book club must offer students ways of working with dense and difficult texts. Students' writing encourages dialogue, group work furthers that dialogue by creating a real audience, and that audience demonstrates the collaborative nature of making sense of the text. And it is important that these elements work together because — as with juggling or the fox-trot — it's how the various critical moments happen at once that is both wonderful and impossible but still true. Book clubs derive much of their usefulness from their longitudinal complexity, an important part of unveiling the intricacies, and glories, of reading.

Because of space restrictions, we can't tell you everything these students did — and didn't do — in their rich and complicated projects. We're not showing you the insightful final analyses that the groups wrote — analyses that teach us a lot about *Paradise*. We're not telling you about the group that didn't come together, the group with the tattler, and the group in which one student took all the credit for the final paper idea. And we're not telling you about how insular these groups were, how students didn't draw on experiences and knowledges outside this class to make meaning of *Paradise*, even though they were encouraged to — and even though we've seen students do so (sometimes excessively) in other book club settings.

We never intended to set up the book club as foolproof. No project is. But we have found few other projects that let us do so much complicated and important literacy work at once: collaborative learning, reading as process, writing as process, theorizing the complexity of meaning making. The book club puts students in dynamic situations as meaning makers, gives them a structure through which to see themselves in action, and provides them with a language to talk about the critical work they're doing so that they can take it with them to their next projects, projects in and out of school.

Toward an End

Book clubs serve a practical function in the college writing classroom: students who are often not particularly proficient readers and are not interested in becoming so get much needed practice in careful reading. And reading helps students become better writers for a host of reasons. First-year writing is usually part of the general education requirements for most colleges and universities, and so it makes sense that the course should help students learn the skills they need to navigate the rest of their course work.

We are unwilling to let reading go from our classrooms because of the role that general education is supposed to play in the lives of our students. What are the liberal arts for students who don't read? Lee teaches at an institution with a new degree in criminal justice and a respected degree in aviation science. How can the liberal arts speak to the future police officers and pilots (both military and commercial)? At her institution, the humanities professors are sometimes skeptical of those majors. But rather than ignore these students, we can teach them to be thoughtful police officers and pilots. And isn't that what we are supposed to do?

Equally important to the mission of general education requirements as part of a liberal arts education — which is often the only way the traditional liberal arts is incorporated into professionalized degree programs — is the understanding of the critical work involved in reading and writing as well as the effects that work has in the world. Paulo Freire tells us that one true word can change the world (75). But what does that mean? What does a true word look like? What sort of criteria do we use to decide? And how does such a word ultimately change the world? Answers to these complex questions are not easy to come by. And teaching our students that these are important questions to ask and that they are not easily answered is the work of first-year writing and general education. To understand reading and writing as highly creative acts of interpretation, steeped in purpose and able to develop critical literacy, takes something more tangible than talk. Reading in the writing classroom, layered with other projects that echo the important themes in our classes, helps us make real both what critical literacy means and how we get it done.

Our practice reclaims reading for the writing classroom. Reading and literature were long seen as fine and delicate, designed for advanced students who were serious about studying the great traditions of Western civilization. But reading is much less rarefied than that. It is, simply, what makes us both human and humane. And so it makes sense that composition classrooms incorporate the reading of literature, that students study literature not for its finer aesthetic qualities but for the practice it gives new writers in the difficult but vital work of critical analysis.

Any compositionist coming through a PhD program, as we did, in the last decade of the twentieth century can recite the cruel and difficult history between literature and composition in English departments, starting at Harvard in the 1890s. But in all that history, there is one question we, as teachers and scholars, come back to over and over again: What have we lost in relinquishing reading in first-year writing over the years because of this battle? Other questions tumble out from there. How has making reading, and in particular literature, a part of a turf war helped us help our students? How has the debate about what students read in our writing classrooms overshadowed how they read — a question that is far more relevant and of infinitely more interest to writing teachers? (As we ask these questions, we are aware that an entire generation of compositionists working to define our discipline, often by not talking about literature, made it possible for us to ask them now.)

We do not write to say that teachers must use literature to teach writing, that nonfiction or genre fiction isn't ripe with possibility to do what we outline above. But we do believe, as Louise Rosenblatt does in *Literature as Exploration*, that reading creative texts (and teachers and readers can decide for themselves what that means) puts students in touch with that particular and elusive critical muscle that allows them to identify with (or not), interpret, and otherwise make sense of their world — not just of the books they read in class. A liberal arts education is supposed to develop this ability.

We didn't set out to reference Rona's mother time and again in this piece, but right is right: a liberal arts education is about not being good at only one thing. Composition can play a clear role in a liberal arts education. Our subject is the complexities, the tools, the mindset, the ethics of critical inquiry, and the various forms such inquiry takes: reading, writing, thinking. Reading is a particularly accessible way to open a conversation about the nature and process of critical inquiry in the classroom. It introduces students to a reading life — to reading life.

Note

1. Of the seventeen students in the class, eleven were women and six were men. Fifteen students were in their first year; two (both women) were in their second year. Three students, all women, were student athletes. Sixteen students identified themselves as white; one as Asian. Eleven students were from Michigan; the others were from Illinois, Vermont, Maryland, New Jersey, and California. All students willingly agreed to be part of this study, and all chose pseudonyms.

Language, Metaphor, and Textuality

Language and Metaphor:
The Ways We Think in Words

Background: First-Year Writing at Indiana University

Christine R. Farris

My editorial collaboration with Judith Anderson would not have been possible without the relationship between literature and composition in the Indiana University Department of English. The history of this relationship includes various initiatives and courses aimed at bridging the gaps between literature and composition, scholarship and teaching, theory and practice. As discussed in our introduction, this history defines our situation. At the graduate level, we have long had a doctoral concentration, not in composition and rhetoric per se, but in composition and literacy studies, which has made possible scholarly projects that juxtapose historical, linguistic, literary, ethnographic, and pedagogical work. At the undergraduate level, for over twenty-five years, Indiana University students have been able to meet the composition proficiency requirement by taking either one semester of elementary composition or two semesters of introduction to the study of literature and writing, typically taught as a large faculty lecture with multiple discussion sections led by graduate associate instructors. There is considerable cross-fertilization between the elementary composition and the literature/composition courses, and interaction among literature faculty members, associate instructors, and composition faculty members, who also teach literature. The elementary composition course stresses critical reading and analytic writing about a variety of cultural texts. It is not unusual to find that strategies emphasized in the composition course for analyzing patterns, binaries, and anomalies in the language and images

---

Judith H. Anderson and Christine R. Farris

of newspaper stories, photographs, film scenes, and critical essays (what Rosenwasser and Stephen call "the method" [44]) have entered the teaching lore of the whole department.

A Preparing Future Faculty (PFF) initiative began my collaboration with Judith. Funded by our graduate school and the Pew Foundation to integrate the teaching and scholarly experiences of doctoral students, the PFF grant enabled another literature colleague, Mary Favret, and me to design, with input from several other faculty members, a semester-long "proseminar" in the teaching of literature and culture, subsequent to one on the teaching of composition.[1] The department felt that if our PhDs were to meet the challenges of hiring English departments, their education would have to forge a stronger connection between research and teaching, as well as between composition and literature, and involve a greater number of faculty members in teacher preparation. Judith volunteered to teach this second proseminar. In it, she collaborated with graduate students in literature, who had already been trained to teach composition, in the design and eventual implementation of a first-year English course for nonmajors that integrated literature and writing and centered on the topic of language and metaphor. We had long conversations about the challenges of the experiment: How might "literary" language form the basis of a course aimed at developing first-year students' critical reading and writing? How much writing could reasonably be assigned to freshmen? And perhaps the biggest challenge, How would we reconfigure the faculty member–graduate student and scholar-teacher relationships and the "ownership" of the new first-year course?

Even though our English department regularly assigns graduate students as assistants for large literature classes, it offered the assistants no systematic preparation to teach literature. Our teacher training, while rigorous and effective, had been tied primarily to the elementary composition courses. Before the first semester of teaching composition, associate instructors attend a week-long orientation, take the first semester-long proseminar with a composition faculty member, and meet in small groups with a senior mentor instructor. Teaching from a common syllabus, these new instructors discuss their pedagogy, assemble teaching portfolios that include case studies of student writers and assignments, and revise the syllabus to make it their own. All the while, through reflective practice, they are contributing to an ever-changing writing curriculum.

In 1994, we had the opportunity to redesign the first-year composition course, the basis of the associate instructor training. I shifted the focus from decontextualized argument to analysis, not of imaginative writing—literature—but of other kinds of representations of gender, race, class, and ethnicity in a variety of texts, both printed and visual. In their other graduate courses, our instructors were becoming increasingly familiar with semiotics and cultural studies, turns in English studies that complicate composition theory and yet can still shape a pedagogy that is responsive to what we and our colleagues across the curriculum find dissatisfying about student writing. As a writing-across-the-curriculum consultant I had discovered that much of what faculty members consider ineffective, boring, and just plain bad about undergraduate writing is rooted in students' cultural misunderstandings: in their perceptions that experience is universally the same for everyone and that cultural texts of all sorts mirror that experience unproblematically. When faculty members are disappointed with student writing in ways that do not have to do with error, it is often because students cannot get beyond merely agreeing or disagreeing, delivering back commonplaces or ventriloquizing the positions of the expert critics they read. Writing research papers that synthesize multiple sources in the manner of academic scholars is not enough to develop in students the tolerance, let alone the desire, for complexity that most faculty members would like to see them demonstrate (Farris, "Too Cool" 98).

The curriculum I designed (and have since improved with my composition colleague John Schilb and many associate instructors) is aimed not only at making the moves of academic writing visible to those who do not necessarily intuit them but also at making students more active, critical subjects, aware of how academic discourse works and how language and visual representations invite them to occupy various and sometimes conflicting positions as readers. It is important that a first-year English course do more than just usher students through the stages of the writing process, regardless of topic, or invite them, as David Bartholomae says, to "invent the university" by patching together the received interpretations of experts. Our aim is that students become more active interpreters of culture as part of their reading and writing processes and that they come to understand the extent to which any texts they construct are located within cultural frameworks. As Robert Scholes, Nancy Comley, and Gregory Ulmer have suggested, and as Judith Anderson's course exemplifies, an awareness that textual forms and language are culturally and socially shaped can empower students when they are given opportunities to "work and play" with texts, both literary and nonliterary, in ways that encourage their "understanding of fundamental textual processes" rather than their "passive submission" to "a collection of 'master' works" (xv).

When you up the ante in first-year English from a set of skills or stages in a process — hard enough for new graduate instructors to teach in the old days — to postmodern notions of reading, writing, and representation, the instructors' work, even with a common syllabus and a great deal of mentoring, gets harder. But as someone responsible for preparing new graduate instructors in the teaching of writing in a department that has a PhD program centering primarily on literature, I wanted, as did cooperating colleagues, to see the teaching preparation program and support system continue and become even more integrated with scholarship throughout English studies, as graduate students moved into the teaching of first-year literature / composition courses and eventually into lower-division, writing-intensive literature courses. Thanks to the successful piloting of faculty members like Judith, advanced graduate students now have the option of enrolling in a second pedagogy seminar (after the one on composition) in preparation for teaching a section of the freshman-level Introduction to the Study of Literature and Writing. As noted earlier, the department has long offered this course as a large lecture with five to six discussion sections. Now, when the course follows the second pedagogy proseminar, the common syllabus is the collaborative product that the instructional team is not just imagining but actually scheduled to teach. So far, about ten different versions of the pedagogy seminar have emerged from various research areas in the department: Literary Representations of Violence; Writing Disaster; Literature and War; Literature and Animal Rights; The Literature of Passing; Language, Metaphor, and Thought; Literature and Medicine; and From Manuscripts to Microchips.

For a director of composition, responsible for training thirty to forty graduate instructors each year, this innovation represents not only an integration of the concerns of English studies but also a possible redivision of labor. What often works against efforts to raise the status of composition studies in English is the arrangement obvious to those first entering the discipline. Key to graduate students' view of teaching as an intellectual enterprise, particularly the teaching of writing, is their awareness of whose capital is tied to pedagogy and first-year English. The ways in which our colleagues and graduate students at Indiana have expanded their scholarly relationships to include pedagogy, formerly the domain only of the writing specialists, have been encouraging. Employing various means of assessment, we remain vigilant that these collaborations still provide valuable reading and writing experiences for first-year students, whose instruction cannot take a backseat to the education of graduate students (Farris and Favret 18). But as we slowly reshape the curricular and institutional space that composition and literature occupy, we can at least begin to imagine these two enterprises on an equal basis under a future professoriate that views the teaching of both as legitimate and satisfying intellectual work.

Foreground: Literature and Writing Instruction at Indiana University
Judith H. Anderson

My story about the first-year course in literature and composition that I taught with five graduate assistants (associate instructors, or AIs) at Indiana University begins with the training in teaching composition the graduate students had already received, which Christine Farris described in the preceding section; it proceeds next to a graduate course on teaching literature with a writing component and concludes with the first-year undergraduate course itself and the graduate students' written reflection on this pedagogical experience. My part in this story, the two middle stages, occupies the remainder of this essay. I would stress here that these middle stages are inseparable: the undergraduate course is the product of the graduate course, where its theoretical and pedagogical underpinnings are found, and it is also where the graduate students' training is actualized. Without the graduate course and the AIs trained in it, the multisectioned undergraduate course I describe would have been unimaginable. Its success validated the training, commitment, and contribution of the AIs every bit as much as it did my initial conception. In short, instead of being freestanding, this first-year course existed within a program and resulted from a process.

Planning and Preparation: Underpinning with Theory and Pedagogy

When I offered a pedagogically oriented graduate course called Language, Metaphor, and Thought, which was to eventuate in an option combining literature and composition for first-year undergraduates, I considered it both practically and conceptually an experiment. Enrollment in the course was limited to six students; the six students and I would each teach a section in the following fall semester. There were to be three fifty-minute section meetings a week in the undergraduate course, plus a weekly lecture of the same duration for all the sections together—a total of one hundred fifty brand new college students. We scheduled the lecture in the early evening to make it more of an event on our residential campus and to enable all seven sections—meeting consecutively from 8:00 to 5:00—to be at the same stage of discussion. The AIs and I lectured about equally (two lectures apiece for them, three for me), intending the lectures as a different type of learning from the discussion sections. The lectures allowed us to model an approach or introduce some of the larger ideas in the course, which then could be treated in textually embedded extensions and in more detailed, hands-on ways in the sections.

Our purpose in the graduate course was to conceive the content of the first-year course, to explore ways of teaching it, and to produce a syllabus. Our discussion of teaching was to continue when we taught the undergraduate course, conferring in weekly two-hour meetings in which we compared teaching experiences and discussed classroom texts, negotiated the next writing assignment proposed (in written detail) by one of us for all sections, and considered optimal ways to relate the sections to the coming week's lecture, whose general focus had already been announced on the syllabus. Given the subject I chose for the first-year course, not an immediate hit such as "best sellers" or "the genre of the comic book," I acknowledged that it would be a challenge to make the course a success, but I also believed that the effort was worth making and could be successful. The place of language in thought, creativity, and the more general production of culture is to me what first-year English should be about.

The focus of our first-year course was squarely on language — on the basics, especially the conceptual ones. I was tired of hearing new undergraduates remark that they had expected college to be less like high school. I wanted to challenge them. Our gamble in the course was that if we could not only persuade students of the fundamental role language plays in thinking but actually make them more aware of their own thinking in language, especially metaphoric language, they would be more attentive to their reading and writing processes. This goal meant putting content and understanding first and expecting students progressively to achieve broader, more lasting results for reading and writing and also to achieve results for writing per se more gradually than in a course devoted primarily or exclusively to composition. The option that included our course carried literature and composition credit in the general education program and required a commitment of two semester courses; the other composition option only required one. That is, our course afforded a whole year to work on composition.

The graduate students who signed up for Language, Metaphor, and Thought were required to have taken the proseminar in the teaching of composition and to have taught at least one semester of composition, and they all were to have had a second semester of it behind them when we taught our undergraduate course. I could thus rely on these students' knowing from instruction and experience how to teach composition. Three of them had considerably more experience in the writing program, and, not surprisingly, I learned as much about teaching writing from my AIs as they did from me. They represented various concentrations in the English department: two Victorianists; one Americanist straddling the nineteenth and twentieth centuries; two early modernists, one minoring in philosophy and the other in drama; and a modernist with a minor in film. All clearly had an interest in the topic.[2] Our different backgrounds, which could have been a problem in another course, proved highly relevant to our success.

I divided the graduate course into three roughly equal emphases: pedagogy, theory, and application, the last being the invention of our first-year syllabus. These emphases overlapped: the pedagogical issues engaged the teaching of texts that highlighted language; we talked about ways of translating theoretical abstractions into terms first-year students might grasp; and our eventual first-year syllabus was designed precisely with such issues in mind. We began by reviewing relevant published textbooks such as *Language Awareness* (Eschholz, Rosa, and Clark), which anthologizes readings about language, and *Text Book* (Scholes, Comley, and Ulmer), which focuses more on literary language and form. We read and talked about the suitability of the readings, evaluated the questions and written exercises included, considered ways of presenting the material to a first-year class, and invented alternative writing assignments, especially imaginative ones designed to provoke an awareness of language as a medium. We used such textbooks to brainstorm but also kept in mind that we would probably use one or more of them in whole or in part in our own course; in the end we did not use these texts, although they would serve excellently in courses somewhat different from what ours turned out to be.

Changing emphasis in the second third of the course, we focused on readings about metaphor, which reflect various theories of language: empiricist and rationalist, speech act, structural, phenomenological, subjectivist, deconstructist, neocognitivist, and so on. Major texts were George Lakoff and Mark Johnson's *Metaphors We Live By* (as a simple representative of cognitive science humanistically conceived) and Sheldon Sacks's collection *On Metaphor*, but we also read extensive selections from Johnson's *Philosophical Perspectives on Metaphor*. We looked into the debate about the etymological basis of metaphor in Paul Ricoeur's *Rule of Metaphor* and Jacques Derrida's "White Mythology," which raises fundamental questions about the relation of language to history, and we topped these off with Derek Attridge's contribution in *Post-structuralism and the Question of History*.[3] Attridge's essay deals at length with Ferdinand de Saussure's ideas about language, with which my graduate students professed acquaintance but from which I would include specific readings if I were to teach the same course again.

Our first faculty guest, a philosopher with a remarkable knack for making logical abstraction exciting to undergraduates, came to us during the pedagogically oriented first third of the course, but our other four faculty guests, all in English, came during the second third to talk about lecturing to first-year students. Their presentations, interspersed with the theoretical reading, kept us in touch with applications. After the presentations about lecturing, our next reading was Johnson's forty-odd-page introductory history of traditional and modern theories of metaphor (the Greeks to the moderns), and we discussed whether and how it might be made into an accessible, engaging lecture for first-year students.

The final third of the course was the high point for all of us. Here, after talking about the general shape of the syllabus and looking at the various syllabi that I had collected from colleagues, we considered each graduate student's nominations for the syllabus: prose fiction, essays and articles, poems, cartoons, advertisements, and so on. Each provided photocopies for all of us to read before our discussion (short novels were excerpted to give us a fair sense of them), and each had a full class day to present her or his texts, reasons for choosing them, and possible approaches to them. I had also distributed a few of my own nominations earlier in the course. Once the presentations were finished, I drafted a fairly detailed syllabus based on them and asked each of the students to rough one out as well, a project whose difficulty they admitted they had underestimated. So had I: since we had accumulated far more possibilities for the syllabus than we could use and since everyone had favored texts, some tough choices, imaginative adjustments, and negotiations were needed first in framing a syllabus and then in agreeing to its final form. The result surprised us all and continued to do so when we actually taught it: what we had was a syllabus far richer than any of us could ever have dreamed of producing alone. The unique result of the process of theorizing content and pedagogy that we had undertaken, this syllabus was fundamental to the success of the undergraduate course.

Our syllabus aside, we still wondered whether our course, now entitled Language and Metaphor: The Ways We Think in Words, would have sufficient enrollment in the fall for us to teach it. Fortunately, our course turned out to be the most popular choice of its peers during registration: it filled quickly. Its success when actually taught led us to teach it again the following year, with the same positive reception. Despite thirty years of teaching at Indiana University, I was surprised that an average mix of first-semester students—drawn from all schools of the university, not just from the College of Arts and Sciences—would respond with as much interest as they did.

Teaching the First-Year Course: Provisional Result of a Continuing Process

Roughly the first third of our undergraduate syllabus focused on language. From the start, we wanted the spotlight on the linguistic medium that not only expresses but also shapes and informs our thinking—on the glue that bonds writing and literature, understood both broadly and narrowly. Our aim was to cultivate habits of mind common to the cultures of composition and literature, which, in accord with current neocognitive theory, I prefer to imagine ambidexterously as the right and left hands of a whole person. Thus our plan was to lay a foundation on which we could erect an increasingly complex structure of reading and digesting, talking and listening, writing and understanding—of making knowledge one's own. Given the abstraction of our focus on language and metaphor, the ways in which we made the topic accessible to beginning college students must, in the interest of understanding and credibility, be treated in sufficient detail. In fact, how we made this topic accessible is the pedagogical crux, the proof of the syllabus pudding, so to speak.[4]

In the fall semester, I gave the first two lectures, which coordinated with work in the sections. Our major text for the first week was the dictionary, and in discussion sections during this week, we used photocopied pages from two full-size desk dictionaries, either of which we had required the students to buy, and also some pages from a 1948 dictionary defining black and white. We worked with the lexical entries, which, I was startled to realize, the first-year students did not understand. The problem came not just with the abbreviation; it involved the basic grammatical concept—certainly the distinction between a transitive and intransitive verb but even that between a noun and verb. Besides demystifying these lexical mysteries, we talked more generally about dictionary definitions: what they consist of, how to describe their range of meaning, whether etymology adds anything to our knowledge, how dictionary writers (or we) decide on pronunciation, the difference between language as a system (*langue*) and as a speech act (*parole*), in what way a word defined in a dictionary actually refers to something outside the dictionary, and what words might have to do with thinking. Our only reading for this week was a brief excerpt from *The Autobiography of Malcolm X* (170–73) in which the author tells how he copied out the pages of an entire dictionary, entry by entry, when he was in prison in order to become capable of communicating in an idiom other than street talk. Malcolm relates how his lexical transcription enabled him to understand books and to think in new ways—sometimes, as our 1948 dictionary suggested, in culturally loaded ways, since words are far from neutral or innocent. Even Malcolm's copying (not highlighting!) each entry, instead of merely reading it, played into our larger conception of the relationship between writing and understanding—grasping, as a neocognitivist like Andy Clark might put it.

The initial lecture was "Words, Dictionaries, and the Mental Lexicon." In the sections immediately before it, we had distributed an exercise that the students were to write for the final section meeting of the week. Entitled "When does the dictionary end?" (a question formulated by the AI Jonathan Hillman), this exercise had four steps: looking up about a dozen specified words in a comprehensive, current dictionary (e.g., *truth, concept, fiction, tree, name, dense, warm, blue*); inventing or hypothesizing an explanation of the etymology of the verb *invest* or *signify* in a brief paragraph; and for two of the nouns listed above, looking up all the main words in the primary definition (the first or first two given). Then, for one of the same nouns, the students were to write a paragraph describing what conclusion or discovery looking up all these words had led to and why. (Students uncertain about a conclusion were invited to look up all the main words in the definitions of the words within the definitions of the two nouns with which they had started.) Many students found the dictionary endless, as well they might have.

Since this initial evening lecture was a novel experience for most of the first-year students, we provided a handout for note taking with questions that highlighted the structure of the lecture:

1. What is a dictionary? What does it have to do with fiction?
2. Alphabetical order: since when and with what implications?
3. What does etymology ("true speech") tell us?
4. Reference: what is this word-thing problem?
5. How is the mental lexicon organized? What role do prototypes play?

The overarching theme of this lecture was the fictiveness or constructed-ness of language — language as a "system of symbolic behavior," as the *American Heritage College Dictionary* puts it — with the dictionary itself as a prime index of the values, attitudes, education, art, and government of a society. In the lecture, I paused over the meaning of *system* — a group of interrelated elements — and glossed *symbolic* simply as "representational." I also asked the students for the meaning of *fiction*, which they hadn't looked up yet, and repeatedly heard variants of "untruth" before hearing anything remotely resembling "imagination." I talked next about the changing mean-ings of words, as evidenced by *black* and *white* in the older and newer lexical entries we had examined in sections and by such a word as *inconvenient*, which in Elizabethan times had a less trivial import than nowadays.

I also spoke about the history of the dictionary since its establishment as a cultural fixture, about four hundred years ago, and especially about alphabetical order as a conspicuous characteristic of it. I used as an over-head a dictionary page showing schematically the development of our alphabet from ancient semitic forms through Greek, Etruscan, and Roman ones to those relatively more recent to stress the fictionality of the alphabet itself, as well as of alphabetical order, which has become like second nature to us. In comparison with alphabetical order, other, older ways of ordering words, such as topics (farming, music), grammar (nouns, verbs), sounds (vowels, consonants), logical categories (genus, species), or hierarchical status (higher to lower) seem more closely to reflect nature or objective reality, and, in comparison with them, the alphabet is much more abstract (Anderson, *Words* 53–70). Here a couple of overheads of seventeenth-century English alphabets whose letters are formed by human bodies, often in comically ungainly poses, came in handy, since they could be glossed as responses to anxiety about the lack of any real connection between language and the objective world (Goldberg 227–28).

The lecture also treated etymology as another feature of the dictionary, and it engaged the popular conception that because etymology gives us the history of a word, through it we are getting back to the thing or action that is the basis of the word—its "truth," so to speak—when all we're really getting back to is another word or words and therefore an earlier stage of language. From this point we segued to a related question that the very existence of a dictionary urges, the question of reference: how does language refer to the world?

Here an overhead illustration of the word-thing problem from Jean Aitchison's *Words in the Mind* was helpful. The illustration consists of a human head looking at a flower in a flowerpot, labeled "thing"; above the head is a thought bubble, in which is a similar but not wholly identical flower, labeled "concept"; and apart from it, under the label "word," is FLOWER in bold type. The illustration shows how words are linked to things by means of concepts. It could mislead by suggesting that a concept is a mental image of the thing, but on close examination, subtle differences between the real flower and the one in the thought bubble suffice to separate them. The picture was useful in showing the difference (and the distance) between word and thing—the space for potential disconnects and misperceptions—and in showing how language might become a self-enclosed system, a world (or thought bubble) of its own.

Returning to the subject of reference and to the dictionary for an example, I covered the potted flower (the object "out there") in the overhead with my hand and noted that when you encounter a word in the dictionary, it exists on the level of the thought bubble. Strictly speaking, it doesn't refer. The thought bubble is language and what is in the thought bubble is inside language. *Flower* is the entry word listed in the dictionary, and the concept *flower* is the meaning or definition of the entry word: both are in the thought bubble, or language. Again strictly speaking, then, a word in a dictionary only refers when a language user directs it at some specific thing—such as a flower growing in a flowerpot—in a specific act, such as speech or writing.

The remainder of the lecture drew on Aitchison's research into the mental lexicon, the dictionary in our heads: its size (forty to fifty thousand words, not counting proper names and idiomatic phrases) and its organization, which is not alphabetical. Some evidence of its organization is based on malapropisms, which, together with a "malaproping" *Frank and Ernest* cartoon, afforded more welcome comedy in a talk as conceptual as this one. Interestingly, all the organizational models point to a selection of words that is comparative or differential, both of their meanings and of their sounds.

One of the most interesting differences between the book dictionary and the mental lexicon involves prototypes, what Aitchison describes (and illustrates pictorially) as little mental models or categories that mix observation, cultural beliefs, and personal interpretations. Whereas a dictionary tells us that peacocks, penguins, sparrows, parrots, robins, and finches are all birds, it doesn't distinguish which of these are "birdier" or more typical. Apparently, people do. Experiments have shown that we classify examples in such categories as birds, vegetables, and furniture according to the extent to which they represent the prototypical form in each category: a robin, a pea, a chair. Of further interest, young children use prototypes peculiar to their limited experience but revise (and normalize) these as they get older. Since prototypes convincingly play a role in our ability to categorize and to think, they are susceptible to stereotyping; what is promising, however, is the fact, evidenced in the cognitive development of children, that our prototypes can change. Clearly, they might be harder to change when we are older, but the cognitive ability to do so is a human endowment. First-year students need hope, as well as critique.

In the discussion section that followed the lecture and concluded the first week, the students handed in their one-page responses to the exercise sheet "When does the dictionary end?" A good number of them (more the second year than the first) concluded that words lead you to other words. Here, we all could talk about deferral and differentiation without the premature burden of an alien terminology, such as Saussure's or Derrida's. We could talk about the way one word turns into another or is like another or the way metaphor keeps sneaking in. We also discussed the definitions of the more difficult words assigned, such as *opaque, warm, dense, blue*, and *pink*, and the etymology of *invest*, the more interesting of the students' options. We ran out of time in the class, rather than out of topics.

The second week provided more of a challenge for relating the lecture to the sections. The lecture, "Naming and Categories," concerned another set of necessary conceptual basics, but the discussion sections and the one-page writing assignment were focused on readings expressing ideas about and attitudes toward language: the first two chapters of Helen Keller's *Story of My Life*, Addie's sole chapter in William Faulkner's *As I Lay Dying*, and the chapter on the language reformers of Jonathan Swift's Academy of Laputa in *Gulliver's Travels*.

While "snippetry" is a dubious practice, the reading selections for this week (and others) were excerpted to ensure a steady focus on language, rather than on the characters, the plot, or some other center of a longer text, for which the students initially yearn, since this is what they are used to dealing with. A key strategy of the course was to focus steadily on language in a sufficient variety of texts and applications to sustain interest. With respect to language, our focus thus ensured that there was nowhere to hide. Keller's autobiography demonstrates the necessity of language to thought and humanity, as we ordinarily understand it, as well as the intellectual liberation of language. Almost as effectively, Faulkner's Addie argues that language is an unnatural barrier between us emotionally and physically that should be bypassed. The contrast between these two texts is electrifying for students. It urges debate and begins to introduce the sorts of contrasts among readings that would later provide prompts for our formal papers.

For Keller's autobiography, we discussed how her teacher tried to make her aware of the ability of language to categorize things by putting a different doll in her lap and how the running water finally led Keller to see that language identifies and distinguishes things. We talked about the blind and deaf Keller's metaphor of a fog for her prelinguistic awareness and her "wordless sensation," as opposed to a thought; about her discovery that "each name gave birth to a new thought"; and about the process of abstraction that she grappled with (21, 23–24). We did a close reading of Addie's brief but difficult chapter, looking at how she defines her identity, her opinion of words, and how it contrasts with Keller's and how she characterizes Anse, her husband, and connects his nothingness with words and specifically with his name.

This second seminal lecture began by relating the contrast between Addie's and Keller's attitudes toward language to the function of words (the human head and the flowerpot) in the preceding lecture. Whereas for Addie, words are "shape[s] to fill a lack," empty substitutes for living, Keller finds through words the ability to think, to divide the world into identifiable parts, and thus to categorize and understand what is in it (164). Anchored in these two short texts, the lecture turned to naming, the process by which we separate the world we experience into knowable parts. Names are words: proper names like Sarah or Jason are just a subcategory of words and work the way other words do. They separate and distinguish us. Insofar as they do, names like Sarah or Jason function much as other names, such as "salt" or "pepper," do. Again Aitchison's studies proved useful, as did an article by William Labov, "The Boundaries of Words and Their Meanings." These sources provided illustrations of the kinds of shapes — vases, cups, mugs, glasses, bowls, plates — that linguists have used to test the human process of distinction and categorization. I had an overhead of five objects like these, with and without handles, and another of roughly twenty containers with handles, varying gradually from one another. Some container shapes were as familiar as a cup and others as odd as a goblet or a tricornered, hollow container with a handle. Pointing at specific shapes, I asked, "What is this?" or "What is this now?," to which the students called out answers. I also asked for the basis of the identifying labels in each example and sometimes pressed further. The point of this game was, first, to demonstrate how language labels and separates things and, second, to suggest how fuzzy, interpretative, and somewhat arbitrary our labels and categories are. To ask these questions was also to double back on the subject of prototypes at the end of the preceding lecture. In my own section the day before, I had similarly asked the students to picture in their minds a Texan. The result: a man in his twenties, tall and athletic, wearing a cowboy hat, boots, and jeans. Point made? Are there not female Texans, for example?

Imperfect as our labels and categories might be, they remain a basic tool of thought and much more: they are shapers, models, and encoders (containers) of thought, and it is on this fundamental point—at once fascinating and unsettling for students—that the lecture focused throughout. As a final way of realizing the significance of names in our culture, we used the last ten to fifteen minutes to show the beginning of the award-winning video *Maya Lin: A Strong Clear Vision*, which is about Maya Lin's designing of the Vietnam War Memorial when Lin was a student of art, architecture, and sculpture at Yale. This memorial consists largely of names in chronological order, by date of death, and the names are inscribed on a reflecting surface of polished black stone. Lin's design therefore reflects our society's interest in recording and distinguishing people and times, but it also shows an interest in blending viewer and monument, past and present. As the video makes dramatically clear, when you look at the monument you are reflected in the polished surface, and the names of the dead are written on your image. The memorial both reflects us and asks us to go beyond the usual borders of ourselves—of our own names, in this instance—to see ourselves in others and others in ourselves.

In the final section meeting of this week, I divided my time between Swift's language projectors and the students' short essays (on the significance of names or on Addie's or Keller's likely response to Swift's Academy of Laputa). For Swift's academy, I came to class with various objects in my office—a stapler, a pen, a mug, some paper and books—and refusing to talk, tried to conduct a conversation with the students. Mercifully, some students began to laugh, and we proceeded to the discussion of Laputa's second major project to reform language. This project, which tries to replace words with things, connected both with Addie's ideas about language and with the anthropomorphic alphabet I had shown in the first lecture. It operates on the opposite assumption from the first Laputan language project; instead of trying to plumb the wisdom hidden within words, it assumes that they are useless. Whereas Keller would have disapproved of this project to eliminate words, she might have found more appealing the concept of a self-sufficient language that is implicit in the academy's first project.

The Remaining Twelve Weeks

Conceptually, the syllabus, our choice and schedule of texts, along with our integration of writing, was the sine qua non of this course. It was extensive in its range of genres and disciplines, a range that was historical, national, and racial. Tightly focused yet widely various, our unusual syllabus enabled us to keep the spotlight on language and more specifically on metaphorical language without our giving the impression that we were repeating ourselves—jumping up and down in one place, as it were. Our choice and schedule of texts gave us both coherence and progress, including an increasing complexity and breadth of disciplinary reference. Our pedagogical approach and methods are what maintained accessibility for beginning college students.

Our course was sectioned into four units: Language and Thought, Metaphor, Cultural Metaphors, and a concluding summation called Word-World. These units are overlapping and their sectioning merely indicates relative emphasis; "thought" is understood to pertain to all four but is specified in the first section, where the connection most needs stressing. Broadly, the focus of the week after "Naming and Categories" was on the colonizing of language, beginning with Gloria Anzaldúa's "How to Tame a Wild Tongue" (55–64), an in-your-face essay guaranteed to stir debate about multilingualism, and then featuring Brian Friel's short, wry, but poignant play *Translations*, which centers on the enforced Englishing of Irish place names in the nineteenth century. (The very title of this play consists of a traditional rhetorical term for metaphor, *translatio*[n], a carrying across or transfer.) The lecture for this week, the first given by an AI, provided historical context for the play and included an effective dramatic reading by two of our students of the final love scene between a British soldier who speaks no Celtic and an Irish woman who speaks no English. The end of the lecture led up to the essay of roughly one page on language and identity for that week. This essay addressed one of two topics. The first invited students to choose a brief passage from *Translations* about language and identity and to analyze how it confirms, complicates, or contradicts Anzaldúa's claim that "ethnic identity is twin skin to linguistic identity" (59). The second underlined thetic words in a passage in *Translations* and asked for a detailed discussion of the passage that evaluates whether what a character describes as intercultural "decoding" is possible or desirable. Both options reflect the view that focused comparative topics foster insight and broaden perspective: they help students work outside, and eventually evaluate, the views they bring to the campus. Several of our subsequent writing prompts similarly began with a discrepancy or contradiction between the assigned texts or a controversial assertion in one of them. Thus they served as springboards for argument and further modeled at least one way of contextualizing it.

For the first month of the course, we assigned short, varied, weekly or occasionally biweekly writing assignments: exercises ranged from the dictionary project to a descriptive paragraph in monosyllables (meant to increase awareness of word choice and borrowed from creative writing courses) to a brief analysis of highly metaphoric lines in a short poem, guided by questions about them, to mini essays, derived from the focus of the week and guided by a topic partly delineated by leading questions or by a debatable statement. Some assignments were challenging; others more fun. There was always a choice and room for originality, but they assumed, with support from cognitive theory, that models, prompts to modify and build on, are fundamental to learning. We read and evaluated these short papers for expression and content, sending the message that the two are inseparable. The brevity of these papers enabled us to respond to writing problems with individual commentary, consultation, and, where appropriate, revision before much was at stake, psychologically or quantitatively. Aside from the enormous advantage of keeping the students writing, our method also ensured that when we turned to longer essays, we were little plagued by the notorious five-paragraph essay, the formula many of our students learn in high school and are reluctant to abandon unless asked to think and write in a different way.

From the colonizing of language we turned to Italo Calvino's short sketches "Two Pounds of Goose Fat" and "The Cheese Museum," which variously remark and exhibit the metaphorical relation of form and content, language and concept, naming and possession. Again, although the students had been introduced to such issues, they had certainly not made them their own, as was evident when the same issues turned up in different guises. We also read a number of (mainly) short poems, which, with Calvino, while we were still in the Language and Thought unit, moved us ever closer to an increasingly inevitable emphasis on metaphor.

Lewis Carroll's *Alice* novels followed, since they everywhere engage cruxes of language and metaphor, and they proved hugely successful. An assignment on shaped poems, including the tale/tail poem of Carroll's mouse (complete with tail rhyme) proved an effective way to show — visually, tangibly — the relation of form to content, a concept otherwise very difficult to grasp, and readily connected to the students' writing. The lecture for this week, by the AI Chris Hokanson, treated Carroll's word games. It began with a thesis statement distributed to the students and pointedly developed the statement by analyzing incremental textual examples, thus becoming an instance of the integration of meaningful form and content.

Metaphor, the second unit of the course, sampled theories of metaphor in ways more accessible to the students at this point than they would have been earlier. We read parts of Lakoff and Johnson's popularized neo-cognitivitism in *Metaphors We Live By* and had lectures on metaphor. We further read, besides poems, part of Lakoff and Mark Turner's application of neocognitivism to poetry, which connects everyday with poetic utterance and concludes with a brief excursion into the metaphoric structure of contemporary ideology. Having explored the strengths and limits of Lakoff and Turner's approach, we concluded with a brief portion of Neil Postman's chapter "The Medium Is the Metaphor," a translation of the form/content dialectic to the mind-numbing, ideological impact of "television culture" in modern America. By thus exploring metaphor in relation to ideology, we were also preparing for our next unit on cultural metaphors. But the highlight of this unit proved, to my utter astonishment, to be Jorge Luis Borges's "Library of Babel," a fascinating but difficult story about the textualization of human existence, including our perceptions of space and history. This short story is sufficiently difficult that, despite its relevance to our course,

I had to be pressured by the AIs to include it. But we had the benefit of an excellent lecture on Borges by Justus Nieland, an informed AI specializing in modernism, that included accessible definitions of modernism and post-modernism, complete with illustrations and film clips (Warhol's *Marilyn Monroe* and the parody of *Psycho* in *The Simpsons*).[5] The students were strikingly engaged, provoked, and excited by Borges's intellectual, ideological, and interpretative challenge to them.

During this second unit of the course, the first formal essay was due, initially in draft form and a week later in its final form. All the instructors had individual conferences with students to discuss their drafts during this period; these conferences were now required, rather than optional and encouraged. This three-page essay was to consider the use of metaphor in any text already read in the course or else in everyday conversation or popular periodicals, newspapers, advertisements, and the like. We wanted the first formal essay to offer a fairly familiar topical option, one with which the students from the School of Business or the Schools of Music, Education, Public and Environmental Affairs or the School of Health, Physical Education, and Recreation would be as comfortable as those majoring in psychology, classics, or the life sciences in the College of Arts and Sciences — not to mention those few who might be thinking about a major in English.

We assigned two more formal essays, each incrementally longer by a page and each focusing more closely on an assigned text or a combination of texts. We also employed various methods such as peer editing and further individual conferences, drafts, and revisions. Our exams were a take-home essay for the mid-term and essay questions distributed in advance for the final.

The penultimate unit of the syllabus, Cultural Metaphors, began with a week on metaphors in science, a popular focus that led students to question the metaphors they excitedly uncovered in their textbooks for science and social science courses. Emily Martin's "The Egg and the Sperm" and Susan Sontag's *AIDS and Its Metaphors* also afforded useful models of beginnings and endings of arguments. We concentrated on the endings of arguments, since students were pretty competent with the beginnings of arguments from our earlier work. The AI's lecture, making use of Thomas Kuhn, engaged metaphors active in scientific paradigm shifts.

As I hope is now evident, in our lectures we pooled our own resources, our own diversity of backgrounds and interests, to show students that reading and writing are at home with—indeed, inseparable from—intellectual stimulation and complexity. We tried to remain focused on language, written and read, and to keep moving, suggesting the range, significance, and interwoven cultural implications of our focus. The doors we could open mattered as much as getting to the other side of the room; there would be more time for crossing the room if there was motivation.

The major part of our section on cultural metaphors, which opened with scientific metaphors, focused on metaphors of blackness and whiteness. Mainly, but not exclusively, it concerned race. It began with a selection from Toni Morrison's criticism in *Playing in the Dark: Whiteness and the Literary Imagination*, which mentions Herman Melville's writing approvingly as an exception to racist norms; then it proceeded to the haunting chapter on whiteness in *Moby-Dick* before turning to the main attraction, *Pudd'nhead Wilson*, a short novel about identity in which Mark Twain casts his ironic and controversial eye on race relations in middle America on the threshold of the Civil War. We also had a day on the African American poets Paul Laurence Dunbar and Langston Hughes (in Bontemps), with Wallace Stevens's "Snow Man" added for another, quirky, complicating perspective on whiteness.

The unit ended with a week on eye-opening political metaphors associated with the founding of America in selections from the letters of John Adams and Abigail Adams[6] and Thomas Paine's *Common Sense*. The AI's lecture related these metaphors to Benedict Anderson's work on the impact of the emergence of print capitalism and imagined communities—a nice tie back to Postman's reflections about television as medium and metaphor. For the final meeting of this unit, each student found a current political metaphor (on the basis of a thesis and keywords) through a Web search and then presented it, with analysis, to his or her discussion section: the Republican elephant and Democrat donkey were particular hits. We often hear that a significant sign of progress in students' education comes with their recognition and development of relationships among their courses.

With the many radiating extensions of our focus on language, we sought to model and provoke this process and to exploit its ability to make connections among texts, paragraphs, and even sentences, whether read or written. To a considerable extent, we succeeded.

We devoted the final unit, Word World, to Paul Auster's *City of Glass*, and we could not have asked for a text better suited to our purpose of summation and culmination. Virtually without exception, the students agreed that they could not have grasped this novel at the outset of the course, and once they got into it, their enthusiasm for it was overwhelming. *City of Glass* parodies a detective novel, which generically relates it to our earlier Twain novel, and with tantalizing ingenuity it draws readers into pursuit of an uncentered signifier. Again like Twain's novel, it features identity and human doubles, and, without sacrificing human character or human engagement, it seamlessly translates these elements into the realm of language. In its receding depths, the relation of word and thing, mind and object, fictive writing and embodied living becomes intensely and wonderfully provoking.

For the last discussion, the reading assignment was one poem of twenty-three short lines, Edwin Muir's "The Animals." This was the only new reading the students had for the whole week, since we wanted time to review the course. Muir's poem is about the biblical fifth day of creation, the day the animals were created and the day before we arrived with our words, or names. It highlights both central concerns of Auster's novel, which makes much of Genesis, and of the entire course: naming and categorization, metaphor, fiction and construction, ethical and political consequences. The conclusive remark on an anonymous course evaluation that I cherish most came in response to the question, "How do you see this course fitting into your education?" The student wrote, "This course is itself an education."

A Brief Reprise

The claim of the course I've described here is finally more conceptual than methodological. This course focuses squarely on what most fundamentally joins writing and reading, literature and culture, and thought and expression—language. The use of English, including but not restricted to its creative use and certainly not to its creative use in traditional literature, is also what most specifically joins the (very) various schools in the university and the various departments in the College of Arts and Sciences to the Department of English. Language, in its literary and rhetorical forms and implications, not only justifies the cooperative union of the two "(sub)cultures" of literature and composition in the field of English but also challenges their separation.

As our introduction explains, this final course in our volume, Language and Metaphor: The Ways We Think in Words, also has characteristics that link it to the distinctive emphases of each of the preceding groups: the humanities programs of the first, the more rhetorical courses of the second, and the more broadly cultural courses of the third. We have found in this course on language and the archtrope metaphor, as these function in the structures of the social and cultural world and in our thinking about this world, a particularly pronounced engagement with textuality and with the literary or rhetorical elements of writing for which faculty members in other disciplines respect our expertise in English (Scholes, *Rise* 20). A focus on language and metaphor gets to the core that is relevant to all disciplinary discourses. Metaphor, too, is fundamental to human culture, whether or not it is true that all human categorization is basically metaphorical, as Lakoff and Johnson have asserted; that metaphors function in a way similar to models, hypotheses, or insight in the sciences, as Max Black long since suggested; or that basic philosophical concepts—indeed language itself—is tropic and translative, as a host of philosophers and literary critics have held since Nietzsche's time.

In the final analysis, the presence of literature in such a course is, perhaps, less an absolute necessity than a significant advantage, as Clyde Moneyhun argues in this volume. Literature is in the composition classroom because it makes textuality in its fullest sense noticeable and engaging, and it does so in a contextualized way that is densely and complexly human. Textuality embodies the linguistic play in which differential structuring enables *"the discourse of the other"* (Berger 16). This discourse is the expression of a collective or structural agency: *différance* . . . or the unconscious, or the unconscious as language, or heteroglossia, or language-games, or the collective discourses shaped by a society's cultural and institutional practices. (16)

Any given course in this mode will proceed from simpler or shorter forms of textuality to relatively more sophisticated ones—from an essay or short poem or *Alice in Wonderland* to *City of Glass*, for example—but its focus will nonetheless remain textual. Textuality certainly involves an attention to surfaces, but it recognizes that surface and substance are intertwined. This knowledge is the special insight that those in the modern (and ancient) languages share, and it distinguishes our expertise from that of other disciplines in a way that cultural studies by itself does not: most departments in the humanities and the social sciences teach cultural studies and teach it well, but "textuality" departments are the ones that attend to the actual, informing medium of expression—to the situated use of language.

Notes

1. My description of the development at Indiana University of the proseminar on the teaching literature unavoidably recalls an article about it that I wrote with Favret (see Farris and Favret).

2. One of the graduate students did not teach the undergraduate course with us in the fall, since she decided to leave the program. A second student, Miguel Powers, successfully taught a version of the course without a lecture at the University of San Diego and at Palomar College (a two-year school) the second year rather than with us. He reported that his course at Palomar College was highly successful, and he has since taught versions of our course at Fullerton College, another two-year school, with continuing success.

3. For discussion of the relation of these works, see Anderson, *Translating*.

4. As in this paragraph, we thought in metaphors ourselves and theorized about the significance of mixed ones, in which some theorists see only confusion and others see minds in process, breaking new ground (Pepper; Goodman; Pesmen).

5. I paired the AIs' lectures with their areas of expertise and suggestions for the syllabus—a definite plus. Our collaborative work on the syllabus made this pairing possible.

6. Letters 43–44, 52, 75, 79, 82, 85, 87, 91, 93–94, 105, 114–15, 118.

Notes on Contributors

Judith H. Anderson, Chancellor's Professor at Indiana University, has published numerous studies of Renaissance literature and culture, including *The Growth of a Personal Voice:* Piers Plowman *and* The Faerie Queene (1976), *Biographical Truth: The Representation of Historical Persons in Tudor-Stuart Writing* (1984), *Words That Matter: Linguistic Perception in Renaissance English* (1996), and *Translating Investments: Metaphor and the Dynamic of Cultural Change in Tudor-Stuart England* (2005). She is coeditor (with Elizabeth Kirk) of *Will's Vision of* Piers Plowman (1990) and (with Donald Cheney and David Richardson) of *Spenser's Life and the Subject of Biography* (1996). She has received five awards from Indiana University that recognize excellence in teaching.

John Cyril Barton is assistant professor of English at the University of Missouri, Kansas City. He has published essays on William Dean Howells and American literary realism, Theodore Dreiser and the criminal justice system, speech-act theory in the work of Derrida and Deleuze and Guattari, and he has a forthcoming publication on the antigallows movement in antebellum America. He received a teaching award in 2001–02, partly in recognition for teaching and helping to design the writing course discussed in this volume.

Allison Berg is associate professor at James Madison College in Michigan State University. She has published *Mothering the Race: Women's Narratives of Reproduction, 1890–1930* (2002), as well as articles on American literature, popular culture, and pedagogy. Her current research focuses on representations of the civil rights movement in history, literature, and film.

Michael P. Clark is professor of English and associate executive vice chancellor for academic planning at the University of California, Irvine. He is a past director of the Humanities Core course there. His publications include books on literary theory and articles on early American literature, the Vietnam War and popular culture in the United States, and the teaching of writing. He edited *The Range of the Aesthetic: The Place of Literature in Theory Today* (2000) and *The Eliot Tracts, with Letters from John Eliot to Thomas Thorowgood and Richard Baxter* (2003). While directing the Humanities Core course described in this volume, he received awards for UC, Irvine, Teaching Innovator of the Year, 1999–2000 and for Excellence in Teaching, School of Humanities.

Helen Emmitt is associate professor of English at Centre College. She has published essays on Ezra Pound, George Eliot, and Margaret Drabble and is currently working on a book about contemporary Irish poetry.

Christine R. Farris is professor of English and director of composition at Indiana University. She is the author of *Subject to Change: New Composition Instructors' Theory and Practice* (1996) and the coeditor (with Chris Anson) of *Under Construction: Working at the Intersections of Composition Theory, Research, and Practice* (1998) and has written articles on composition and cultural studies, teacher preparation, and writing across the curriculum. She edited a special issue of *WPA: Journal of the Council of Writing Program Administrators* on changes in the first-year writing curriculum. At Indiana University, she has received the President's Award for Distinguished Teaching, as well as three other teaching awards.

Tamara A. Goeglein, associate dean of the faculty and associate professor of English at Franklin and Marshall College, has published scholarly essays examining the influence of dialectical and rhetorical manuals, particularly Ramist manuals, on early modern English poetics. She is currently writing a series of essays on the Renaissance emblem book.

Faye Halpern, for four years a preceptor in the Expository Writing Program of Harvard University, is now assistant professor of English at the University of Calgary. She has published essays on persuasion and organized panels around the theme "Deception in the Writing Classroom," for various CCCC conventions. Her current book project puts the nineteenth-century "scribbling women" writers in the context of professional male orators and rhetoricians.

Douglas Higbee, a doctoral student in English at the University of California, Irvine, is currently writing a dissertation on British veterans of the First World War and their relation to postwar British culture and society.

Andre Hulet is a graduate of the Programs in Writing at the University of California, Irvine. His poetry has appeared in *Faultline* and other journals. He currently resides and works in Portland, Oregon.

Rona Kaufman is assistant professor of English at Pacific Lutheran University, where she teaches composition, rhetoric, and creative nonfiction; directs the Writing Center; and is director of faculty development for the First-Year Experience Program. She is the coeditor of *Placing the Academy: Essays on Landscape and Academic Identity* (2007). Other work has appeared in *JAC* and *Interdisciplinary Studies in Literature and the Environment*.

Elizabeth Losh is writing director of the Humanities Core course at the University of California, Irvine, where she also conducts research on writing by biliterate students and on the application of new technologies to the teaching of composition. She has published essays about government Web sites and military-funded video games. She is currently working on a book about digital rhetoric that focuses on the representation of public institutions in cyberspace. For her part in the curricular redesign of the UCI Humanities Core course described in this volume, she received the award for Outstanding Commitment to TA Professional Development and Undergraduate Education in 2001.

Daniel Manheim is professor and chair of English at Centre College. He has published essays on Henry Adams and Emily Dickinson, and his current work focuses on Dickinson's poetic development.

Clyde Moneyhun is associate director of the Program in Writing and Rhetoric at Stanford University. He has coedited *Living Languages: Contexts for Reading and Writing* (with Nancy Buffington and Marvin Diogenes, 1997) and *Crafting Fiction: In Theory, in Practice* (with Marvin Diogenes, 2002). His book "Arguing with Power: A Brief Rhetoric of Argument" is forthcoming.

Mark Rasmussen is associate professor of English at Centre College. He has published essays on Chaucer and Spenser and has edited the collection *Renaissance Literature and Its Formal Engagements* (2002). His current work considers the genre of poetic complaint from classical antiquity to the Renaissance.

Milton Reigelman is J. Rice Cowan Professor of English and director of overseas programs at Centre College. He is the author of *The Midland: A Venture in Literary Regionalism* (1975), as well as of essays on Melville, Faulkner, George Eliot, John Le Carré, and Ed McClanahan.

Lori Robison is associate professor of English and codirector of the Composition Program at the University of North Dakota. She has published articles on the construction of race in the postbellum United States and is currently working on the book "Domesticating Difference: Gender, Race, and the Birth of a New South."

Jeanne Marie Rose is assistant professor of English and composition coordinator at Penn State University, Berks. While completing her dissertation at the University of Rochester, she was an adjunct faculty member at Rochester Institute of Technology. She currently studies the institutional status of composition, with emphasis on the role of the administrator of the writing program.

Gordon W. Thompson was Bain-Swiggett Professor and former chair of English (twice) at Earlham College. His publications include "Ancient Wholes and Modern Fragments" (1983) and "Quaker Educational Values for a Diverse Community: A Jewish View," which appeared in *The Inward Teacher: Essays to Honor Paul Lacey* (2002). He retired in 2005.

Lee Torda is associate professor of English and coordinator of the Writing Program at Bridgewater State College. She has written the instructor's manual for *Fieldworking: Reading and Writing Research* (1997) and is currently archiving teacher stories at Bridgewater, the oldest state normal school in the United States.

Margaret Vandenburg, senior lecturer in English at Barnard College, is director of First-Year English: Reinventing Literary History and former associate director of the Writing Program. Her published work includes critical essays on Hemingway, Barnes, and Eliot, as well as a historical novel featuring the avant-garde salon of Gertrude Stein. In 2004, she received the Emily Gregory Award from Barnard College for excellence in teaching.

Maryanne Ward is professor of English and a former director of the Humanities Program at Centre College. She has published articles on nineteenth-century fiction.

Helen M. Whall is associate professor of English at the College of the Holy Cross. She is a former director of the First-Year Program and the College Honors Program and a recent recipient of the Holy Cross Distinguished Teaching Award. She has published essays on Shakespeare and the Renaissance as well as the book *To Instruct and Delight: Didactic Method in Five Tudor Dramas* (1988). She is currently preparing a book on the role of the joke and the jest in Shakespeare's comedies.

Philip White is associate professor of English and chair of writing at Centre College. He has published critical essays on Shakespeare and on contemporary poetry, and his poems have appeared in various magazines and journals.

Eric A. Wolfe is assistant professor of English at the University of North Dakota. His current book project is "The Lure of the Voice: Constituting the National Subject in the Early United States."

Works Cited

Achebe, Chinua. "Dead Men's Path." *Charters* 10–12.

Adams, John, and Abigail Adams. *Familiar Letters of John Adams and His Wife Abigail Adams during the Revolution*. Ed. Charles Frances Adams. Boston: Houghton, 1875.

Ahmed, Leila. *A Border Passage: From Cairo to New York—A Woman's Journey*. New York: Farrar, 1999.

Aitchison, Jean. *Words in the Mind: An Introduction to the Mental Lexicon*. 2nd ed. Oxford: Blackwell, 1994.

Alvarez, Julia. *How the García Girls Lost Their Accents*. Chapel Hill: Algonquin, 1991.

———. *In the Time of the Butterflies*. Chapel Hill: Algonquin, 1994.

Anderson, Benedict. *Imagined Communities: Reflections on the Origin and Spread of Nationalism*. London: Verso, 1983.

Anderson, Judith H. *Translating Investments: Metaphor and the Dynamic of Cultural Change in Tudor-Stuart England*. New York: Fordham UP, 2005.

———. *Words That Matter: Linguistic Perception in Renaissance English*. Stanford: Stanford UP, 1996.

Anzaldúa, Gloria. *Borderlands / La Frontera: The New Mestiza*. San Francisco: Aunt Lute, 1987.

Attridge, Derek. "Language as History / History as Language: Saussure and the Romance of Etymology." *Post-structuralism and the Question of History*. Ed. Attridge, Geoff Bennington, and Robert Young. Cambridge: Cambridge UP, 1987. 183–211.

Atwood, Margaret. *"Bluebeard's Egg" and Other Stories*. 1983. Boston: Houghton, 1986.

———. "Happy Endings." *Charters* 47–49.

Auster, Paul. *City of Glass*. New York: Penguin, 1987.

———. "Ghosts." *The New York Trilogy*. New York: Penguin, 1990. 159–232.

Babel, Isaac. "My First Goose." *Charters* 51–53.

Bakhtin, Mikhail. "The Problem of Speech Genres." *"Speech Genres" and Other Late Essays*. Trans. Vern W. McGee. Ed. Caryl Emerson and Michael Holquist. Austin: U of Texas P, 1986. 60–102.

Banks, Russell. *The Sweet Hereafter*. New York: Harper, 1991.

Barnes, Julian. *A History of the World in 10½ Chapters*. London: Picador, 1989.

Barth, John. *Chimera*. 1972. New York: Fawcett, 1993.

Barthes, Roland. *Image-Music-Text*. Trans. Stephen Heath. New York: Hill, 1977.

Bartholomae, David. "Inventing the University." *When a Writer Can't Write: Studies in Writer's Block and Other Composing Process Problems*. Ed. Mike Rose. New York: Guilford, 1985. 134–65.

———. "Response." *College Composition and Communication* 46 (1995): 84–87.

———. "Writing with Teachers: A Conversation with Peter Elbow." *College Composition and Communication* 46 (1995): 62–71.

Bartholomae, David, and Anthony Petrosky, eds. *Ways of Reading: An Anthology for Writers*. 7th ed. Boston: Bedford–St. Martin's, 2005.

Bawarshi, Anis. "The Genre-Function." *College English* 62 (2000): 335–60.

Bazerman, Charles. "The Life of Genre, the Life in the Classroom." *Genre and Writing: Issues, Arguments, Alternatives*. Ed. Wendy Bishop and Hans Ostrom. Portsmouth: Boynton, 1997. 19–26.

———. "Systems of Genres and the Enactment of Social Intentions." Freedman and Medway 79–101.

Beaumont, Matt. *E: A Novel*. London: Dutton, 2000.

Belknap, Robert L. *Tradition and Innovation: General Education and the Reintegration of the University*. New York: Columbia UP, 1977.

Bell, Daniel. *The Reforming of General Education: The Columbia College Experience in Its National Setting*. New York: Columbia UP, 1966.

Belsey, Catherine. *Critical Practice*. London: Methuen, 1980.

Berger, Harry, Jr. "Phaedrus and the Politics of Inscription." *Situated Utterances: Texts, Bodies, and Cultural Representations*. New York: Fordham UP, 2005. 415–54.

Berlin, James. *Rhetoric and Reality: Writing Instruction in American Colleges, 1900–1985*. Carbondale: Southern Illinois UP, 1987.

———. *Rhetorics, Poetics, and Cultures: Refiguring College English Studies*. Urbana: NCTE, 1996.

———. *Writing Instruction in Nineteenth-Century American Colleges*. Carbondale: Southern Illinois UP, 1984.

Berthoff, Ann E. *The Making of Meaning: Metaphors, Models, and Maxims for Writing Teachers*. Portsmouth: Boynton, 1981.

Bialostosky, Don H. "Romantic Resonances." *College Composition and Communication* 46 (1995): 92–96.

Bizzell, Patricia. *Academic Discourse and Critical Consciousness*. Pittsburgh: U of Pittsburgh P, 1992.

———. "Cognition, Convention, and Certainty: What We Need to Know about Writing." *Pre-Text* 3.3 (1982): 213–43.

Bizzell, Patricia, and Bruce Herzberg, eds. *Negotiating Difference: Cultural Case Studies for Composition*. Boston: Bedford–St. Martin's, 1996.

Black, Max. *Models and Metaphors: Studies in Language and Philosophy*. Ithaca: Cornell UP, 1962.

Bleich, David. *Know and Tell*. Portsmouth: Boynton, 1998.

Bloom, B. S., ed. *Taxonomy of Educational Objectives. Handbook I: Cognitive Domain*. London: Longman, 1956.

Bohannan, Laura. "Miching Mallecho: That Means Witchcraft." *From the Third Programme*. Ed. John Morris. London: Nonesuch, 1956. 174–89.

Böll, Heinrich. "Like a Bad Dream." Charters 134–38.

Bontemps, Arna, ed. *Negro American Poetry*. New York: Noonday, 1990.

Booth, Wayne. *A Rhetoric of Irony*. Chicago: U of Chicago P, 1974.

Borges, Jorge Luis. "The Library of Babel." *Ficciones*. Trans. Emecé Editores. Ed. Anthony Kerrigan. New York: Grove, 1962. 79–88.

Boyer Commission on Educating Undergraduates in the Research University. "Reinventing Undergraduate Education: A Blueprint for America's Research Universities." 1998. 28 August 2000 <http://notes.cc.sunysb.edu/Pres/boyer.nsf>.

Brody, Miriam. *Manly Writing: Gender, Rhetoric, and the Rise of Composition*. Carbondale: Southern Illinois UP, 1993.

Brontë, Emily. *Wuthering Heights*. Oxford: Oxford UP, 1999.

Brooks, Cleanth. *The Well Wrought Urn*. New York: Harcourt, 1947.

Bruffee, Kenneth. *Collaborative Learning: Higher Education, Interdependence, and the Authority of Knowledge*. Baltimore: Johns Hopkins UP, 1993.

———. "Collaborative Learning and the 'Conversation of Mankind.'" *College English* 46 (1984): 635–52.

———. "Liberal Education and the Social Justification of Belief." *Liberal Education* 68 (1982): 95–114.

Calvino, Italo. "The Cheese Museum." Calvino, *Mr. Palomar* 71–75.

———. *Mr. Palomar*. Trans. William Weaver. New York: Harcourt, 1985.

———. "Two Pounds of Goose Fat." Calvino, *Mr. Palomar* 67–70.

Campbell, John, and Joseph Voelker. "Imagining the Future Citizen." *Liberal Education* 89 (2003): 46–53.

Carnes, Mark C., ed. *Novel History: Historians and Novelists Confront America's Past (and Each Other)*. New York: Simon, 2001.

Carr, Edward Hallett. *What Is History?* New York: Vintage, 1961.

Carroll, Lee Ann. *Rehearsing New Roles: How College Students Develop as Writers*. Carbondale: Southern Illinois UP, 2002.

Carroll, Lewis. *Alice's Adventures in Wonderland* and *Through the Looking Glass*. New York: Bantam, 1992.

Carter, Angela. *"The Bloody Chamber" and Other Stories*. London: Virago, 1979.

Castronovo, Russ. "Framing the Slave Narative/Framing Discussion." *Approaches to Teaching* Narrative of the Life of Frederick Douglass. Ed. James C. Hall. New York: MLA, 1999. 42–48.

Certeau, Michel de. *The Practice of Everday Life*. Trans. Steven Randall. Berkeley: U of California P, 1984.

Chandler, Raymond. *The Big Sleep*. 1939. New York: Vintage, 1992.

Charters, Ann, ed. *The Story and Its Writer: An Introduction to Short Fiction*. 3rd ed. Boston: Bedford–St. Martin's, 1991.

Chaucer, Geoffrey. *The Canterbury Tales*. Trans. Nevill Coghill. 1992. New York: Barnes, 1994.

Chauncey, George. *Gay New York: Gender, Urban Culture, and the Makings of the Gay Male World, 1890–1940*. New York: Basic, 1994.

Cisneros, Sandra. "Woman Hollering Creek." *Woman Hollering Creek*. New York: Vintage, 1991. 43–56.

The Civil War. Dir. Ken Burns. Videocassette. PBS, 1989.

Cixous, Hélène, and Catherine Clément. *The Newly Born Woman*. 1975. Trans. Betsy Wing. Minneapolis: U of Minnesota P, 1980.

Clark, Andy. *Being There: Putting Brain, Body, and World Together Again*. Cambridge: MIT P, 2001.

Clark, Michael P., and Elizabeth Losh. *Humanities Core Course Exploration and Discovery Guide and Writer's Handbook*. New York: Forbes Custom, 1999.

Clifford, John, and John Schilb. "Composition Theory and Literary Theory." *Perspectives on Research and Scholarship in Composition*. Ed. Ben W. McClelland and Timothy R. Donovan. New York: MLA, 1985. 45–67.

Connors, Robert J. *Composition-Rhetoric: Background, Theory, and Pedagogy*. Pittsburgh: U of Pittsburgh P, 1997.

Conrad, Joseph. *Heart of Darkness*. Ed. Paul B. Armstrong. New York: Norton, 1988.

Coover, Robert. "The Gingerbread House." Coover, *Pricksongs* 61–75.

———. "J's Marriage." Coover, *Pricksongs* 112–19.

———. *Pricksongs and Descants*. New York: Dutton, 1969.

Course Descriptions for Literature. 2003. Coll. of Liberal Arts, Rochester Inst. of Technology. 27 Mar. 2003 <http://www.rit.edu/%7E690www/langlit/lang.html>.

Cox, James M. "Attacks on the Ending and Twain's Attack on Conscience." Graff and Phelan 305–11.

Crafts, Hannah. *The Bondwoman's Narrative*. New York: Warner, 2002.

Crain, Jeanie C. "Comment on 'Two Views on the Use of Literature in Composition.'" *College English* 55 (1993): 678–79.

Crane, Gregory. "Deep Reading in the Digital Age." Univ. of California, Irvine, Humanitech and Humanities Center Talk. 27 Feb. 2001.

Cripps, Thomas. "Historical Truth: An Interview with Ken Burns." *American Historical Review* 100 (1995): 741–64.

Cross, Timothy. *An Oasis of Order: The Core Curriculum at Columbia College*. New York: Office of the Dean, Columbia Coll., 1995.

Crowley, Sharon. *Composition in the University: Historical and Polemical Essays*. Pittsburgh: U of Pittsburgh P, 1998.

Cuddon, J. A. "Detective Story." *A Dictionary of Literary Terms*. Rev. ed. New York: Penguin, 1979. 182–84

Culler, Jonathan. *On Deconstruction: Theory and Criticism after Structuralism*. Ithaca: Cornell UP, 1982.

Cutright, Marc, ed. *Strengthening First-Year Student Learning at Doctoral/Research-Extensive Universities*. Brevard: Policy Ctr. on the First Year of College, 2002.

Dante. *Inferno*. Trans. Michael Palma. New York: Norton, 2002.

Davis, Natalie Zemon. "AHR Forum: *The Return of Martin Guerre*: 'On the Lame.'" *American Historical Review* 93 (1988): 572–603.

Davis, Rebecca Harding. *Life in the Iron Mills*. Ed. Cecelia Tichi. Boston: Bedford, 1998.

DeLillo, Don. *Libra*. New York: Penguin, 1991.

Derrida, Jacques. "Différance." 1968. *Margins of Philosophy*. Trans. Alan Bass. Chicago: U of Chicago P, 1982. 1–27.

———. "White Mythology: Metaphor in the Text of Philosophy." Trans. F. C. T. Moore. *New Literary History* 6 (1975): 5–74.

Desjardin, Thomas A. *Stand Firm Ye Boys from Maine*. Oxford: Oxford UP, 1995.

Doctorow, E. L. *Ragtime*. New York: Random, 1978.

Donne, John. *The Complete Poems of John Donne*. Ed. Roger E. Bennett. Chicago: Packard, 1942.

Douglas, Ann. *Terrible Honesty: Mongrel Manhattan in the 1920s*. New York: Farrar, 1995.

Douglass, Frederick. *Narrative of the Life of Frederick Douglass*. New York: Penguin, 1997.

Downing, David B., Claude Mark Hurlbert, and Paula Mathieu, eds. *Beyond English, Inc.: Curricular Reform in a Global Economy*. Portsmouth: Boynton, 2002.

Doyle, Arthur Conan. "A Scandal in Bohemia." *The Complete Sherlock Holmes*. Vol. 1. Garden City: Doubleday, 1960. 161–75.

Duffin, Kathy. "An Overview of the Academic Essay." Teaching Materials for the Harvard University Writing Center, 1998.

Dunn, Katherine. *Geek Love*. New York: Vintage, 2002.

Eagleton, Terry. *Literary Theory: An Introduction*. Minneapolis: U of Minnesota P, 1983.

Elbow, Peter. "Being a Writer vs. Being an Academic: A Conflict in Goals." *College Composition and Communication* 46 (1995): 72–83.

———. "The Cultures of Literature and Composition: What Could Each Learn from the Other?" *College English* 64 (2002): 533–46.

———. "The War between Reading and Writing—and How to End It." *Rhetoric Review* 12.1 (1993): 5–23.

———. *Writing without Teachers*. Oxford: Oxford UP, 1973.

Eliot, T. S. The Waste Land *and Other Poems*. 1934. San Diego: Harcourt, 1962.

Ellison, Ralph. *Invisible Man*. New York: Random, 2002.

Emig, Janet. "Writing as a Mode of Learning." *College Composition and Communication* 28 (1977): 122–28.

Erdrich, Louise. *Love Medicine*. New York: Holt, 1993.

Eschholz, Paul, Alfred Rosa, and Virginia Clark, eds. *Language Awareness: Readings for College Writers*. 8th ed. Boston: Bedford–St. Martin's, 2000.

Euripides. *Medea*. Cambridge: Cambridge UP, 2002.

Farris, Christine R. "Giving Religion, Taking Gold: Disciplinary Cultures and the Claims of Writing across the Curriculum." *Cultural Studies in the English Classroom*. Ed. James Berlin and Michael J. Vivion. Portsmouth: Boynton, 1992. 112–22.

———. "Too Cool for School? Composition as Cultural Studies and Reflective Practice." *Preparing College Teachers of Writing: Histories, Theories, Programs, Practices*. Ed. Betty P. Pytlik and Sara Liggett. New York: Oxford UP, 2002. 97–107.

Farris, Christine R., and Chris M. Anson. "Introduction: Complicating Composition." *Under Construction: Working at the Intersections of Composition Theory, Research, and Practice*. Logan: Utah State UP, 1998. 1–7.

Farris, Christine R., and Mary Favret. "Teaching the Teaching of Literature." *Peer Review: Journal of the Association of American Colleges and Universities* 6 (2004): 16–18.

Faulkner, William. *As I Lay Dying*. New York: Random, 1964.

———. *Essays, Speeches, and Public Letters*. Ed. James B. Meriwether. New York: Random, 1965. 119–20.

Findlay, Robert. "AHR Forum: *The Return of Martin Guerre*: 'The Refashioning of Martin Guerre.'" *American Historical Review* 93 (1988): 553–71.

Fish, Stanley. "Anti-foundationalism, Theory Hope, and the Teaching of Composition." *Doing What Comes Naturally: Change, Rhetoric, and the Practice of Theory in Literary and Legal Studies*. Durham: Duke UP, 1989. 342–55.

———. *Professional Correctness: Literary Studies and Political Change*. Oxford: Clarendon, 1995.

Fletcher, Stephanie. *E-Mail: A Love Story*. New York: Fine, 1996.

Foley, Helene. *The Homeric Hymn to Demeter: Translation, Commentary, and Interpretive Essays*. Princeton: Princeton UP, 1994.

Foucault, Michel. *The Archeology of Knowledge and the Discourse on Language*. Trans. A. Sheridan Smith. New York: Pantheon, 1972.

———. *L'ordre du discours*. Paris: Gallimard, 1971.

Freedman, Aviva, and Peter Medway, eds. *Genre and the New Rhetoric*. London: Taylor, 1994.

Freire, Paulo. *Pedagogy of the Oppressed*. New York: Continuum, 1993.

Friel, Brian. *Translations*. London: Faber, 1981.

Gadamer, Hans-Georg. *Truth and Method*. New York: Continuum, 1975.

Gamer, Michael. "Fictionalizing the Disciplines: Literature and the Boundaries of Knowledge." *College English* 57 (1995): 281–86.

Ganter, Granville. "The Art of Prophecy: Interpretive Analysis, Academic Discourse, and Expository Writing." *Composition Studies* 29.1 (2001): 63–79.

García Márquez, Gabriel. *Love in the Time of Cholera*. Trans. Edith Grossman. New York: Penguin, 1999.

Gates, Henry Louis, Jr., and Nellie Y. McKay. "The Literature of Slavery and Freedom." Gates and McKay 127–36.

———, eds. *Norton Anthology of African American Literature*. New York: Norton, 1997.

———. "Preface: Talking Books." Gates and McKay xxvii–xxxvi.

Gilbert, Sandra M., and Susan Gubar. "A Feminist Reading of Gilman's *The Yellow Wallpaper*." Charters 1446–48.

Gilman, Charlotte Perkins. "On the Reception of 'The Yellow Wallpaper.'" *The Yellow Wallpaper*. Ed. Dale M. Bauer. Boston: Bedford–St. Martin's, 1998. 349–51.

———. "Undergoing the Cure for Nervous Prostration." Charters 1449–50.

———. "The Yellow Wallpaper." Charters 528–41.

Goldberg, Jonathan. *Writing Matter: From the Hands of the English Renaissance*. Stanford: Stanford UP, 1990.

Goodman, Nelson. *Ways of Worldmaking*. Indianapolis: Hackett, 1978.

Graff, Gerald. Afterword. Young and Fulwiler *When* 324–33.

———. *Beyond the Culture Wars: How Teaching the Conflicts Can Revitalize American Education*. New York: Norton, 1992.

———. *Clueless in Academe: How Schooling Obscures the Life of the Mind*. New Haven: Yale UP, 2003.

———. "Disliking Books at an Early Age." *Falling into Theory: Conflicting Views on Reading Literature*. Ed. David H. Richter. 2nd ed. Boston: Bedford–St. Martin's, 2000. 41–48.

———. *Professing Literature*. Chicago: U of Chicago P, 1987.

Graff, Gerald, and James Phelan, eds. Adventures of Huckleberry Finn: *A Case Study in Critical Controversy*. Boston: Bedford, 1995.

Greenblatt, Stephen. "Culture." *Critical Terms for Literary Study*. Ed. Frank Lentricchia and Thomas McLaughlin. Chicago: U of Chicago P, 1990. 225–32.

Guillory, John. *Cultural Capital: The Problem of Literary Canon Formation*. Chicago: U of Chicago P, 1993.

Hairston, Maxine. "Breaking Our Bonds and Reaffirming Our Connections." *College Composition and Communication* 36 (1985): 272–82.

———. "Diversity, Ideology, and Teaching Writing." *College Composition and Communication* 43 (1992): 179–93.

———. "The Winds of Change: Thomas Kuhn and the Revolution in the Teaching of Writing." *College Composition and Communication* 33 (1982): 76–88.

Hammett, Dashiell. *The Maltese Falcon*. New York: Vintage, 1989.

Harris, Joseph. "The Idea of Community in the Study of Writing." *College Composition and Communication* 40 (1989): 11–22.

———. "Meet the New Boss, Same as the Old Boss: Class Consciousness in Composition." *College Composition and Communication* 52 (2000): 43–68.

———. *A Teaching Subject: Composition since 1966.* Upper Saddle River: Prentice, 1997.

Hartwig, D. Scott. *A Killer Angels Companion.* Gettysburg: Thomas, 1996.

Harvey, Gordon. "Premises of the Program." Internal doc. for the Harvard Univ. Expository Writing Program. 2000.

Haswell, Richard. "Documenting Improvement in College Writing: A Longitudinal Approach." *Written Communication* 17 (2000): 307–52.

Hemingway, Ernest. "A Clean, Well-Lighted Place." *"The Snows of Kilimanjaro" and Other Stories.* 1937. New York: Macmillan, 1961. 29–33.

———. *The Green Hills of Africa.* New York: Scribner's, 1935.

Henderson, Brian. "The Civil War: 'Did It Not Seem Real?'" *Film Quarterly* 44 (1991): 2–14.

Homer. *Odyssey.* London: Penguin, 2003.

Horner, Winifred, ed. *Composition and Literature: Bridging the Gap.* Chicago: U of Chicago P, 1983.

Hourani, Albert. *History of the Arab Peoples.* Cambridge: Belknap P–Harvard UP, 2002.

Hurston, Zora Neale. *Their Eyes Were Watching God.* New York: Harper, 1998.

Irving, John. "Trying to Save Piggy Sneed." *Trying to Save Piggy Sneed.* New York: Arcade, 1996. 5–23.

Iser, Wolfgang. *The Act of Reading: A Theory of Aesthetic Response.* Baltimore: Johns Hopkins UP, 1978.

Jackson, Shirley. "The Lottery." New York: Farrar, 1949.

Jacobs, Harriet. *Incidents in the Life of a Slave Girl.* Ed. L. Maria Child. New York: Washington Square, 2003.

Jameson, Fredric. *The Political Unconscious: Narrative as a Socially Symbolic Act.* Ithaca: Cornell UP, 1981.

Jay, Gregory S. "Comment on 'Two Views on the Use of Literature in Composition.'" *College English* 55 (1993): 673–75.

Johnson, Alex. "Why Isaac Bashevis Singer, Truman Capote, Joseph Conrad, and Virginia Woolf (among Others) Were Having a Bad Morning." *How Writers Teach Writing.* Ed. Nancy Kline. New York: Prentice, 1992. 157–72.

Johnson, Mark, ed. *Philosophical Perspectives on Metaphor*. Minneapolis: U of Minnesota P, 1981.

Jordan, June. "Nobody Mean More to Me Than You and the Future Life of Willie Jordan." *On Call*. Boston: South End, 1985. 123–40.

Joseph, Philip. "The Verdict from the Porch: Zora Neale Hurston and Reparative Justice." *American Literature* 74 (2000): 455–83.

Joyce, James. *Portrait of the Artist as a Young Man*. Oxford: Oxford UP, 2000.

Joyce, Michael. *Of Two Minds: Hypertext Pedagogy and Poetics*. Ann Arbor: U of Michigan Press P, 1995.

Kaplan, Marion. *Between Dignity and Despair: Jewish Life in Nazi Germany*. New York: Oxford UP, 1998.

Kaplan, Nancy. "Literacy beyond Books: Reading When All the World's a Web." *The World Wide Web and Contemporary Cultural Theory*. New York: Routledge, 2000. 207–34.

Keats, John. *The Poetical Works of John Keats*. Ed. H. Buxton Forman. 7th ed. London: Reeves, 1902.

Keller, Helen. *The Story of My Life*. New York: Grosset, 1905.

Kent, Thomas, ed. *Post-process Theory: Beyond the Writing-Process Paradigm*. Carbondale: Southern Illinois U P Popular, 1999.

Kingston, Maxine Hong. *The Woman Warrior*. New York: Random, 1975.

Klein, Kathleen Gregory, ed. *Diversity and Detective Fiction*. Bowling Green: Bowling Green State UP, 1999.

Knight, Leon. "Comment on 'Two Views on the Use of Literature in Composition.'" *College English* 55 (1993): 676–78.

Komunyakaa, Yusef. *Thieves of Paradise*. Middletown: Wesleyan UP, 1998.

Kroll, Barbara. "The Rhetoric/Syntax Split: Designing a Curriculum for ESL Students." *Journal of Basic Writing* 9.1 (1990): 40–55.

Krumholz, Linda. "The Ghosts of Slavery: Historical Recovery in Toni Morrison's *Beloved*." *Toni Morrison's* Beloved: *A Casebook*. Ed. William L. Andrews and Nellie McKay. New York: Oxford UP, 1999. 107–25.

Kundera, Milan. *The Book of Laughter and Forgetting*. Trans. Michael Henry Heim. New York: Harper, 1994.

Labov, William. "The Boundaries of Words and Their Meanings." *New Ways of Analyzing Variation in English*. Ed. Charles-James Nice Bailey and Roger W. Shuy. Washington: Georgetown UP, 1973. 340–73.

Lahiri, Jhumpa. *The Interpreter of Maladies: Stories*. Boston: Houghton, 1999.

Lakoff, George, and Mark Johnson. *Metaphors We Live By.* Chicago: U of Chicago P, 1980.

Lakoff, George, and Mark Turner. *More Than Cool Reason: A Field Guide to Poetic Metaphor.* Chicago: U of Chicago P, 1989.

Landow, George P. *Hypertext: The Convergence of Contemporary Critical Theory and Technology.* Baltimore: Johns Hopkins UP, 1992.

"Language." *American Heritage College Dictionary.* 3rd ed. 1992.

Latosi-Sawin, Elizabeth. "Comment on 'Two Views on the Use of Literature in Composition.'" *College English* 55 (1993): 675–76.

Laurence, David. "The Latest Forecast." *ADE Bulletin* 131 (2002): 14–19.

Leavitt, David. "The Way I Live Now." Charters 1470–71.

Lee, Li-Young. "Persimmons." *PoetryFoundation.org.* 10 Oct. 2006 <http://www.poetryfoundation.org/archive/poem.html?id=171753>.

LeFevre, Karen Burke. *Invention as a Social Act.* Carbondale: Southern Illinois UP, 1987.

Limerick, Patricia Nelson. *The Legacy of Conquest: The Unbroken Past of the American West.* New York: Norton, 1987.

Lindemann, Erika. "Freshman Composition: No Place for Literature." *College English* 55 (1993): 311–16.

———. "Three Views of English 101." *College English* 57 (1995): 287–302.

Long, Elizabeth. "Textual Interpretation as Collaborative Action." *The Ethnography of Reading.* Ed. Jonathan Boyarin. Berkeley: U of California P, 1993. 180–207.

Lorde, Audre. "The Master's Tools Will Never Dismantle the Master's House." *Essays and Speeches.* Trumansburg: Crossing, 1984. 110–13.

Lowell, Robert. "Skunk Hour." *Poets.org.* Academy of American Poets. 10 Oct. 2006 <http://www.poets.org/viewmedia.php/prmMID/15279>.

Luvaas, Jay, and Harold W. Nelson, eds. *The U.S. Army War College Guide to the Battle of Gettysburg.* Carlisle: South Mountain, 1987.

Lyotard, Jean-François. *The Postmodern Condition: A Report on Knowledge.* Trans. Geoff Bennington and Brian Massumi. Minneapolis: U of Minnesota P, 1988.

Macdonald, Gina, and Andrew Macdonald. "Ethnic Detectives in Popular Fiction: New Directions for an American Genre." 60–113.

Machiavelli, Niccolo. *The Prince.* London: Penguin, 2003.

Macrorie, Ken. *Telling Writing.* 1970. Rochelle Park: Hayden, 1980.

Mailloux, Steven. *Reception Histories.* Ithaca: Cornell UP, 1998.

Malamud, Bernard. *The Magic Barrel.* New York: Farrar, 2003.

Malcolm X and Alex Haley. *The Autobiography of Malcolm X.* New York: Ballantine, 1992.

Martin, Emily. "The Egg and the Sperm: How Science Has Constructed a Romance Based on Stereotypical Male-Female Roles." *Signs* 16 (1991): 485–501.

Marx, Leo. "Mr. Eliot, Mr. Trilling, and *Huckleberry Finn.*" Graff and Phelan 290–305.

Maya Lin: A Strong Clear Vision. Santa Monica. American Film Foundation, 1994.

McCarthy, Nan. *Chat.* New York: Pocket, 1995.

———. *Connect.* New York: Pocket, 1996.

———. *Crash.* New York: Pocket, 1998.

McCaughey, Robert. *Stand, Columbia: A History of Columbia University in the City of New York, 1754–2004.* New York: Columbia UP, 2003.

McCulloch, Samuel Clyde. *Instant University: The History of the University of California, Irvine, 1957–93.* Irvine: U of California, Irvine, 1966.

McCullough, David Willis. "Designs on the Teacups." Rev. of *Lucy,* by Ellen Feldman. *New York Times Book Review* 12 Jan. 2003: 5.

McLeod, Susan H., ed. *Strengthening Programs for Writing across the Curriculum.* San Francisco: Jossey-Bass, 1988.

McQuade, Donald. "Composition and Literary Studies." *Redrawing the Boundaries: The Transformation of English and American Literary Studies.* Ed. Stephen Greenblatt and Giles Gunn. New York: MLA, 1992. 482–519.

Melville, Herman. *Moby-Dick.* New York: Grosset, 1925.

Millay, Edna St. Vincent. "I, being born a woman." *The Harp-Weaver and Other Poems.* New York: Harper, 1923. 70.

Miller, Carolyn. "Genre as Social Action." Freedman and Medway 23–42.

Miller, Susan. *Textual Carnivals.* Carbondale: Southern Illinois UP, 1991.

Mishima, Yukio. "Three Million Yen." Charters 996–1006.

Morrison, Toni. *Beloved.* London: Picador, 1988.

———. *The Bluest Eye.* New York: Penguin, 2000.

———. *Paradise.* New York: Penguin, 1999.

———. *Playing in the Dark: Whiteness and the Literary Imagination.* Cambridge: Harvard UP, 1992.

Mosley, Walter. *White Butterfly.* New York: Norton, 1992.

Muir, Edwin. "The Animals." *One Foot in Eden.* London: Faber, 1956. 16.

Murray, Donald. "Finding Your Own Voice: Teaching Composition in an Age of Dissent." *College Composition and Communication* 20 (1969): 118–23.

National Resource Center for the First-Year Experience and Students in Transition. *The 2000 National Survey of First-Year Seminar Programs: Continuing Innovations in the Collegiate Curriculum.* Monograph 35. Columbia: U of South Carolina, 2002.

Nelson, Cary, ed. *Will Teach for Food: Academic Labor in Crisis.* Minneapolis: U of Minnesota P, 1997.

Oates, Joyce Carol. "Where Are You Going, Where Have You Been?" Ed. Elaine Showalter. New Brunswick: Rutgers UP, 1994. 23–50.

O'Brien, Tim. *Going after Cacciato.* New York: Delacorte, 1978.

———. *The Things They Carried.* Boston: Houghton, 1990.

———. "The Things They Carried." Charters 1069–83.

Olsen, Tillie. "I Stand Here Ironing." *Tell Me a Riddle.* New York: Delta, 1994. 1–12.

Olson, Gary A. "Toward a Post-process Composition: Abandoning the Rhetoric of Assertion." Kent 7–15.

Orwell, George. "Politics and the English Language." 1936. *"Shooting an Elephant" and Other Essays.* New York: Harcourt, 1950. 77–92.

Paine, Thomas. *Common Sense. From Revolution to Republic: A Documentary Reader.* Ed. Alan Rogers and Alan Lawson. Cambridge: Schenkman, 1976. 93–116.

Palahniuk, Chuck. *Fight Club.* New York: Holt, 1997.

Paretsky, Sara. *Indemnity Only.* New York: Random, 1982.

Pepper, Stephen C. *World Hypotheses: A Study in Evidence.* Berkeley: U of California P, 1961.

Pesmen, Dale. "Reasonable and Unreasonable Worlds: Some Expectations of Coherence in Culture Implied by the Prohibition of Mixed Metaphor." *Beyond Metaphor: The Theory of Tropes in Anthropology.* Ed. James W. Fernandez. Stanford: Stanford UP, 1991. 213–43.

Peterson, Linda H. "The English Literature Seminar as Writing across the Curriculum." Young and Fulwiler *When* 261–70.

Plath, Sylvia. *Ariel.* 1965. New York: Harper, 1999.

———. "Black Rook in Rainy Weather." *Collected Poems.* Ed. Ted Hughes. New York: Harper, 1981. 56–57.

———. "Daddy." Plath, *Ariel* 56–59.

———. "Lady Lazarus." Plath, *Ariel* 6–9.

———. "Metaphors." *Crossing the Water: Transitional Poems.* New York: Harper, 1971.

Plato. *Republic.* Trans. Paul Shorey. Cambridge: Harvard UP, 1943.

——. *Symposium.* Trans. Christopher Gill and Desmond Lee. New York: Penguin, 2006.

Poe, Edgar Allan. "The Purloined Letter." *The Complete Tales and Poems.* New York: Random, 1938. 208–22.

Postman, Neil. "The Medium Is the Metaphor." *Amusing Ourselves to Death: Public Discourse in the Age of Show Business.* New York: Penguin, 1985. 3–15.

Pratt, Mary Louise. "Arts of the Contact Zone." Bartholomae and Petrosky 513–34.

Reed, Ishmael. "I am a Cowboy in the Boat of Ra." *New and Collected Poems, 1964–2006.* New York: Carroll, 2006. 21–23.

Reither, James A. "Motivating Writing Differently in a Literary Studies Classroom." Young and Fulwiler *When* 47–62.

Rich, Adrienne. "As if Your Life Depended on It." *What Is Found There: Notebooks on Poetry and Politics.* New York: Norton, 1993. 32–33.

——. *Diving into the Wreck: Poems 1971–72.* New York: Norton, 1973.

——. "When We Dead Awaken: Writing as Re-Vision." 1971. *On Lies, Secrets, and Silence: Selected Prose, 1966–1978.* New York: Norton, 1979. 33–49.

Richards, I. A. *Practical Criticism.* 1929. New York: Harcourt, n.d.

Ricoeur, Paul. *The Rule of Metaphor: Multi-disciplinary Studies of the Creation of Meaning in Language.* Trans. Robert Czerny. Toronto: U of Toronto P, 1979.

Ristroph, Alice. "Writing in Moral Reasoning 22: Justice." Teaching Materials for the Course. n.d.

Rodriguez, Richard. *Hunger of Memory: The Education of Richard Rodriguez.* New York: Bantam, 1983.

Rohman, D. Gordon, and Albert O. Wlecke. *Pre-writing: The Construction and Application of Models for Concept Formation in Writing.* US Office of Educ. Cooperative Research Project No. 2174. East Lansing: Michigan State U, 1964.

Rose, Jeanne Marie. "'B Seeing U' in Unfamiliar Places: ESL Writers, E-Mail Epistolaries, and Critical Computer Literacy." *Computers and Composition* 21 (2004): 237–49.

Rosenberg, Rosalind. *Changing the Subject: How the Women of Columbia Shaped the Way We Think about Sex and Politics.* New York: Columbia UP, 2004.

Rosenblatt, Louise. *Literature as Exploration.* 5th ed. New York: MLA, 1995.

——. "Towards a Transactional Theory of Reading." *Journal of Reading Behavior* 1.1 (1969): 31–49.

Rosenwasser, David, and Jill Stephen. *Writing Analytically.* 4th ed. Boston: Thomson, 2006.

Rushdie, Salman. *Shame*. New York: Vintage, 1984.

Saadawi, Nawal el. *God Dies by the Nile*. Trans. Sherif Hetata. London: Zed, 1985.

Sacks, Sheldon, ed. *On Metaphor*. Chicago: U of Chicago P, 1978.

Salih, Tayeb. *A Season of Migration to the North*. Trans. Denys Johnson-Davies. London: Penguin, 2003.

Salvatori, Mariolina. "Conversations with Texts: Reading in the Teaching of Composition." *College English* 58 (1996): 440–54.

———. "Towards a Hermeneutics of Difficulty." *Audits of Meaning: A Festschrift in Honor of Ann E. Berthoff*. Ed. Louise Z. Smith. Portsmouth: Boynton, 1988. 80–95.

Schilb, John, and John Clifford, eds. *Making Literature Matter: An Anthology for Readers and Writers*. 3rd ed. Boston: Bedford–St Martin's, 2005.

Scholes, Robert E. Preface. Scholes, Comley, and Ulmer iii–vi.

———. *The Rise and Fall of English*. New Haven: Yale UP, 1998.

———. *Textual Power: Literary Theory and the Teaching of English*. New Haven: Yale UP, 1985.

Scholes, Robert E., Nancy R. Comley, and Gregory Ulmer, eds. *Text Book: Writing through Literature*. 3rd ed. New York: Bedford–St. Martin's, 2002.

Seitz, James. "Changing the Program(s): English Department Curricula in the Contemporary Research University." Downing, Hurlbert, and Mathieu 151–63.

Selfe, Cynthia. "Technology and Literacy: The Perils of Not Paying Attention." *College Composition and Communication* 50 (1999): 411–35.

Shaara, Michael. *The Killer Angels*. New York: Ballantine, 1974.

Shakespeare, William. *Hamlet*. Ed. Stephen Greenblatt. New York: Norton, 1997.

———. Sonnet 65. *Riverside Shakespeare*. 2nd ed. Ed. G. Blakemore Evans et al. Boston: Houghton, 1997. 1855.

Shelley, Mary. *Frankenstein*. Ed. Johanna M. Smith. Boston: Bedford–St. Martin's, 1992.

Showalter, Elaine. *Teaching Literature*. Malden: Blackwell, 2003.

———. "What Teaching Literature Should Really Mean." *Chronicle of Higher Education* 17 Jan. 2003: B7.

Shuker-Haines, Timothy, and Martha M. Umphrey. "Gender (De)Mystified: Resistance and Recuperation in Hard-Boiled Female Detective Fiction." *The Detective in American Fiction, Film, and Television*. Ed. Jerome H. Delamater and Ruth Prigozy. Westport: Greenwood, 1998. 71–82.

Sommers, Nancy, and Laura Saltz. "The Novice as Expert: Writing the Freshman Year." *College Composition and Communication* 56 (2004): 123–48.

Sontag, Susan. Illness as Metaphor *and* AIDS and Its Metaphors. 1978. New York: Doubleday, 1990.

———. "The Way We Live Now." Charters 1179–93.

Spellmeyer, Kurt. *Common Ground: Dialogue, Understanding, and the Teaching of Composition.* Englewood Cliffs: Prentice, 1993.

Stein, Gertrude. *Everybody's Autobiography.* New York: Random, 1937.

Stevens, Wallace. *Collected Poetry and Prose.* 1954. New York: Lib. of America, 1997.

A Student Guide to Writing at UCI. Ed. Ray Zimmerman. 8th ed. Boston: Pearson Custom, 2000.

Swift, Jonathan. Gulliver's Travels *and Selected Writings in Prose and Verse.* Ed. John Hayward. Bloomsbury: Nonesuch, 1934.

Tan, Amy. *The Joy Luck Club.* New York: Vintage, 1991.

Tang, Chung Man. "In Memory of Myself." *A Student's Guide to First-Year Composition.* Ed. N. Buffington, A. Crocket, and P. Ryder. Minneapolis: Burgess, 1996. 390–404.

Tate, Gary. "Notes on the Dying of a Conversation." *College English* 57 (1995): 303–09.

———. "A Place for Literature in Freshman Composition." *College English* 55 (1993): 317–21.

Teller, Astro. *Exegesis.* New York: Vintage, 1997.

Thomas, Brook. "Teaching the Conflicts in the Humanities Core Course at the University of California, Irvine." *College Literature* 21 (1994): 120–35.

Trachte, Kent. *First-Year Residential Seminars at F[ranklin] and M[arshall]: A Brief History.* Unpublished document. 12 July 1994.

Trimbur, John. "Consensus and Difference in Collaborative Learning." *College English* 51 (1989): 602–16.

TuSmith, Bonnie. "Benefit of the Doubt: A Conversation with John Edgar Wideman." *Conversations with John Edgar Wideman.* Ed. TuSmith. Jackson: UP of Mississippi, 1998. 195–219.

Twain, Mark. *Pudd'nhead Wilson.* New York: Airmont, 1966.

Walton, Priscilla L., and Manina Jones. *Detective Agency: Women Rewriting the Hard-Boiled Tradition.* Berkeley: U of California P, 1999.

Ward, Geoffrey. *The Civil War.* New York: Knopf, 1990.

Wharton, Edith. *The House of Mirth.* New York: Scribner's, 1922.

White, Hayden. *The Content of the Form: Narrative Discourse and Historical Representation*. Baltimore: Johns Hopkins UP, 1987.

———. "The Value of Narrativity in the Representation of Reality." White, *Content* 1–25

Wideman, John Edgar. *All Stories Are True*. New York: Vintage, 1992.

Wilson, August. *The Piano Lesson*. New York: Plume, 1990.

Winterson, Jeanette. *Sexing the Cherry*. London: Vintage, 1990.

Woolf, Virginia. *To the Lighthouse*. Ed. Sandra Kemp. London: Routledge, 1994.

Wordsworth, William. "Nuns Fret Not." *Norton Introduction to Poetry*. 7th ed. Ed. J. Paul Hunter. New York: Norton, 1998. 257.

———. "Wordsworth's Prefaces of 1800 and 1802." *Lyrical Ballads: Wordsworth and Coleridge*. Ed. R. L. Brett and A. R. Jones. London: Methuen, 1963. 235–66.

"WPA Outcomes Statement for First-Year Composition." *WPA: Writing Program Administration* 23.1–2 (1999): 59–66.

Wright, Richard A. "Between Laughter and Tears." Rev. of *Their Eyes Were Watching God*, by Zora Neale Hurston. *New Masses* (Oct. 1937): 22+.

———. *Native Son*. New York: Harper, 1998.

Young, Art, and Toby Fulwiler. Introduction. Young and Fulwiler, *When* 1–11.

———, eds. *When Writing Teachers Teach Literature: Bringing Writing to Reading*. Portsmouth: Boynton, 1995.

Index